DICTIONARY
OF
BRITISH-INDIAN DATES

DICTIONARY
OF
BRITISH-INDIAN DATES

BEING

A COMPENDIUM OF ALL THE DATES ESSENTIAL TO THE STUDY OF THE HISTORY OF BRITISH RULE IN INDIA

GYAN

Published by

Gyan Publishing House
5, Ansari Road
Daryaganj, New Delhi-110002
Phone: 011-47034999, 9811692060
E-mail: books@gyanbooks.com

Distribution Network
gyanbooks.com
India, USA, Canada, UK, Australia, France

ISBN : 978-81-212-6356-6 (PB)
First Published, 1866

2nd Impression 2022

Printed at: Gyan Press, Delhi.

DICTIONARY OF BRITISH-INDIAN DATES

DICTIONARY

OF

BRITISH-INDIAN DATES

BEING

A COMPENDIUM OF ALL THE DATES ESSENTIAL
TO THE STUDY OF THE HISTORY OF
BRITISH RULE IN INDIA

DICTIONARY

OF

BRITISH-INDIAN DATES.

ABDUL KHALIK, second son of Tippoo, surrendered with his brother to Lord Cornwallis as hostages, February 26, 1792.

—— were restored to their father 1794.

—— after the fall of Seringapatam, Abdul surrendered himself a second time to the British, May 5, 1799.

ABERCROMBIE, General, taken prisoner by the French when on an expedition against the Mauritius, 1810.

—— recaptured the same day, October 1810.

—— received the surrender of the Island, November 1, 1810.

ABERCROMBY, Sir R., K.C.B., Governor of Bombay, from January 21, 1790, to November 26, 1792; Commander-in-Chief in India, from October 28, 1793, to April 30, 1797.

ACTS of the Legislative Council of India. First called Acts, 1834.

ACT 1 of 1834. Concerning the power of the Governor-General and Vice-Presidents. Passed November 20.

—— 2. Concerning the powers of the Secretaries of the Government of India. Passed November 20.

1835.

ACT 1. Concerning the obedience due from the Officers of the Government of Madras to the Governor. Passed January 7.

—— 2. For placing Assam, Arracan, and Tenasserim under the control of the Sudder Dewanny Adawlut, of the Nizamut Adawlut, and of the Sudder Board of Revenue. Passed January 12.

—— 3. Concerning the Revenue of conquered and ceded Provinces. Passed February 19.

—— 4. Relating to Calcutta Justices of the Peace. Passed March 13.

—— 5. Relating to Madras Moonsiff's Fees. Passed March 13.

—— 6. Relating to Cossyah Hills and Cachar. Passed March 13.

—— 7. Concerning the power of the Governor of Bengal and Agra to transfer certain duties to any Sessions Judge. Passed June 8.

—— 8. Concerning Bengal Revenue. Passed June 8.

—— 9. Concerning Salt Department, Bengal and Cuttack. Passed July 6.

—— 10. Concerning Publication of Acts in 'Government Gazette.' Passed July 6.

—— 11. Concerning Liberty of the Press. Passed Aug. 3.

—— 12. Concerning certain Regulations in Madras Code to be rescinded. Passed August 3.

—— 13. Concerning Sudder Fouzdarry Adawlut, Bombay. Passed August 3.

—— 14. Concerning the power of the Governor of Bombay to appoint Military Officers to Civil employ. Passed August 3.

—— 15. Concerning Witnesses, Madras Courts, repealing Regulation 5 of 1802. Passed August 3.

—— 16. Concerning Bengal Ryots and Indigo Contracts: rescinding Sections 2 and 3 of Regulation 5 of 1830. Passed August 3.

—— 17. Concerning Gold and Silver Coinage. Passed August 17.

ACT 18. Concerning Chuprass or Badges: repealing Clause 8, Section 9, of Regulation 11, 1806, and Clause 4, Section 30, of Regulation 20, 1817. Passed November 9.

—— 19. Concerning the power of Assistant Judges, Bombay. Passed November 9.

—— 20. Concerning Bombay Police Regulations. Passed November 23.

—— 21. Concerning Issue of Copper Coins, Bengal. Passed December 7.

1836.

ACT 1. Concerning Lighthouse Fees in the Island of Perim. Passed January 4.

—— 2. Concerning Bombay Customs duties and repealing Regulation 3 of 1834, except the repealing Clauses. Passed January 11.

—— 3. For abolishing Bombay Cattle-duty. Passed February 8.

—— 4. Concerning Insolvent Debtors. Passed February 22.

—— 5. Concerning the enforcement of Decrees, Bengal. Passed March 7.

—— 6. Concerning Madras Criminal Law. Passed March 7.

—— 7. Concerning Bombay Taxes, and confirming Acts under Regulations 3 and 4 of 1817—7 of 1818—4 of 1821—19, 20, and 21 of 1827—15 of 1828—2 and 13 of 1831—1 and 10 of 1833, and Regulations 19 and 32 of 1827. Passed March 28.

—— 8. Concerning the eligibility to office of Principal Sudder Ameen, Sudder Ameen and Moonsiff, Bengal. Passed March 28.

—— 9. Concerning the power of a Commanding Officer to administer Oaths. Passed April 11.

—— 10. Concerning Indigo Contracts, Bengal, and repealing Clause 3, Section 5 of Regulation 6, 1823. Passed April 11.

—— 11. Concerning the non-exemption of any person from Civil Courts, &c., and repealing Section 107 of 53 George III. Passed May 9.

Act 12. Concerning execution of Decrees of the Nawab of Furruckabad. Passed May 23.

—— 13. Concerning Coinage. Passed May 23.

—— 14. Concerning Bengal Customs and repealing Regulations imposing Transit and Town Duties and Import Duty on sea goods, except on the Jumna and any frontier line, and concerning Duties on Western Salt. Passed May 30.

—— 15. Concerning Subathoo. Passed June 13.

—— 16. Concerning appointment of Vakeels, Madras. Passed June 20.

—— 17. Concerning Territories of the Begum Sumroo. Passed June 20.

—— 18. Concerning Tolls, Bombay. Passed September 5.

—— 19. Concerning Bank of Bengal. Passed September 19.

—— 20. Concerning Divisions of Estates, Bengal. Passed September 19.

—— 21. Concerning creation of new Zillahs, and alteration of existing Zillahs, Bengal. Passed September 19.

—— 22. Concerning Eastern Canal Tolls, Bengal, and repealing Regulation 7, 1810, and parts of Regulation 18, 1806. Passed September 26.

—— 23. Concerning Zemindarees of Goomsur and Soorada, Madras. Passed October 10.

—— 24. Concerning Madras and Bombay Sudder Ameens and other Officers. Passed October 10.

—— 25. Concerning Warehousing Ports. Passed October 31.

—— 26. Concerning appointment of Superintendent of Governor-General's Camp. Passed November 7.

—— 27. Concerning Vakeels, Madras, and repealing Regulation 5, 1817. Passed November 7.

—— 28. Concerning Assessments, Madras. Passed November 7.

—— 29. Concerning the number of Sudder Ameens, Madras: also regarding Fees. Passed November 14.

—— 30. Concerning Punishment for Thuggee. Passed November 14.

ACT 31. Concerning Madras Regulation, relating to Grants of Money or Land. Passed November 28.

—— 32. Relating to Importation of Foreign Sugar, Bengal. Passed November 28.

1837.

ACT 1. Relating to Calcutta Justices of the Peace. Passed February 6.

—— 2. Concerning Bombay Bhore Ghaut Tolls and repealing Regulation 9 of 1830, and Regulation 11 of 1831, and Act 18 of 1836. Passed February 6.

—— 3. Concerning the Transferring of Appeals from one Zillah to another, Bengal. Passed March 13.

—— 4. Empowering British Subjects to hold Land. Passed April 17.

—— 5. Concerning Bengal Emigration. Passed May 1.

—— 6. Concerning Cuttack Revenue. Passed May 1.

—— 7. Concerning power of Queen's Criminal Courts to grant a Free Pardon, &c. Passed May 1.

—— 8. Concerning Travancore. Passed May 8.

—— 9. Concerning Testamentary powers of Parsees. Passed May 15.

—— 10. Relating to Claims to Land in Prince of Wales Island, Singapore, and Malacca, and repealing Regulations 1 and 9 of 1830 of the Local Government, and Regulation 1 of 1831 of the Vice-President in Council. Passed May 22.

—— 11. Concerning Bombay Code and repealing Acts 1 and 2 of Regulation 1, 1820. Passed May 29.

—— 12. Concerning the City of Calcutta. Passed June 5.

—— 13. Concerning Courts Martial, Bombay. Passed June 5.

—— 14. Concerning Foreign Bottoms. Passed June 12.

—— 15. Concerning Bengal Police-tax. Passed June 19.

—— 16. Concerning Bengal Customs and modifying Act 14 of 1836. Passed July 3.

—— 17. Concerning Post-Office and repealing Regulation 11 of 1830. Passed July 24.

—— 18. Concerning Committal and Trial for Thuggee. Passed August 7.

Act 19. Concerning Evidence by Convicted Persons. Passed August 7.

—— 20. Concerning Transmission of immovable Property, Prince of Wales Island, Singapore, and Malacca. Passed September 11.

—— 21. Concerning Declarations as Substitution for Oaths. Passed September 25.

—— 22. Concerning Madras Revenue. Passed September 25.

—— 23. Concerning the power of Principal Sudder Ameens in cases of Perjury, Madras. Passed October 2.

—— 24. Concerning Bengal Police; Powers of Session Judges; Revision of Proceedings. Passed October 2.

—— 25. Concerning Appeals, Bengal, and repealing so much of Clause 2, Section 31 of Regulation 7, 1822, and Section 19 of Regulation 8, 1831, as provides that certain suits shall not be cognisable by any Sudder Ameen or Moonsiff. Passed October 2.

—— 26. Concerning extra powers of Governor-General of India. Passed October 16.

—— 27. Concerning Bombay Salt Duties. Passed November 8.

—— 28. Concerning Bengal Stamp Officers and repealing part of Section 7, Regulation 10, 1829, directing that Manager of Stamp Duties be a Covenanted Servant. Passed November 20.

—— 29. Concerning Bengal Judicial and Revenue Language. Passed November 20.

—— 30. Concerning Madras Police. Passed November 20.

—— 31. Concerning Coinage and suspending Act 17 of 1837. Passed November 20.

—— 32. Concerning Emigration and repealing Act 5 of 1837. Passed November 20.

—— 33. Concerning Madras Police. Passed November 20.

—— 34. Concerning Exemption of Europeans and Americans from Trial, &c., by the Ameen, Madras, and repealing Section 6 of Regulation 8, 1827. Passed November 20.

ACT 35. Concerning Decrees, Madras; and repealing certain previous Acts. Passed November 20.

—— 36. Concerning Madras Criminal Law. Passed November 20.

—— 37. Concerning Bombay Political Offences and repealing so much of Section 26, Regulation 13, 1827, as requires certain Courts to refer to Governor-General on trial of Political Offences. Passed November 20.

—— 38. Concerning Bengal Local Agents under Regulation 19, 1810. Passed November 20.

1838.

ACT 1. Concerning Bombay Customs:—(1) Repealing all Regulations of Bombay Code passed prior to 1827, except Sections 1, 2, 3 of Regulation 6, 1799, and Clause 2, Section 7 of Regulation 9, 1800, and Sections 14, 17, 20, 21, 25 of Regulation 1, 1805, and Regulation 2 of 1810, and Regulation 6 of 1814. (2) Repealing chapters 1, 2, 4, 6, 8, 9 of Regulation 20, 1827, with the Appendices A, B, C, E, H, I, J, K; also Regulation 2, 1831, Regulation 13, 1831, Regulation 1, 1832, Regulation 4, 1833, Regulation 4, 1834, and all parts of Regulations levying transit or inland Customs Duties; also Act 2, 1836. Passed January 3.

—— 2. Concerning Salt Customs, North-Western Provinces. Passed January 5.

—— 3. Concerning Madras and Cochin Criminal Judge, and repealing Act 8, 1837. Passed January 5.

—— 4. Concerning Perjury, Bombay. Passed January 29.

—— 5. Concerning Bengal Bonded Warehouse Association. Passed March 14.

—— 6. Bombay Commissions of Inquiry into Malversation. Passed March 19.

—— 7. Certain powers of Judge of Zillah or City Courts, Bengal. Passed April 23.

—— 8. Bombay Tolls. Passed April 23.

—— 9. Concerning power of Session Judges to impose Fines, Bombay. Passed April 30.

—— 10. Concerning Administration of Kumaon, N.W. P.,

and repealing Regulation 10, 1817, of Bengal Code. Passed April 30.

ACT 11. Concerning the Remuneration of Ameens for effecting the Partition of Estates, Bengal, repealing Section 15 of Regulation 19, 1814. Passed May 14.

—— 12. Concerning Madras Zillah Judges. Passed May 21.

—— 13. Bengal. G.-in-C. may extend Regulation 12 of 1833 to certain Courts. Passed May 21.

—— 14. Concerning Madras Revenue. Passed July 16.

—— 15. Concerning Bombay Regulations, and repealing Clause 1 Section 35 of Regulation 12, 1827. Passed July 16.

—— 16. Jurisdiction of Courts, Bombay. Passed July 23.

—— 17. Jurisdiction of Courts, Madras. Passed August 13.

—— 18. Concerning Sureties, Bombay. Passed August 20.

—— 19. Concerning Coasting Vessels, Bombay, repealing Sections 20 and 21 of Regulation 20 of 1827. Passed August 27.

—— 20. Concerning Post-Office, repealing Section 8, Act 17, 1837. Passed August 27.

—— 21. Concerning Coinage. Passed August 27.

—— 22. Jurisdiction of Courts, Bengal. Passed September 10.

—— 23. Concerning Madras Code, and repealing part of Section 3 of Regulation 4, 1831. Passed September 17.

—— 24. Concerning the Bank of Bengal and repealing Section 3 of Act 19, 1836, and any other provisions of that Act which prescribe or imply that the Capital Stock of the Bank of Bengal shall not exceed 75 lakhs. Passed September 24.

—— 25. Concerning Wills, &c., and repealing Statute 32, H. 8, cap. 1; 34 and 35 H. 8, cap. 5; 10 Car. 1, Section 2, cap. 2 (1.), Sections 5 and 6, 12, 19, 20, 21, and 22 of the Statute of Frauds, 29 Car. 2, cap. 3; 7 W. 3, cap. 12 (1.), Section 14 of 4 and 5 Anne, cap. 16; 6 Anne, cap. 10 (1.), Section 9 of 14 Geo. 2, cap. 2 v.; 25 Geo. 2, cap. 6; 25 Geo. 2, cap. 11 (1.) Passed October 8.

ACT 26. Concerning the power of Governor-General in Council to alter place of Trial, Madras. Passed October 8.

—— 27. Concerning Principal Sudder Ameens, Bengal, and repealing part of Clause 1 Section 18 of Regulation 5, 1831, referring suits preferred to a Provincial Sudder Ameen, in which the Vakeels of his Court shall be a party. Passed October 22.

—— 28. Concerning Perjury. Passed November 5.

—— 29. Concerning Bengal and Cuttack Salt Department, and repealing Sections 59, 60, and 61 of Regulation 10, 1819. Passed November 12.

—— 30. Bengal Registration of Deeds. Passed November 19.

—— 31. Concerning Criminal Law, and repealing Sections 59, 60, 61, 80, 81, 82, 84, 85, 90 (part), 114, 117, 119, and 123 of Statute 9, George IV. c. 74. Passed December 3.

—— 32. Powers of Justices of the Peace, Bengal. Passed December 10.

1839.

ACT 1. Concerning Distress for Rent, Bengal, repealing all Regulations giving Authority to Persons by right of Office to sell Property for Arrears of Rent. Passed February 4.

—— 2. Concerning Summary Jurisdiction. Passed February 4.

—— 3. Concerning the non-exemption of Persons, on account of birth or descent, from the jurisdiction of Revenue Courts or Moonsiffs in matters of rent. Passed February 18.

—— 4. Concerning Summary Jurisdiction in Prince of Wales Island, Malacca, and Singapore. Passed March 18.

—— 5. Do. do. do. Passed March 18.

—— 6. Concerning Bank of Bengal. This Act rescinds and cancels the Charter of the Bank of Bengal, dated

May 29, 1823, and Act 19, 1836, and 24, 1838. Passed March 18.

ACT 7. Concerning Madras Tahseeldars, repealing Section 23, Regulation 28, 1802, and annulling all Commissions appointed under it. Passed March 18.

—— 8. Concerning certain lapsed Villages, Bombay. Passed April 8.

—— 9. Concerning Suits in *formâ pauperis,* Bengal. Passed April 15.

—— 10. Concerning Felony in Prince of Wales Island, Singapore, and Malacca. Passed April 15.

—— 11. Abolishing Institution Fees on Appeal to Privy Council. Passed April 22.

—— 12. Concerning Assessment of Property, Prince of Wales Island, Singapore, and Malacca, repealing Regulation 1, 1827, of Governor in Council of Prince of Wales Island. Passed April 29.

—— 13. Concerning Madras Port Duties. Passed May 20.

—— 14. Concerning Emigration, repealing Acts 32 of 1837 and No. 5 of 1837. Passed May 27.

—— 15. Concerning Madras Sugar Customs. Passed June 10.

—— 16. Concerning Assessment and Collection of Rents, Prince of Wales Island, Singapore, and Malacca. Passed June 10.

—— 17. Concerning Rates of Postage. Passed July 1.

—— 18. Concerning Thuggee. Passed July 15.

—— 19. Concerning Criminal Trials, Bombay. Passed July 22.

—— 20. Concerning Revenue, Bombay. Passed July 29.

—— 21. Concerning Calcutta and River Hooghly, annulling the authority of Justice of the Peace to sentence for felony under any bye-law for Calcutta, and repealing an Ordinance, passed 26th July 1814, registered in Supreme Court November 11, 1814. Passed August 26.

—— 22. Concerning Prisoners' Counsel Act. Passed September 9.

ACT 23. Authorising sentences of Imprisonment, with or without hard labour, by Courts-Martial. Passed Sept. 23.

—— 24. Concerning Administration of Justice and Collection of Revenue, Ganjam and Vizagapatam, repealing Act 23 of 1836. Passed October 2.

—— 25. Concerning Collectors as Magistrates, Bombay, repealing Regulation 4, 1831, Clause 4, Section 11, and Clause 3, Section 27 of Regulation 16, 1827 ; Clause 4, Section 16, Regulation 17, 1827 ; Clause 2, Section 8, Regulation 12, 1827 ; so far as they relate to the penal jurisdiction of Collectors or Magistrates. Passed November 25.

—— 26. Concerning Bengal Public Officers : repeals such parts of Section 10, Regulation 5, 1793, and Section 10, Regulation 4, 1803, as relate to charges of corruption ; and Section 8, Regulation 6, 1793 ; Section 8, Regulation 5, 1803 ; Clauses 9, 10, 11, and such parts of Section 9, Regulation 13, 1793, as relate to Covenanted Servants ; Clauses 9, 10, 11, and such parts of Section 12, Regulation 12 of 1803, as relate to Covenanted Servants ; Section 4, and following Sections of Regulation 8, 1806 ; also Regulation 10, 1806, except that part relating to Security required ; also Regulation 17, 1813, Regulation 8, 1817, and Sections 5 and 6 of Regulation 8, 1825, and all parts of Regulations extending the same. Passed December 2.

—— 27. Concerning Calcutta Court of Requests. Passed December 16.

—— 28. Concerning Buildings in Bombay and Colaba : repeals first 12 Articles of Regulation 3, 1812, and 18th, 25th, and all following Articles of same Regulation ; also 1st, 2d, 5th, and 7th Articles of Regulation 3, 1815. Passed December 16.

—— 29. Concerning Dower. Passed December 16.

—— 30. Concerning Law of Inheritance. Passed December 16.

—— 31. Concerning offences against the Mint. Passed December 23.

—— 32. Concerning Interest. Passed December 30.

1840.

ACT 1. Regulating the Procedure on Trials referred to the Court of Fouzdaree Adawlut, Madras. Passed January 27.

—— 2. Concerning Execution of Sentences of Imprisonment passed by Courts-Martial. Passed February 10.

—— 3. Concerning Incorporation of a Bank at Bombay. Passed February 17.

—— 4. Relating to Bengal Magistrates in affrays arising out of disputed possession of land: repeals Regulation 49, 1793; Regulation 14, 1795; Regulation 32, 1803, Section 5; Regulation 6, 1813; Regulation 15, 1824; Regulation 2, 1829, and so much of any Regulation extending the above, &c. Passed February 17.

—— 5. Concerning Judicial Oaths of Hindoos and Mohammedans. Passed February 24.

—— 6. Concerning Law of Bills of Exchange. Passed March 2.

—— 7. Concerning the offices of Deputy and Assistant Register to Bengal Sudder Courts. Passed March 30.

—— 8. Concerning Madras Punchayets. Passed April 13.

—— 9. Madras English Law Amendment: extends part of 3 and 4 Will. 4, cap. 42—viz., Sections 26, 29, 39, 40, 41, to the Territories of the E.I.C. Passed April 20.

—— 10. Relating to Pilgrim Taxes and Superintendence of the Temple of Juggernath, and repealing such parts of Section 31, Regulation 12, 1805, Section 4, Regulation 27, 1793, as provide for their continuance; also Regulation 4, 1806; Regulation 5, 1806, Section 9; Regulation 6, 1808; Regulation 4, 1809, Section 4; Regulation 4, 1810; Regulation 11, 1810, and Regulation 18, 1810. Passed April 20.

—— 11. Concerning Bombay Criminal Law. Passed April 20.

—— 12. Concerning Assessment, George Town, Singapore, and Malacca. Passed June 8.

—— 13. Concerning English Law Factors' Act. Passed June 29.

ACT 14. Rendering a Written Memorandum necessary to the validity of certain Promises and Engagements. Passed June 29.

—— 15. Relating to Bombay—extending Regulation 15 of 1827, and 13 of 1830, to the Agents of Foreign Sovereigns, Bombay. Passed June 29.

—— 16. Concerning Transported Convicts. Passed August 3.

—— 17. Concerning Salt Laws, Madras. Passed August 10.

—— 18. Concerning Licences, Bombay. Passed August 10.

—— 19. Concerning Appeals in *formâ pauperis*, Bengal. Passed September 14.

—— 20. Relating to Auction Purchasers of Assessed Estates, Bengal. Passed October 19.

—— 21. Concerning Bengal Suits. Passed October 19.

—— 22. Relating to Punishment of Vagrants in Calcutta, Madras, and Bombay. Passed November 23.

—— 23. Concerning Execution of Process, Bengal. Passed November 30.

—— 24. Relating to Municipal Rates, Calcutta. Passed December 7.

—— 25. Concerning Abkaree Revenue, Bengal. Passed December 28.

1841.

ACT 1. Concerning Bengal Revenue. Passed April 12.

—— 2. Concerning Licences, Bombay. Passed May 10.

—— 3. Concerning Trial for Larceny, Bombay: repeals Art. 1 Title 14, and Art. 3 Title 15 of Rule, Ordinance and Regulation 2, 1827. Passed May 10.

—— 4. Concerning Bombay rate of charge for Carriages. Passed May 17.

—— 5. Concerning State Offences. Passed May 31.

—— 6. Concerning Importation of Rum into Bengal. Passed June 7.

—— 7. Concerning Examination of absent Witnesses, repealing all Regulations for taking Evidence of absent Witnesses. Passed June 14.

ACT 8. Concerning English Law Interpleader. Passed June 21.

—— 9. Concerning Abkaree Revenue, Bengal. Passed June 28.

—— 10. Concerning Ship Registers. Passed July 5.

—— 11. Concerning Military Courts of Requests: repeals all Regulations concerning Military Courts of Requests. Passed July 5.

—— 12. Concerning Bengal Revenue Sale Law: repeals Section 2, Regulation 14, 1793, Section 2, Regulation 3, 1794, Regulation 11, 1822, except Sections 36 and 38, and Regulation 7, 1830. Passed July 19.

—— 13. Concerning Bonded Warehouses. Passed August 16.

—— 14. Relates to Regulation of Markets, Bombay and Colaba. Passed August 23.

—— 15. Relates to giving Security, Calcutta: repeals Section 7 of Regulation 9 of 1819. Passed August 23.

—— 16. Concerning taking of Oaths of Qualification by Justices of the Peace. Passed August 30.

—— 17. Concerning Appeals, Security for Costs of Bengal. Passed August 30.

—— 18. Concerning Exportation of Military Stores. Passed August 30.

—— 19. Concerning Protection of Property against wrongful possession in cases of Successors. Passed September 6.

—— 20. Concerning Collection of Debts on Successions. Passed September 6.

—— 21. Concerning Local Nuisances. Passed September 6.

—— 22. Concerning Municipal Rates, Town of Madras. Passed October 11.

—— 23. Concerning Importation of Rum, Madras. Passed October 11.

—— 24. Concerning Illusory Appointments, Transfer of Estates, &c. Passed October 18.

—— 25. Concerning Contempts in Equity. Passed October 18.

ACT 26. Concerning Law Amendment. Passed October 18.

—— 27. Concerning unclaimed Dividends on Insolvent Estates. Passed October 18.

—— 28. Concerning Camp-Followers. Passed November 15.

—— 29. Concerning dismissal of Suits and Appeals, Bengal and Madras: repeals Clause 2, Section 27, Regulation 23, 1814, of the Bengal Code, and Clause 2, Section 26, Regulation 6, 1816, of the Madras Code. Passed December 13.

—— 30. Represses Obstructions to Justice: repealing Section 42, further proviso in Section 74, Regulation 23, 1814, Clauses 2 and 3, Sections 5 and 6 of Regulation 12, 1825. Passed December 20.

—— 31. Touching Bengal Criminal Appeals, repealing those parts of Bengal Code which concern the powers, &c., of Criminal Courts in respect to Appeals. Passed December 20.

1842.

ACT 1. Concerning Opium Sale, Calcutta. Passed January 10.

—— 2. Concerning extraordinary Powers of Governor-General during his absence from the Council. Passed March 28.

—— 3. Concerning Petty Thefts. Passed July 22.

—— 4. Concerning Boat Regulations, Madras Roads. Passed July 22.

—— 5. Concerning Bombay and Colaba Licences. Passed July 29.

—— 6. Concerning annexation of Territory, Bombay: repeals Regulation 29, 1827, and Regulation 7, 1830, as to specified Villages. Passed August 5.

—— 7. Concerning Costs of Translations, Bengal: repeals Section 5 of Regulation 19, 1797, and Regulation 4 of 1803. Passed August 19.

—— 8. Concerning Madras and Bombay Legislative Acts. Passed September 2.

—— 9. Concerning Conveyance of Freehold Estates. Passed September 2.

ACT 10. Municipal and Sanitary, Bengal. Passed October 14.

—— 11. Concerning Importation of Foreign Sugar. Passed October 21.

—— 12. Concerning Military Bazars. Passed October 28.

—— 13. Concerning Bombay Revenue. Passed October 28.

—— 14. Concerning abatement of Nuisances, Bombay and Colaba. Passed November 25.

—— 15. Concerning Emigration to the Mauritius. Passed December 2.

—— 16. Concerning Bengal Leases. Passed December 16.

—— 17. Concerning Bombay Revenue Commissioners: repeals Part 8, Regulation 5, 1830. Passed December 16.

—— 18. Concerning Criminal Cases connected with Collection of Revenue, Bombay. Passed December 23.

1843.

ACT 1. Concerning Unregistered Titles: repeals all Provisions in any Regulation touching notice of Unregistered Conveyances, &c. &c. Passed January 27.

—— 2. Concerning Bengal Appeals to Sudder Dewanny Adawlut. Passed February 1.

—— 3. Concerning Special Appeals. Passed February 1.

—— 4. Concerning Appeals from Justices of the Peace. Passed March 24.

—— 5. Concerning Abolition of Slavery. Passed April 7.

—— 6. Concerning Courts of Ameens and Moonsiffs, &c., Bengal: (3) repeals parts of Regulation 23, 1814, forbidding Sudder Ameens and Moonsiffs from requiring Security, &c.: (6) repeals Clause 2, Section 13, Regulation 23, 1814, and Clause 4, Section 5, Regulation 5, 1831. Passed April 21.

—— 7. Concerning Appeals, Madras: (5) rescinds Section 7, Regulation 7, 1827: (24) rescinds Section 3, Regulation 8, 1816: (28) rescinds Section 2, Regulation 13, 1832. Passed April 28.

ACT 8. Concerning Provincial Courts of Appeal, Madras. Passed April 28.

—— 9. Concerning Incorporation of Bank of Madras. Passed June 14.

—— 10. Concerning the Administration of Justice, and Collection of Revenue, Madras. Passed July 15.

—— 11. Concerning Bombay Hereditary Officers, rescinding Sections 17 and 18, Regulation 16, 1827. Passed July 22.

—— 12. Concerning Judicial Language. Passed July 29.

—— 13. Concerning Madras Public Officers, repealing Regulation 3, 1809 ; 2, 1810 ; 6, 1818 ; and 18, 1822, Passed July 29.

—— 14. North-Western Provinces, Manufacture of Salt and Customs, (1) repealing Regulation 16, 1829, Act 2, 1838, part of Regulation 9, 1810, and other stated parts of other Regulations. Passed August 5.

—— 15. Concerning Uncovenanted Deputy Magistrates. Passed August 5.

—— 16. Concerning the offering of Rewards for the apprehension of Offenders, repealing Sections 2 and 3, Regulation 9, 1808, and Sections 16 and 17, Regulation 16, 1810. Passed August 12.

—— 17. Concerning Official Trustees. Passed August 19.

—— 18. Concerning Thuggee and Dacoity in Allied States. Passed September 9.

—— 19. Concerning Registration of Deeds : repeals Act 1, 1843, except the repeals of notice of existence of unregistered instruments. Passed October 28.

—— 20. Concerning extraordinary powers of Governor-General. Passed October 30.

—— 21. Concerning Emigration to Mauritius. Passed November 11.

—— 22. Concerning Jurisdiction of Zillah Courts, Bengal : repeals recited parts of Section 17, Regulation 3, 1793. Passed November 18.

—— 23. Concerning Jurisdiction of Zillah Courts, Bengal : repeals recited parts of Section 12, Regulation 2,

1803, and of Regulations extending the same. Passed November 18.

ACT 24. Concerning Punishment of Dacoity. Passed November 18.

—— 25. Concerning False Marks on Foreign Manufactures. Passed November 23.

1844.

ACT 1. Securing certain Immunities and Privileges to His Highness the Nabob of the Carnatic, his Family, and Retinue. Passed January 20.

—— 2. Concerning Appeals to Her Majesty in Council. Passed February 17.

—— 3. Legalising Corporal Punishment in cases of Petty Larceny. Passed March 2.

—— 4. Concerning Bengal Police, Dacoity, &c.: repeals Regulation 9, 1808. Passed March 2.

—— 5. Suppressing Private Lotteries. Passed March 2.

—— 6. Concerning Madras Export and Import Duties: (1) repeals such parts of Regulation 10, 1803; 1, 3, and 6, 1812; Regulation 3, 1821, and of any others as impose inland Transit or Town Duties: (2) repeals Regulation 9, 1803, except Sections 55 to 70 inclusive; Regulation 11, 1803; Regulation 14, 1808; Regulation 15, 1808, except Section 5; Regulation 2, 1812, except Sections 15 and 17; Regulation 4, 1812; such parts of Regulation 1, 1813, as relate to Spirits, Duties, and Drawback; Regulation 2, 1816; Regulations 2 and 3, 1818; Regulations 4 and 7, 1819, with their Schedules, except so far as they rescind other Regulations and other Provisions imposing Sea Customs Duties. Passed March 16.

—— 7. Concerning Competency of Witnesses. Passed April 6.

—— 8. Concerning Native Military Prisoners. Passed April 9.

—— 9. Concerning Institution of Suits before Principal Sudder and Sudder Ameens. Passed April 13.

—— 10. Concerning Sentences for Murder. Passed May 11.

ACT 11. Concerning Supreme Court, Calcutta. Passed May 18.

—— 12. For securing an exact Discipline in the Indian Navy. Passed May 25.

—— 13. Concerning Coinage ; Trisoolee Pice cease to be a legal tender, Benares. Passed June 15.

—— 14. Concerning Transportation for Life. Passed July 6.

—— 15. Concerning Customs Duties. Passed July 6.

—— 16. Concerning Bombay Salt Duties : (1) repeals Section 1, Act 27, 1837 ; (3) repeals Section 43, Act 1, 1838 ; (5) repeals specified parts of Schedules A and B, Act 1, 1838. Passed July 27.

—— 17. Concerning Collection of the Revenue of the State of Colaba. Passed August 10.

—— 18. Concerning Superintendence of Bengal Jails : repeals all former Regulations and Acts concerning the control of the same. Passed September 7.

—— 19. Abolishing Town Duties, Mokauts, &c., in the Bombay Presidency. Passed September 14.

—— 20. Relating to Advances made to Agents. Passed October 26.

—— 21. Regulating Emigration to Jamaica, British Guiana, and Trinidad. Passed November 16.

—— 22. Concerning Copper Coinage. Passed December 28.

1845.

ACT 1. To amend Act 12, 1841. Concerning Sale of Lands for Arrears of Rent, &c. Passed January 11.

—— 2. Punishment of Adultery in Bombay Presidency. Passed January 18.

—— 3. Courts of Appeal ; Security of Costs from Appellant. Passed February 15.

—— 4. Regarding Registration of Deeds. Passed March 1.

—— 5. Concerning Examination and Appointment of Hindoo and Mohammedan Law Officers. Passed March 22.

—— 6. Issue of Commissions of Peace. Passed April 5.

—— 7. Water-Rent, Tolls, and Dues on Canals in the North-West Provinces. Passed April 12.

Act 8. For amending Section 75, and Chapter 17 of Regulation 4, 1827, of the Bombay Code. Passed April 19.

—— 9. For amending certain Schedules of Import Duties, and for repealing Act 15 of 1844. Passed May 17.

—— 10. Empowering Courts to issue Warrants in cases of failure to serve Summons. Passed May 17.

—— 11. Touching the Collection and Disbursement, &c., of Public Funds intended for Police and Municipal Purposes in the Islands of Bombay and Colaba. Passed May 24.

—— 12. Authorising the Employment of the Uncovenanted Assistant Register of the Sudder Dewanee, and Sudder Foujdaree Adawlut of Bombay, on the Duties of Register. Passed June 7.

—— 13. For the Extension of Power of the Supreme Court of Judicature at Bombay, with reference to the Enrolment of Attorneys. Passed June 28.

—— 14. Concerning appointment of Nazirs in the Moonsiffs' Courts. Passed July 12.

—— 15. Concerning Privileges of Native Officers and Soldiers in respect of Judicial and Revenue Proceedings. Passed August 16.

—— 16. Concerning readmission of Appeals after dismission, under Act 29 of 1841. Passed August 16.

—— 17. Concerning Attendance of Witnesses in the Moonsiffs' Courts, Bengal. Passed August 16.

—— 18. Concerning Punishment of Offences by Convicts under Sentence of Imprisonment for Life. Passed August 23.

—— 19. Concerning Incorporation of Assam Company. Passed August 30.

—— 20. Concerning Articles of War for Native Officers and Soldiers. Passed September 6.

—— 21. Concerning Agents for the Suppression of the Meriah Sacrifices, Orissa. Passed September 13.

—— 22. Concerning Powers of Governor-General in certain cases when absent from his Council. Passed September 20.

—— 23. To enable the Union Bank of Calcutta to sue

and be sued in the name of the Secretary or Treasurer of the Company. Passed November 22.

ACT 24. Concerning Court of Trial for the Officers of the Pilot Service. Passed November 22.

—— 25. Regulating the time of sailing of Ships carrying Emigrants from Madras to Jamaica, British Guiana, and Trinidad. Passed December 20.

—— 26. Licences for Sale of Liquors in Calcutta. Passed December 27.

—— 27. Power of Assistant Magistrates to decide Cases under Provision of Act 4, 1840. Passed December 27.

—— 28. Concerning Improvement in Administration of Justice and Despatch of Business, &c., in the Supreme Court of Fort St George. Passed December 27.

—— 29. Empowering Government of Bombay to appoint Joint Zillah or Joint Session Judges. Passed December 27.

—— 30. Enabling Session Judges in Madras to award Fines in Compensation to Injured Persons. Passed December 27.

—— 31. Concerning Exemption of Soldiers' and Others' Pensions from Attachment by Process of the Courts of the E.I.C. Passed December 27.

—— 32. For modifying Regulation 1 of 1820 of Madras Code relative to the Manufacture of Spirituous Liquors by Distillation. Passed December 27.

1846.

ACT 1. Concerning Appointment and Remuneration of Pleaders in the Courts of the E.I.C. Passed January 7.

—— 2. Concerning unscrewed Cotton exported from Continent of India, and imported at Bombay. Passed January 7.

—— 3. Concerning Establishment and Maintenance of Field Boundary Marks in the Bombay Presidency. Passed January 7.

—— 4. Concerning Sale of Land in Bengal. Passed January 7.

Act 5. Act for placing the Police of Surat under the Magistrate. Passed December 5.

—— 6. Concerning Administration of the Government in Bhuttee Territory. Passed December 5.

—— 7. Concerning Diet Money for Witnesses in petty cases. Passed December 5.

—— 8. Concerning duration of the existing Settlement of the North-west Provinces. Passed December 5.

—— 9. Authorising the Government of Fort St George to provide Regulations for the Ports, &c., in the Territories subject thereto. Passed December 5.

—— 10. Regulating Proceedings in certain cases of Distraint for Rent. Passed December 5.

—— 11. Concerning Exemption from General Regulations of Part of Candeish and the Zillah Ahmednuggur. Passed December 12.

1847.

Act 1. For the Establishment and Maintenance of Boundary Marks in the North-west Provinces of Bengal. Passed January 30.

—— 2. Explaining certain parts of the Oath Act, Act 5 of 1840. Passed February 13.

—— 3. Providing for the Appointment of Constables and Peace Officers at Settlements in the Straits. Passed February 19.

—— 4. To authorise the Governor in Council of Fort St George to appoint any Military Officer a Magistrate. Passed April 10.

—— 5. To facilitate the Execution of Justice in Territories not subject to General Regulations. Passed April 10.

—— 6. Concerning Copper Currency in Penang, Singapore, and Malacca. Passed May 1.

—— 7. To regulate Distraint for Small Rents in Calcutta. Passed May 1.

—— 8. Concerning Emigration of Labourers from Madras to Mauritius. Passed May 8.

—— 9. Regarding Assessment of Lands gained from the Sea or Rivers in the provinces of Bengal, Behar, and Orissa. Passed May 8.

ACT 10. For amending Act 30 of 1836, regarding Punishment of Thuggee. Passed June 19.

—— 11. To authorise reception of Convicts from Hong-Kong. Passed August 7.

—— 12. Repealing the Law authorising the Impositions of Fines on Moonsiffs and Sudder Ameens. Passed August 21.

—— 13. Repealing Act 14 of 1839, in as far as it relates to the Emigration of the Natives of India to Ceylon. Passed August 21.

—— 14. Repealing Section 3, Regulation 4, 1793, and Section 3, Regulation 3, 1803, of the Bengal Code for Transcription of Plaints. Passed August 28.

—— 15. For the Survey of Lands in Calcutta. Passed September 11.

—— 16. Constituting Commissioners for the Town of Calcutta. Passed October 23.

—— 17. For remedying a defect in the Law regarding undiscovered defaults in the Prosecution of Suits and Appeals. Passed November 6.

—— 18. Concerning Informalities in Registration of Deeds. Passed November 27.

—— 19. For making Amendments in certain Articles of War for the Government of Native Officers and Soldiers in the Military Service of the E.I.C. Passed December 18.

—— 20. To encourage learning in the Territories of the E.I.C. by enforcing the right called Copyright. Passed December 18.

—— 21. Concerning Administration of Justice in Bombay, Despatch of Business, &c. Passed December 18.

—— 22. To enable Commissioners who may be appointed under Act 16, 1847, to purchase and hold property for the Improvement of the Town of Calcutta. Passed December 18.

—— 23. For the amendment of Act, 31 of 1838, concerning Criminal Law. Passed December 31.

1848.

Act 1. Concerning Forgery. Passed January 22.

—— 2. Concerning Commissioners for the Town of Calcutta, their Powers, Privileges, and Duties. Passed February 26.

—— 3. Concerning the meaning to be attached to the words Thug and Thuggee, Murder by Thuggee, when used in the Acts of the Council of India. Passed February 26.

—— 4. Concerning the regulation of Coroners' Juries. Passed February 26.

—— 5. Concerning Mochulkas Penal Recognisances. Passed March 4.

—— 6. Concerning equalisation of Duties on Goods in British and Foreign Bottoms. Passed March 4.

—— 7. Exempting certain Free Ports from the operation of Section 3 Act 6 of 1848, and otherwise to amend that Act, touching Drawbacks or Exportation. Passed March 25.

—— 8. To modify the provisions of Sections 9, 10, 11, and 13, of Regulation 5, 1812, of the Bengal Code, concerning realisation of Revenue and Rent. Passed March 25.

—— 9. For repealing Acts 12 of 1839 and 12 of 1840, concerning Funds for Municipal purposes in Prince of Wales Island, Singapore, and Malacca. Passed March 25.

—— 10. For annexing the lapsed State of Mandvee to Bombay Presidency. Passed April 8.

—— 11. For the Punishment of Wandering Gangs of Thieves and Robbers. Passed May 20.

—— 12. Concerning Jurisdiction of the Calcutta Court of Commissioners for the Recovery of Small Debts. Passed May 27.

—— 13. Concerning the Time within which a Suit may be brought to contest the Awards of the Revenue Authorities in Bengal. Passed June 10.

—— 14. To enable the Supreme Court of Calcutta to issue Commissions for taking Affidavits. Passed June 17.

ACT 15. Forbidding Trading by the Officers of the Supreme Court. Passed June 17.

—— 16. For the removal of certain Restrictions on the Salt Trade. Passed July 1.

—— 17. Concerning Stamp Duties, instead of Institution Fees, &c. Passed August 26.

—— 18. For the Administration of the Estate of the late Nawaub of Surat. Passed August 26.

—— 19. Concerning revision of Sentences of subordinate Criminal Courts in the Presidency of Bengal and Madras. Passed September 2.

—— 20. Enforcing attendance of Proprietors and Farmers of Land, &c., before Collectors of Land Revenue in the Lower Provinces of Bengal Presidency. Passed September 23.

—— 21. An Act for Preventing Wagers. Passed October 10.

—— 22. To simplify Indictment for Forgery. Passed October 10.

—— 23. To amend a Clerical Error in Act 25, 1840. Passed December 10.

—— 24. Concerning Power of Governor-General when absent from the Council of India. Passed October 10.

—— 25. For the Restoration of the Jaghire of Bunganapilly. Passed November 25.

—— 26. To extend to the Straits the Act for regulating Coroners' Juries. Passed December 30.

—— 27. To amend Act 12 of 1844 concerning Indian Navy. Passed December 30.

1849.

ACT 1. For Punishment of Offences committed in Foreign States. Passed January 27.

—— 2. Abolishing Practice of Branding and Exposing Convicts. Passed January 27.

—— 3. Confirming an Agreement between certain Shareholders and Creditors of the Union Bank, Calcutta. Passed February 10.

—— 4. For the Safe Custody of Criminal Lunatics. Passed February 10.

ACT 5. Defining Duties of Customs and Excise. Passed March 3.

—— 6. Concerning Military and Naval Pensions, Superannuation Allowances. Passed March 17.

—— 7. Concerning Appointment of Administrator-General in Bengal. Passed April 7.

—— 8. Concerning Police Magistrates, Madras, their Penal Jurisdiction. Passed May 12.

—— 9. Enabling one Magistrate in the Presidency of Fort St George to exercise the powers of two Justices. Passed May 12.

—— 10. For appointing a Commissioner of Revenue at Madras. Passed May 26.

—— 11. For securing the Abkaree Revenue of Calcutta. Passed August 11.

—— 12. Concerning Sudder Adawlut, Bombay. Passed August 11.

—— 13. For the prevention of Salt-Smuggling, Calcutta. Passed August 18.

—— 14. To punish tampering with the Army or Navy. Passed August 25.

—— 15. For amending Law concerning Stamped Material in use in the Presidency of Bombay. Passed October 26.

1850.

ACT 1. For confirming the Title to Lands in Calcutta taken for Public Purposes. Passed January 11.

—— 2. To amend and extend to Madras and Bombay Act No. 7, 1849. Passed January 11.

—— 3. Concerning the Jurisdiction of the Courts of Sudder Ameens and District Moonsiffs in the Presidency of Fort St George. Passed January 11.

—— 4. For the amendment of Procedure in cases of Appeal to the Sudder Court. Passed February 15.

—— 5. Concerning Freedom of the Coasting Trade of India. Passed March 8.

—— 6. For enabling Commander-in-Chief to pardon Military Offences. Passed March 15.

—— 7. Defining the Law as to the Removal of Prisoners. Passed March 15.

Act 8. Amending Law concerning certain powers of Zillah and City Judges and Principal Sudder Ameens in cases of Appeal. Passed March 15.

—— 9. Recovery of Small Debts in Calcutta, Madras, and Bombay. Passed March 15.

—— 10. Declaring Aden a Free Port. Passed March 15.

—— 11. To amend Act 10, 1841, concerning Registration of Ships. Passed March 15.

—— 12. For avoiding Loss by the default of Public Accountants. Passed March 22.

—— 13. For punishing Breaches of Trust. Passed Mar. 22.

—— 14. Justices of the Peace in the Straits, their Jurisdiction. Passed March 22.

—— 15. To extend operations of Sections 10 and 12, Regulation 26, 1814, of the Bengal Code. Passed April 4.

—— 16. Restitution of Stolen Property. Passed April 4.

—— 17. Taking Land in Bombay and Colaba for Public purposes. Passed April 4.

—— 18. For the protection of Judicial Officers. Passed April 4.

—— 19. Concerning the Binding of Apprentices. Passed April 11.

—— 20. For settling the Boundaries of the Tributary Mehals of Cuttack. Passed April 11.

—— 21. Extending the principle of Section 9, Regulation 7, 1832, of the Bengal Code throughout the Territories of the E.I.C. Passed April 11.

—— 22. For providing for exercise of certain Powers by the Governor-General when absent from the Council of India. Passed April 13.

—— 23. For securing the Land Revenue of Calcutta. Passed June 8.

—— 24. For better defining the special Duty levied on Tobacco in Bombay. Passed June 8.

—— 25. Concerning forfeiture to Government of Deposits made on incomplete Sales of Land under Regulation 8, 1819, and Act 4, 1846. Passed June 14.

—— 26. To enable Improvements to be made in Towns. Passed June 21.

ACT 27. For the registry of Merchant Seamen. Passed June 21.

—— 28. For the encouragement of Merchant Seamen. Passed June 21.

—— 29. To amend Act 31, 1838, for the prevention of Poisoning. Passed August 2.

—— 30. Concerning Act 1, 1846, and Act 4, 1850, on Safe Custody of Criminal Lunatics. Passed August 9.

—— 31. For protecting the Salt Revenue in Bombay. Passed August 9.

—— 32. To repeal Act 15 of 1836 concerning Subathoo. Passed August 16.

—— 33. Concerning Sale of Putnee Tenures in Bengal. Passed August 23.

—— 34. For the better Custody of State Prisoners. Passed August 23.

—— 35. For regulating the Bombay Ferries. Passed September 6.

—— 36. To amend the 113th Article of War for the Native Army. Passed October 4.

—— 37. Concerning inquiries into the behaviour of Public Servants. Passed November 1.

—— 38. Allowing Counsel to all Persons on Trial of Offences. Passed November 1.

—— 39. Concerning Commissioners for Improvement of the Town of Calcutta. Passed November 22.

—— 40. For the Licensing of Pawnbrokers in Prince of Wales Island, Singapore, and Malacca. Passed November 22.

—— 41. Concerning landing of decrepit Beggars in Prince of Wales Island, Singapore, and Malacca. Passed November 22.

—— 42. Concerning additional facilities for Public Works in Bengal. Passed December 20.

—— 43. For the regulation of Joint-Stock Companies. Passed December 27.

—— 44. For consolidating Board of Customs, Salt and Opium, and the Sudder Board of Revenue in Lower Bengal. Passed December 27.

ACT 45. Concerning the Jurisdiction of Coroners. Passed December 27.

1851.

ACT 1. For the Appropriation of Fines levied under Act 24, 1845. Passed February 7.

—— 2. To amend Regulation 13, 1810, of the Bengal Code for the Trial of Appeals ; touching powers of Judges of Sudder, Dewanny, Adawlut. Passed April 11.

—— 3. To amend Regulation 10, 1819, and Act 29, 1838, for preventing the unlawful Manufacture and Transportation of Salt. Passed April 11.

—— 4. Uncovenanted Deputy Magistrates, Duties of Deputy and Assistant Magistrates, Bombay. Passed April 25.

—— 5. For the relief of certain Sufferers by the Insolvency of Sir Thomas Turton, Bart. Passed June 6.

—— 6. Respecting certain Land in Bombay, called Forest Land. Passed June 6.

—— 7. Concerning execution of Decrees, Bombay. Passed June 13.

—— 8. Concerning Tolls on Public Roads and Bridges. Passed July 6.

—— 9. For the prevention of Gambling in Bombay. Passed July 11.

—— 10. To amend Act 20, 1841, for the Administration of Personal Estate of deceased Persons. Passed July 18.

—— 11. Concerning Custody of Registers of Deeds in Bengal Presidency. Passed September 26.

—— 12. For securing the Land Revenue of Madras. Passed November 14.

—— 13. To amend Act No. 5 of 1851. Passed November 21.

—— 14. Concerning Excise Revenue on Spirituous Liquors and Intoxicating Drugs in Prince of Wales Island, Singapore, and Malacca. Passed November 21.

—— 15. Concerning suppression of Frauds in respect of Cotton, Bombay. Passed November 21.

—— 16. Concerning Receivers of Stolen Property. Passed December 26.

1852.

ACT 1. Customs Laws concerning Bombay. Passed January 2.

—— 2. Concerning Collection of Land Customs on certain Foreign Frontiers of the Presidency of Bombay. Passed June 2.

—— 3. To amend the Law concerning Drugs, Spirituous Liquors, &c. &c., Bombay Territories. Passed January 16.

—— 4. Concerning Law relating to Emigrant Vessels and Emigration of Labourers. Passed January 16.

—— 5. Concerning Law entitled an Act of Marriage for India. Passed January 16.

—— 6. For defraying the Cost of a Lighthouse on Pedra Brunca. Passed January 30.

—— 7. For amending Act 17 of 1840, concerning Salt Laws in the Madras Presidency. Passed February 6.

—— 8. For remunerating the Sheriffs of Calcutta, Madras, and Bombay, for the execution of Mofussil Process within the Jurisdiction of the Supreme Court, under Act 23, 1840. Passed February 6.

—— 9. For repealing Regulation 1 of 1832 of Bengal Code. Passed February 6.

—— 10. Concerning Commissioner for the Improvement of the Town of Calcutta. Passed February 6.

—— 11. Concerning adjudication of Titles to certain Estates claiming to be wholly or partially rent-free in the Presidency of Bombay. Passed February 13.

—— 12. For repealing Act 2 of 1848, and concerning power of Calcutta Commissioners. Passed February 20.

—— 13. Concerning Calcutta Police. Passed February 27.

—— 14. Extending Provisions of Acts 24 of 1841 and 17 of 1843 to the Straits Settlement. Passed February 27.

—— 15. For amending Law concerning Evidence. Passed March 12.

—— 16. For the Administration of Justice in Her Majesty's Courts in the Territories of the E.I.C. Passed March 12.

—— 17. To diminish delay and expense in Her Majesty's Courts in the Territories of the E.I.C. Passed March 12.

Act 18. Concerning Pleaders in the Lower Provinces of Bengal. Passed March 19.

—— 19. Securing the Abkarry Revenue, Madras. Passed March 19.

—— 20. Concerning Land needed for Public purposes in the Presidency of Fort St George. Passed March 27.

—— 21. Concerning Employment of uncovenanted Deputy Collectors in the Presidency of Bombay. Passed April 16.

—— 22. Concerning Summary Suits for Arrears of Rent, Sales of Putnee Talooks and other tenures. Passed April 30.

—— 23. Concerning certain powers of the Governors in Council of Bombay and Madras concerning Fines, Amercements, &c. Passed May 7.

—— 24. Concerning Act 14, 1839, to prevent crimping Coolies for Emigration. Passed May 14.

—— 25. Concerning Decrees made in Appeal. Passed May 14.

—— 26. Concerning mode of Procedure in the Courts of the Sudder Ameens and Moonsiffs in the Presidency of Fort William, powers of Principal Sudder Ameens. Passed May 14.

—— 27. For conferring certain powers on Patels and other heads of villages in the Bombay Presidency. Passed July 2.

—— 28. For relieving the Court of Sudder Fouzdaree Adawlut at Bombay from the Superintendence of Police. Passed July 2.

—— 29. Concerning Circuits of Judicial Commissioners, Bombay. Passed July 2.

—— 30. For the naturalisation of Aliens. Passed July 16.

—— 31. To repeal Clause 17, Section 16, Regulation 20, 1617, of the Bengal Code respecting remuneration of Darogaht. Passed August 13.

—— 32. To facilitate the Prosecution of certain Ministerial and Police Officers for certain Criminal Acts. Passed August 20.

Act 33. To enforce Judgments in Places beyond the Jurisdiction of the Courts pronouncing the same. Passed August 21.

—— 34. Concerning prevention of Gambling in Prince of Wales Island, Singapore, and Malacca. Passed September 10.

—— 35. For the abolition of the Poll-Tax and Levying a Tax on Land covered by houses in Arracan and the Towns of Akyab and Kyouk Phyoo. Passed October 1.

1853.

Act 1. Providing for the punishment of Juvenile Thieves in the Presidencies of Fort St George and Bombay. Passed February 4.

—— 2. Concerning the liabilities of all Her Majesty's Subjects to the same Jurisdiction as Natives in respect of Public and Police Duties, &c., and Public charges incident to the holders of land or their local agents. Passed February 4.

—— 3. Relating to the belongings of the G.I.P.R.C. in the Presidency of Bombay. Passed March 11.

—— 4. For the abolition of the Government monopoly of Tobacco in the Provinces of Coimbatore, Malabar, and Canara. Passed March 11.

—— 5. To amend Act 4 of 1839 concerning Prince of Wales Island, &c. Passed March 18.

—— 6. Relating to Summary Suits for Arrears of Rent, Sales of Putnee Talooks, &c., Sales of Land in satisfaction of Summary Decrees for Rent, &c. Passed April 15.

—— 7. To extend the Jurisdiction of Magistrates in certain Offences not felony under the 53d George 3, Cap. 155, Section 105. Passed April 15.

—— 8. For bringing the state of Colaba under the Laws of the Presidency of Bombay. Passed April 15.

—— 9. To amend Act 6 of 1853. Passed April 22.

—— 10. To amend Act 22 of 1836 touching navigation of Boats on the Hooghly. Passed July 15.

—— 11. For the removal of Nuisances, &c., below High-water Mark in the Islands of Bombay and Colaba. Passed July 15.

ACT 12. Supplemental to Act 111 of 1853, concerning the G.I.P.R. Company. Passed July 22.

—— 13. For bringing certain Territories under the Acts and Regulations in force in the Bombay Presidency. Passed July 29.

—— 14. Concerning the collection and distribution of the effects of Officers, Seamen, and others dying in the Marine Service of the H.E.I.C. Passed October 2.

—— 15. For the amendment of Procedure in Cases of regular Appeal to the Sudder Courts in the Presidency Fort William. Passed October 28.

—— 16. For amending the Law of Special Appeals. Passed November 18.

—— 17. To repeal Regulation 7 of 1816, and concerning the Law to be in force respecting Land granted to Maharajah Jeswunt Rao. Passed November 18.

—— 18. Concerning Sale of Spirituous Liquors in Cantonments. Passed December 2.

—— 19. Concerning Law of Evidence in Civil Courts, Bengal. Passed December 2.

—— 20. To amend Law relating to Pleaders in Courts of the E.I.C. Passed December 8.

—— 21. Providing for the exercise of certain Powers by the Governor-General when absent from the Council of India. Passed December 8.

1854.

ACT 1. To amend the Law for facilitating the acquisition of Land needed for Public Purposes within the Town of Madras. Passed February 3.

—— 2. To abolish the Office of Assessor to the Court of Petty Sessions at Bombay. Passed February 3.

—— 3. To amend the 38th Article of War for the Native Army. Passed February 3.

—— 4. Relating to the execution of Sentences in Petty Cases by Superintendent of Bazaars in Bombay. Passed February 3.

—— 5. To amend Act 5 of 1838 relating to the Bengal

Bonded Warehouse Association. Passed February 10.

Act 6. To amend the Practice and Course of Proceeding in the Equity side of the Supreme Courts in India. Passed February 10.

—— 7. For the apprehension within the Territories under the Government of the H.E.I.C. of Persons charged with the commission of heinous Offences beyond the Limits of the said Territories, and for delivering them up to Justice, and to provide for the Execution of Warrants in Places out of the Jurisdiction of the Authorities issuing them. Passed February 17.

—— 8. To explain and amend Act 10 of 1851 and 20 of 1841. Passed February 17.

—— 9. Relating to Appeals in the Civil Courts of the East India Company. Passed February 17.

—— 10. For regulating the powers of Assistants to Magistrates and of Deputy Magistrates appointed under Act 15 of 1843. Passed February 24.

—— 11. To amend Act 21 of 1835 and Act 22 of 1844, and to authorise the issue of Half-pice. Passed March 3.

—— 12. For conferring Criminal Jurisdiction upon District Moonsiffs at Madras. Passed March 10.

—— 13. To repeal Act 6 of 1852, and to make provision for defraying the Cost of the Lighthouse on Pedra Branca, and for maintaining the same; and also a Floating Light established in the Straits of Malacca, to the West of Singapore, and for the establishment and maintenance of such further Lights in or near to the said Straits as may be deemed expedient. Passed April 7.

—— 14. To continue the operation of Act 19 of 1845 until the 30th day of April 1855. Passed April 15.

—— 15. An Act to facilitate the Proceedings of the Commissioners appointed to inquire into certain Matters connected with the Position of Sir James Brooke, H.M.'s Commissioner and Consul-General in Borneo. Passed July 21.

—— 16. To amend Regulation 11 of 1831 of the Bengal Code. Passed July 28.

ACT 17. An Act for the Management of the Post-Office, for the Regulation of the Duties of Postage, and for the Punishment of Offences against the Post-Office. Passed August 12.

—— 18. An Act relating to Railways in India. Passed August 12.

—— 19. For removing the Prohibition against the Importation of Foreign Sugar. Passed August 26.

—— 20. To amend Regulation 13 of 1833 of the Bengal Code.

—— 21. To amend the Law relating to the several Banks of Bengal, Madras, and Bombay.

—— 22. To repeal certain parts of the 53 Geo. 3, c. 155; of Section 2, Regulation 15 of 1806 of the Bengal Code; and of Regulation 4 of 1809 of the Madras Code. Passed September 23.

—— 23. For the suppression of Outrages in the District of Malabar in the Presidency of Fort St George. Passed October 28.

—— 24. To prohibit Possession of certain Offensive Weapons in Malabar. Passed October 28.

—— 25. An Act for discontinuing the practice of issuing Warrants for the Payment of Money from the Treasuries of the Collectors. Passed November 4.

—— 26. For making better Provision for the Education of Male Minors, subject to the Superintendence of the Court of Wards. Passed November 11.

—— 27. To amend the Law relating to the Nazim of Bengal. Passed November 11.

—— 28. An Act to continue the Commissioners for the Improvement of the Town of Calcutta pending the consideration of an Act to amend Act 10 of 1852. Passed November 18.

—— 29. To prohibit the Exportation of Saltpetre to certain Ports in Europe. Passed November 18.

—— 30. To provide for the Levy of Duties of Customs in the Arracan, Pegu, Martaban, and Tenasserim Provinces. Passed December 2.

—— 31. To abolish real Actions and also Fines and common Recoveries, and to simplify the modes of conveying Lands in cases to which the English Law is applicable.

ACT 32. To facilitate Inquiries respecting the alleged use of Torture in the Presidency of Fort St George.

—— 33. To extend the Provisions of Act No. 12 of 1843. Passed December 23.

—— 34. For regulating the establishment and management of Electric Telegraphs in India. Passed December 23.

1855.

ACT 1. For providing for the exercise of certain Powers by the Governor-General during his absence from the Council of India. Passed February 2.

—— 2. For the further improvement of the Law of Evidence. Passed February 2.

—— 3. For the better prevention of Desertion from the Indian Navy. Passed February 2.

—— 4. For incorporating for a further period and for giving further Powers to the Assam Company. Passed February 10.

—— 5. To assimilate the Process of Execution on all sides of H.M.'s Supreme Courts, and to extend and amend the Provisions of Act 25 of 1841. Passed February 17.

—— 6. To extend the operation of, and regulate the mode of executing, Writs of Execution in H.M.'s Supreme Courts of Judicature. Passed February 17.

—— 7. An Act to amend the Law of Arrest on mesne Process in Civil Actions in H.M.'s Courts of Judicature, and to provide for the Subsistence of Prisoners confined under Civil Process of any of the said Courts. Passed February 17.

—— 8. To amend the Law relating to the Office and Duties of Administrator-General. Passed February 17.

—— 9. For the amendment of Procedure in Cases of regular Appeal to the Sudder Court in Madras. Passed March 21.

ACT 10. An Act to amend the Law relating to the Attendance and Examination of Witnesses in the Civil Courts of the East India Company, in the Presidencies of Fort St George and Bombay, and to amend the Provisions of X. L. Act 19 of 1853. Passed April 14.

—— 11. An Act relating to mesne Profits, and to improvements made by Holders under Defective Titles in Cases to which the English Law is applicable. Passed April 14.

—— 12. An Act to enable Executors, Administrators, or Representatives to sue and be sued for certain Wrongs. Passed April 14.

—— 13. An Act to provide Compensation to Families for Loss occasioned by the Death of a Person caused by Actionable Wrong. Passed April 14.

—— 14. An Act for the better regulation of Military Bazaars in the Presidency of Fort St George. Passed April 14.

—— 15. An Act to amend Regulation 3 of 1833 of the Bombay Regulations. Passed April 14.

—— 16. To amend the Law in force in the Presidency of Bombay concerning the use of Badges. Passed April 14.

—— 17. To improve the Law relating to the Copper Currency in the Straits. Passed June 23.

—— 18. To remove Doubts relating to the power to grant Pardons and Reprieves and remissions of Punishments in India. Passed June 23.

—— 19. To amend the Law relating to District Moonsiffs in the Presidency of Fort St George. Passed August 18.

—— 20. For the establishment and maintenance of Boundary Marks in the Presidency of Fort St George. Passed August 18.

—— 21. For making better Provision for the Education of Male Minors and the Marriage of Male and Female Minors subject to the Superintendence of the Court of Wards in the Presidency of Fort St George. Passed September 1.

ACT 22. For the regulation of Ports and Port-Dues. Passed September 1.

—— 23. To amend the Law relating to the Administration of the Estates of Deceased Persons charged with Money by way of Mortgage. Passed September 1.

—— 24. To substitute Penal Servitude for the Punishment of Transportation in respect of European and American Convicts, and to amend the Law relating to the Removal of such Convicts. Passed September 1.

—— 25. To empower the Session Judge of Coimbatore to hold Sessions at Ootacamund in the Neilgherry Hills. Passed September 29.

—— 26. To facilitate the Payment of Small Deposits in Government Savings Banks to the Representatives of Deceased Depositors. Passed October 13.

—— 27. To enable the Banks of Bengal, Madras, and Bombay to transact certain Business in respect of Government Securities and Shares in the said Banks. Passed October 13.

—— 28. For the repeal of the Usury Laws. Passed October 13.

—— 29. For amending Act No. 6 of 1844. Passed November 17.

—— 30. To repeal Section 7 of Act No. 28 of 1839. Passed November 17.

—— 31. Relating to the Emigration of Native Labourers to the British Colonies of St Lucia and Grenada. Passed December 1.

—— 32. Relating to Embankments. Passed December 1.

—— 33. To prohibit the Exportation of Saltpetre except in British Vessels bound to the Ports of London or Liverpool. Passed December 8.

—— 34. To explain and amend Act No. 33 of 1852. Passed December 15.

—— 35. To abolish the levy of Customs Duty on the Import of Cotton into the North-west Provinces of the Presidency of Bengal. Passed December 15.

—— 36. To empower Officers of Customs and Land Revenue to search Houses and other Enclosed Places for

Contraband Salt in the North-west Provinces. Passed December 22.

ACT 37. To remove from the operation of the General Laws and Regulations certain Districts inhabited by Sonthals and others, and to place the same under the Superintendence of an Officer to be specially appointed for that purpose. Passed December 22.

—— 38. An Act to provide for the Trial and Punishment of Rebellion and other Offences committed within certain Districts in which Martial Law has lately been proclaimed. Passed December 22.

1856.

ACT 1. To prevent the Sale or Exposure of Obscene Books or Pictures. Passed January 1.

—— 2. To enable Magistrates and certain other Officers to take cognisance of certain Offences without requiring a Written Comptery. Passed February 1.

—— 3. To amend Act 11 of 1849, and Act 19 of 1852. Passed February 8.

—— 4. To prevent malicious and wanton Destruction of Cattle. Passed February 8.

—— 5. To give effect to Act 23 of 1854, from the time of its promulgation in the district of Malabar, and to extend the application thereof in future. Passed February 22.

—— 6. For granting Exclusive Privileges to Inventors. Passed February 28.

—— 7. To enable the Bombay Government to provide for a due Supply of Water for Public Use in the Islands of Bombay. Passed February 28.

—— 8. For the better control of Jails in the Presidency of Fort St George and Bombay. Passed March 14.

—— 9. Amending the Law relating to Bills of Lading. Passed April 11.

—— 10. For repealing Article (122) of War for Native Army, and substituting a new Article in lieu thereof. Passed April 11.

—— 11. For the better prevention of Desertion by European Soldiers from the Land Forces of Her Majesty and the East India Company in India. Passed April 11.

Act 12. To amend the Law respecting the enlargement of Ameens by the Civil Courts in the Presidency of Fort William. Passed May 9.

—— 13. For regulating the Police of the Towns of Calcutta, Madras, and Bombay, and in the several Stations in the Settlements of Prince of Wales Island, Singapore, and Malacca. Passed June 13.

—— 14. For the conservancy and improvement of the Towns of Calcutta, Madras, and Bombay, and the several Stations of the Settlement of Prince of Wales Island, Singapore, and Malacca. Passed June 13.

—— 15. To remove all legal obstacles to the Re-marriage of Hindoo Widows. Passed July 25.

—— 16. To authorise the Levy of Port-Dues and Fees at the present rate for a further period of Twelve Months. Passed August 9.

—— 17. To provide for the Execution of Criminal Process in places out of the jurisdiction of the Authority issuing the same. Passed August 23.

—— 18. Relating to the administration of Public Revenues in the Town of Calcutta. Passed August 23.

—— 19. To enable the power of the Governor-General of India in Council to suspend the operation of certain Acts relating to the Emigration of Native Labourers. Passed September 17.

—— 20. To make better provision for the appointment and maintenance of Police Chowkedars in Cities, Towns, Stations, Suburbs, and Bazaars in the Presidency of Fort William in Bengal. Passed November 14.

—— 21. To consolidate and amend the Law relating to the Abkaree Revenue in the Presidency of Fort William in Bengal. Passed November 22.

—— 22. For establishing a Toll on Boats and Timber passing through the Kurrateya River in the district of Bengal. Passed December 5.

—— 23. For recovering arrears of Revenue under Rejotwar Settlement in the Madras Presidency. Passed December 5.

—— 24. To provide for the Dissolution of the Bengal

Mariners' and General Widows' Fund Society, and the distribution of the Funds belonging thereto. Passed December 12.

ACT 25. For comprising in one Act the provisions necessary for the Assessment and Collection of Municipal Rates and Taxes in the Towns of Calcutta, Madras, and Bombay, and the several Stations of the Settlement of Prince of Wales Island, Singapore, and Malacca. Passed December 19.

—— 26. For appointing Municipal Commissioners, and for levying Rates and Taxes in the Town of Madras. Passed December 20.

—— 27. For appointing Municipal Commissioners, and for levying Rates and Taxes in the several Stations of the Settlement of Prince of Wales Island, Singapore, and Malacca. Passed December 20.

——28. For appointing Municipal Commissioners, and for levying Rates and Taxes in Calcutta. Passed December 26.

—— 29. Concerning the taking of Oaths of Office by Registers of Deeds. Passed December 26.

1857.

ACT 1. To prevent the Overcrowding of Vessels carrying Native Passengers in the Bay of Bengal. Passed January 17.

—— 2. To establish and incorporate a University at Calcutta. Passed January 24.

—— 3. Relating to Trespasses by Cattle. Passed January 31.

—— 4. To amend the Law relating to the Duties payable on Tobacco, and the Retail Sale and Warehousing thereof in Bombay. Passed February 9.

—— 5. To confer certain powers on the Oriental Gas Company (Limited). Passed February 13.

—— 6. For the acquisition of Land for Public Purposes. Passed May 1.

—— 7. For the more extensive employment of Uncovenanted Agency in the Revenue and Judicial Departments of the Presidency of Fort St George. Passed May 1.

Act 8. To amend Act 19 of 1847 (Extry.) Passed May 16.

—— 9. To repeal Act 6 of 1856. Passed May 23.

—— 10. To amend Act 37 of 1855. Passed May 20.

—— 11. For the Prevention, Trial, and Punishment of Offences against the State. Passed May 30.

—— 12. To authorise the Arrest and Detention within the Ports of the Straits of Junks or Native Vessels suspected to be Piratical. Passed May 29.

—— 13. To consolidate and amend the Law relating to the Cultivation of the Poppy and the Manufacture of Opium in the Presidency of Fort William in Bengal. Passed June 6.

—— 14. To make further provision for the Trial and Punishment of certain Offences relating to the Army, and of Offences against the State. Passed June 6.

—— 15. To regulate the establishment of Printing Presses, and to restrain in certain cases the circulation of Printed Books and Paper (Extry.) Passed June 13.

—— 16. To make temporary provision for the Trial and Punishment of Heinous Offences in certain Districts (Extry.) Passed June 13.

—— 17. To provide temporarily for the Apprehension and Trial of Native Officers and Soldiers for Mutiny and Desertion. Passed June 20.

—— 18. Relating to the issuing of Writs or Process against certain Members of the Family, Household, and Retinue of his late Highness the Nabob of the Carnatic (Extry.) Passed July 4.

—— 19. For the incorporation and regulation of Joint-Stock Companies and other Associations, either with or without limited liability of the Members thereof. Passed July 10.

—— 20. To amend Act 9 of 1850. Passed July 10.

—— 21. To make better provision for the order and good Government of the Suburbs of Calcutta, and of the Station of Howrah. Passed July 10.

—— 22. To establish and incorporate a University at Bombay. Passed July 18.

ACT 23. To provide for the good order and discipline of certain Volunteer Corps, and to invest them with certain powers. Passed July 18.

—— 24. To authorise the levy of Port-Dues and Fees at the present rates for a further period of Six Months. Passed July 31.

—— 25. To render Officers and Soldiers in the Native Army liable to Forfeiture of Property for Mutiny, and to provide for the adjudication and recovery of forfeitures of property in certain cases. Passed August 8.

—— 26. For regulating Ferries, the Straits Settlement of Prince of Wales Island, Singapore, and Malacca. Passed September 5.

—— 27. To establish and incorporate a University at Madras. Passed September 5.

—— 28. Relating to the Importation, Manufacture, and Sale of Arms and Ammunition, and for regulating the right to keep or use the same. Passed September 11.

—— 29. To make better provision for the Collection of Land Customs on certain Foreign Frontiers of the Bombay Presidency. Passed September 11.

—— 30. For the levy of Port-Dues and Fees in Calcutta. Passed October 23.

—— 31. For the levy of Port-Dues and Fees in Bombay. Passed October 23.

—— 32. To amend Articles of War for Native Army. Passed November 28.

—— 33. To make further provision relating to Foreigners. Passed December 5.

—— 34. Relating to the Sale of Gunja in Bombay Presidency. Passed December 5.

—— 35. For the levy of Port-Dues in the Ports of Moulmein, Rangoon, Kyouk Phyoo, Akyab, and Chittagong. Passed December 14.

1858.

ACT 1. To make lawful Compulsory Labour for the prevention of mischief by Inundation, and to carry on certain Works of Irrigation in the Presidency of Fort St George. Passed January 20.

ACT 2. For the levy of Port-Dues in certain Ports in the Province of Cuttack. Passed January 20.

—— 3. To amend the Law relating to the arrest and detention of State Prisoners. Passed January 23.

—— 4. For providing for the exercise of certain powers by the Governor-General when absent from the Council of India. Passed January 28.

—— 5. For the punishment of certain Offenders who have escaped from Gaol, and of those who have harboured the same. Passed January 29.

—— 6. To authorise the Impressment of Artizans and Labourers for the erection of Buildings for European Troops, and other Military Purposes. Passed January 29.

—— 7. For the levying of Port-Dues, Fees, &c., in the Ports of the Presidency of Fort St George. Passed March 1.

—— 8. For the levying of Port-Dues in the Port of Kurrachee. Passed March 12.

—— 9. For levying Port-Dues in certain Ports within the limits of the Gulf of Cambay. Passed March 19.

—— 10. To authorise the Confiscation of Villages, the imposition of Fines, and the forfeiture of certain Offices in cases of Rebellion and other Crimes committed by Inhabitants of Villages, or by Members of Tribes ; and also to provide for the punishment of Proprietors of Land who neglect to assist in the suppression of Rebellion or in the apprehension of Rebels, Mutineers, or Deserters. Passed March 19.

—— 11. To authorise the Infliction of Corporal Punishment in certain cases. Passed April 4.

—— 12. For raising Funds for making and repairing Roads in the Suburbs of Calcutta and the Station of Dowrah. Passed April 4.

—— 13. For the Punishment of Persons who unlawfully possess or conceal Arms or other Government Property belonging to Her Majesty or the East India Company. Passed April 4.

ACT 14. To extend the Provisions of Act 21 of 1855 in the Presidency of Fort St George to Minors now subject to the Superintendence of the Court of Wards. Passed April 9.

—— 15. For the levy of Port-Dues in Aden. Passed April 14.

—— 16. To extend Act 25 of 1855. Passed April 14.

—— 17. To repeal the Laws relating to the levy of Light Dues at Ports within the limits of the Gulf of Cambay. Passed April 20.

—— 18. For the regulation of certain Ports within the Presidency of Fort St George. Passed April 27.

—— 19. To provide for the authentication of Stamped Paper issued from the Stamp Office in Calcutta. Passed May 11.

—— 20. To facilitate the recovery of Land and other real Property of which possession may have been wrongfully taken during the recent disturbances in the Provinces of the Presidency of Bengal. Passed May 18.

—— 21. For the regulation of Native Passenger Ships and Steam Vessels intended to convey Passengers on Coasting Voyages. Passed May 25.

—— 22. To continue in force for a further period Acts 14 of 1857, 16 of 1857, and 17 of 1857; and to authorise, in certain cases, the Transportation of Offenders sentenced to Imprisonment. Passed June 2.

—— 23. For bringing the District of Kurnool under the Laws of the Presidency of Fort St George. Passed June 12.

—— 24. To continue for Six Months the Privileges granted by Act 1 of 1844 to certain members of the Family, Household, and Retinue of his late Highness the Nabob of the Carnatic. Passed June 22.

—— 25. For appointing Municipal Commissioners, and for raising a Fund for Municipal Purposes in the Town of Bombay. Passed July 7.

—— 26. To make further provision for the Trial and Punishment of Offences against the State. Passed July 7.

ACT 27. To continue in force for a further period of Six Months Act 4 of 1858, for providing for the exercise of certain Powers by the Governor-General during his absence from the Council of India. Passed July 27.

—— 28. For the maintenance of a Police Force for the Port of Madras. Passed July 31.

—— 29. For the relief of Persons who, in consequence of the recent disturbances, have been prevented from instituting or prosecuting Suits or Appeals in the Civil Courts of the North-west Provinces within the time allowed by Law. Passed July 31.

—— 30. To provide for the Administration of the Estate and for the Payment of the Debts of the late Nabob of the Carnatic. Passed August 24.

—— 31. To make further provision for the Settlement of Land gained by Alluvion in the Presidency of Fort William in Bengal. Passed August 24.

—— 32. For bringing the Fort of Tanjore and the adjacent Territory under the Laws of the Presidency of Fort St George. Passed August 24.

—— 33. To amend Act 12 of 1844 for better securing the observance of an exact Discipline in the Indian Navy. Passed September 11.

—— 34. To regulate proceedings in Lunacy in Courts of Judicature established by Royal Charter. Passed September 14.

—— 35. To make better provision for the care of the Estates of Lunatics not subject to the Jurisdiction of the Supreme Courts of Judicature. Passed September 14.

—— 36. Relating to Lunatic Asylums. Passed September 14.

—— 37. To continue certain Privileges and Immunities to the Family and Retinue of his late Highness the Nabob of the Carnatic. Passed October 5.

—— 38. To repeal Regulation 5 of 1832 of the Bengal Code, and to make certain provisions rendered necessary by the transfer of the Delhi Territory to the Administration of the Chief Commissioner of the Punjab. Passed December 11.

ACT 39. For the better recovery of Arrears of Revenue under Ryotwar Settlements in the Madras Presidency. Passed December 11.

—— 40. For making better provision for the care of the Persons and Property of Minors in the Presidency of Fort William in Bengal. Passed December 11.

—— 41. To amend Regulation 10 of 1829 of the Bengal Code for the collection of Stamp Duties. December 30.

1859.

ACT 1. For the amendment of the Law relating to Merchant Seamen. Passed January 25.

—— 2. To amend Act 30 of 1858 to provide for the Administration of the Estate, and for the Payment of the Debts of the late Nabob of the Carnatic. Passed February 5.

—— 3. For conferring Civil Jurisdiction in certain cases upon Cantonment Joint Magistrates, and for constituting those Officers Registers of Deeds. Passed February 7.

—— 4. To make further Provision for the Removal of Prisoners. Passed February 10.

—— 5. To empower the Holders of Ghatwalee Lands in the District of Beerbhoom to grant Leases extending beyond the period of their own possession. Passed March 4.

—— 6. To alter the Duties of Customs on Goods Imported or Exported by Sea. Passed March 14.

—— 7. To empower the Governor of Bombay in Council to appoint a Magistrate for certain districts within the Zillah Ahmedabad.

—— 8. For simplifying the Procedure of the Courts of Civil Judicature not established by Royal Charter. Passed March 22.

—— 9. To provide for the Adjudication of Claims to Property seized or forfeited. Passed April 30.

—— 10. To amend the Law relating to the Recovery of Rent in the Presidency of Fort William in Bengal. Passed April 29.

—— 11. To improve the Law relating to Sales of Land

for Arrears of Revenue in the Lower Provinces under the Bengal Presidency. Passed May 4.

ACT 12. To make better Provision for the Trial of Pilots, at the Presidency of Fort William in Bengal, for Breach of Duty. Passed May 4.

—— 13. To provide for the Punishment of Breaches of Contract by Artificers, Workmen, and Labourers in certain cases. Passed May 4.

—— 14. To provide for the Limitation of Suits. Passed May 4.

—— 15. For granting exclusive Privileges to Inventors. Passed May 17.

—— 16. To explain Act 30 of 1858 to provide for the Administration of the Estate and for the Payment of the Debts of the late Nabob of the Carnatic. Passed June 18.

—— 17. To amend the Law for the realisation of Revenue from Abkaree in the Island of Bombay. Passed July 16.

—— 18. To amend the Law relating to Offences declared to be punishable on conviction before a Magistrate. Passed July 25.

—— 19. An Act to continue in force until the end of the year 1859 Act 28 of 1857, relating to the importation, manufacture, and sale of Arms and Ammunition, and for regulating the right to keep or use the same. Passed August 12.

—— 20. For the suppression of Outrages in the District of Malabar in the Presidency of Fort St George. Passed August 31.

—— 21. For providing for the exercise of certain Powers by the Governor-General during his absence from his Council. Passed September 3.

—— 22. To amend Act 1 of 1852 for the consolidation and amendment of the Laws relating to the Customs under the Presidency of Bombay. Passed September 3.

—— 23. To alter the Rates of Duty on Goods Imported or Exported by Land from certain Foreign Territories into or from the Presidencies of Madras and Bombay respectively. Passed September 3.

ACT 24. For the better regulation of the Police within the Territories subject to the Presidency of Fort St George. Passed September 6.

—— 25. To prevent the Overcrowding of Vessels carrying Native Passengers in the Bay of Bengal. Passed December 14.

—— 26. To continue in force for a further period Act 28 of 1857. Passed December 14.

—— 27. To continue in force for a further period Acts 14 of 1857, 16 of 1857, and 17 of 1857. Passed December 14.

—— 28. To revive and continue in force for a further period Act 33 of 1857, to make further provision relating to Foreigners. Passed December 26.

1860.

ACT 1. To empower the Governor-General in Council to increase the Rate of Duty on Salt imported into the North-western Provinces of the Presidency of Bengal. Passed January 11.

—— 2. To amend the Law relating to the Carriage of Passengers by Sea. Passed January 15.

—— 3. To empower Sessions Judges to pass Sentence in certain cases without reference to the Sudder Court. Passed January 16.

—— 4. To amend Act 8 of 1859 for simplifying the Procedure of the Courts of Civil Judicature not established by Royal Charter. Passed January 23.

—— 5. To amend Act 3 of 1857 relating to Trespasses by Cattle. Passed February 8.

—— 6. To amend Act 19 of 1847, Articles of War for the Native Army. Passed February 23.

—— 7. To enable Joint-Stock Banking Companies to be formed on the principle of Limited Liability. Passed February 24.

—— 8. For regulating the establishment and management of Electric Telegraphs in India. Passed March 12.

ACT 9. To make Provision for the speedy determination of certain Disputes between Workmen engaged in Railway and other Public Works and their Employers. Passed March 12.

—— 10. To amend Act 7 of 1859, to alter the Duties of Customs on Goods Imported or Exported by Sea. Passed March 12.

—— 11. To enforce the fulfilment of Indigo Contracts, and to provide for the appointment of a Commission of Inquiry. Passed April 9.

—— 12. Relating to the Emigration of Native Labourers to the British Colony of St Vincent. Passed April 26.

—— 13. To repeal certain Laws relating to the Jurisdiction of the Zillah Court of Furruckabad. Passed April 26.

—— 14. To provide for the Execution of Process within the premises occupied by H.M. the King of Oude. Passed April 26.

—— 15. To amend and extend Act 22 of 1836, relating to the levy of a Toll on Boats, Rafts, and Floats passing through the Circular and Eastern Canals. Passed April 26.

—— 16. To amend Act 14 of 1856. Passed April 26.

—— 17. To repeal Act 5 of 1858, for the punishment of certain Offenders who have escaped from Jail, and of Persons who shall knowingly harbour such Offenders, and to make certain provisions in lieu thereof. Passed April 26.

—— 18. To continue in force for a further period of Three Months Act 21 of 1859 for providing for the exercise of certain powers by the Governor-General during his absence from his Council. Passed April 26.

—— 19. To amend Act 22 of 1855 for the regulation of Ports and Port-Dues ; and Act 7 of 1858, for the levy of Port-Dues at Ports within the Presidency of Fort St George. Passed May 1.

—— 20. For settling Promissory Notes of the Government of India, producing an annual income of one lac of rupees, and a mansion-house and hereditaments called

Mazagon Castle, in the Island of Bombay, late the property of Sir Jamsetjee Jejeebhoy, Baronet, deceased, so as to accompany and support the title and dignity of a baronet, lately conferred on him and the heirs-male of his body by Her present Majesty Queen Victoria, and for other purposes connected therewith. Passed May 1..

ACT 21. For the Registration of Literary, Scientific, and Charitable Societies. Passed May 21.

—— 22. To remove certain Tracts on the Eastern Border of the Chittagong District from the Jurisdiction of the Tribunals established under the general Regulations and Acts. Passed May 21.

—— 23. To amend Act 21 of 1856, to consolidate and amend the Law relating to the Abkaree Revenue in the Presidency of Fort William in Bengal. Passed May 23.

—— 24. For the solemnisation of Marriages in India by Ordained Ministers of the Church of Scotland. Passed May 23.

—— 25. For the levy of Port-Dues in the Port of Bassein. Passed May 23.

—— 26. To amend Act 8 of 1855 relating to the Office and Duties of Administrator-General. Passed May 31.

—— 27. For facilitating the collection of Debts on Successions, and for the security of Parties paying Debts to the Representatives of deceased Persons. Passed June 25.

—— 28. For the establishment and maintenance of Boundary Marks, and for facilitating the settlement of Boundary Disputes in the Presidency of Fort St George. Passed June 29.

—— 29. To continue in force Act 28 of 1857. Passed June 30.

—— 30. To remove the Pergunnahs of Koonch and Calpee in Zillah Jalour from the operations of the General Regulations. Passed July 5.

—— 31. Relating to the manufacture, importation, and sale of Arms and Ammunition, and for regulating the right to keep and use the same, and to give power of disarming in certain cases. Passed July 17.

ACT 32. Relating to Emigration to the British Colony of Natal. Passed July 24.

—— 33. For imposing Duties on Profits arising from Property, Professions, Trades, and Offices. Passed July 24.

—— 34. To indemnify Officers of Government and other Persons in respect of Fines and Contributions levied, and acts done by them during the late disturbances. Passed August 2.

—— 35. Relating to the Transportation of Convicts. Passed August 2.

—— 36. To consolidate and amend the Law relating to Stamp Duties. Passed August 2.

—— 37. To repeal Act 16 of 1859. Passed August 11.

—— 38. To explain Act 30 of 1858, to provide for the Administration of the Estate and for the Payment of the Debts of the late Nabob of the Carnatic. Passed August 11.

—— 39. To amend Act 32 of 1860, for imposing Duties on Profits arising from Property, Professions, Trades, and Offices. Passed August 18.

—— 40. To amend Act 36 of 1860. Passed September 11.

ADDIBOR, Gulstone, Esq., Governor of Bombay from 1700 to 1709.

AFFGHANISTAN. Shah Soojah restored to his throne by the British, May 8, 1839.

—— storm of Ghuznee, July 23, 1839.

—— Dost Mahomed surrenders himself, 1840.

—— outbreak at Cabul, Nov. 2, 1841.

—— British agree to evacuate Affghanistan, and treaty signed, Dec. 11, 1841.

—— murder of Sir W. Macnaghten, Dec. 23, 1841.

—— British army began to retreat, Jan. 6, 1842.

—— —— totally destroyed, Jan. 13, 1842.

—— —— was reinforced at Peshawur, April 1842.

—— Khyber Pass forced, April 6, 1842.

AFFGHANISTAN, Affghans defeated at Jugdulluck, Sept. 8, 1842.

—— British colours hoisted on the Bala-Hissar at Cabul, Sept. 16, 1842.

—— Istaliff taken, Sept. 29, 1842.

—— British army return to Ferozepore, Dec. 17, 1842.

AGRA fort and town occupied by General Lake, Oct. 17, 1803.

—— residents compelled to take refuge in the fort, and kept in a state of siege by the Neemuch mutineers from 2d July to the 10th of October 1857.

—— Battle of Agra; Kotah contingent repulsed, July 5, 1857.

AHMEDABAD, in Goojerat, taken by assault by Colonel Goddard, in 1780, but was given back to the Mahrattas; reverted to the British on the overthrow of the Peishwa in 1818.

AHMEDNUGGUR captured by General Wellesley in August 1803, but was afterwards returned to the Peishwa, and finally surrendered to the H.E.I.C., June 13, 1817.

AHMUTZ, Colonel, employed by Governor-General and Council to resist process of the Supreme Court, 1779.

AISLABIE, WILLIAM, General of Bombay from 1709 to 1724.

AJMERE ceded to the H.E.I.C., 1817.

AKBAR, born 1543; began to reign 1556; died 1605.

ALEXANDER THE GREAT invaded India, B.C. 327.

ALI HUSSEIN appointed, by the will of the Nabob of the Carnatic, heir of his property and the government of the Carnatic, 1801.

ALIPORE great jail built, 1810.

ALIWAL, battle of, Jan. 28, 1846.

ALLAHABAD seized by the Vizier of Oude, 1753.

—— was surrendered to the British, February 1765.

—— a portion reserved for the Emperor Shah Allum, but the whole passed by treaty to the H.E.I.C. in 1801.

—— native troops mutinied at this station on the 4th of June 1857, when the European inhabitants fled to the fort, which was relieved on June 11 by Colonel Neill.

ALLAHABAD declared the capital of the North-west Provinces in May 1858.

—— Treaty of 1765.

ALLEE MOHUN, right of tribute ceded to the British, 1821.

ALLOWALLEE, confiscation of, 1848.

ALLYGHUR taken from the French, 4th September 1803.

ALMEYDA FRERE, first Portuguese Viceroy in India, landed 1505.

ALMORAH taken by Colonel Nicholls, April 25, 1815.

ALOMPRA drove the Peguans from Burmah and founded a dynasty, 1753.

ALWERDI KHAN, Nabob of Bengal; died April 1756.

ALWUR, treaty at, between Rao Rajah and H.E.I.C., 1803.

AMBOOR defended by Captain Calvert against Hyder Ali, 1767.

—— surrendered to Hyder Ali, January 1781.

AMBOYNA taken by the British, 1796; again in 1810.

—— restored to the Dutch, 1814.

—— massacre of, February 27, 1622-23.

AMEER SINGH was refused his claim to be Rajah of Tanjore, 1798.

—— treaty concluded between the British Government and the real heir, the adopted son of Ameer's elder brother, in 1798.

—— and the administration of Tanjore assumed by the British, October 20, 1799.

AMHERST, Lord, arrived in Calcutta as Governor-General, August 1, 1823.

—— commenced the first war with Burmah, Mar. 5, 1824.

—— quelled a mutiny at Barrackpore, November 2, 1824.

—— concluded a treaty with the King of Oude, 1825.

—— created an Earl in 1826.

—— concluded a treaty with Siam, July 20, 1826.

—— British Government relations with Nagpore, settled Dec. 1826.

—— quitted India, March 10, 1828.

AMHERST began to be built, 1826.

ANDAMAN ISLANDS, measures adopted for clearing them and making a settlement, 1793.

—— declared to be too unhealthy, and settlement withdrawn, 1796.

—— made a penal settlement, 1858.

ANDERSON, Hon. G. W., Governor of Bombay from 27th April 1841 to 9th June 1842.

ANDERSON, Mr D., concluded a treaty with the Mahrattas, 1780 ; it was afterwards set aside.

ANGOOL became tributary to the English in 1804.

ANGRIA, the pirate, was seized with his wife and family, and all the stores he had taken from the H.E.I.C., 1756.

ANJAR ceded to the English, 1816.

—— new treaty of, 1822.

—— all claim given up by H.E.I.C., 1832.

ANNESLEY, Governor of Bombay from 1692 to 1698.

ANTGURH made tributary to the British, 1804.

APPA SAHIB ascended the musnud of Nagpore in 1817.

—— dethroned and sent to the British provinces in 1818.

ARCOT-TOWN taken by Clive, August 30, 1751.

—— besieged and taken by Hyder Ali, October 30, 1780.

—— Nabob of, defeated by the French, 1744 ; died, 1748.

AREENG or AURUNG, battle of, October 7, 1804.

ARGAUM, battle of, 28th November 1803.

ARIKERA, near this place Lord Cornwallis obtained a victory over Tippoo Sahib, May 14, 1791.

ARMEGON, factory built by the H.E.I.C., 1628.

ARNALLA FORT taken by General Goddard in 1781.

ARRACAN, earthquakes in, 1763 and 1833.

—— annexed by the British, January 2, 1826.

ARTHUR, Sir G., Bart., Governor of Bombay from June 9, 1842, to August 6, 1846.

ASHTEE, battle of, February 19, 1818.

ASIATIC SOCIETY founded by Sir William Jones, 1784.

ASSAM ceded by the Burmese to the British, February 1826.

—— a portion of Upper Assam, however, was not finally annexed until 1838.

ASSEERGURH taken from Scindia by Colonel Stevenson, 1803.

—— restored to him by treaty, 1803.

—— surrendered to General Doveton, 9th April 1819.

ATTOCK FORTRESS erected by Akbar, 1581.

AUCHMUTY, Sir SAMUEL, Commander-in-Chief, Madras, September 27, 1810; appointed to command an expedition sent against Batavia, 1811.

AUCKLAND, Lord, Governor-General from March 4, 1836, to February 28, 1842; died 1849.

AUNGIER, GERALD, President of Surat and of Bombay, 1669.

AURUNGABAD, English convoy made prisoners at, October 4, 1804.

AURUNGZEBE appointed to rule the Deccan, 1638.

—— obtained the Imperial throne, 1658; born 1614; died 1707.

AVA, British Ambassador sent to, 1855.

AZIM, the grandson of Aurungzebe, sold the villages of Chuttanuttee and Calcutta to the British in 1700.

AZIMGHUR yielded by treaty to the H.E.I.C., November 10, 1801.

AZIMOOL DOWLAH raised by the British Government to the musnud of Arcot in 1801.

AZOFF AL DOWLAH became Nawab Vizier of Oude in January 1775; died 1797.

B

BAGHAT, Ghoorkas expelled from, 1815.

—— under British rule, 1849.

BAHAWULPORE, Khan of, voluntarily placed himself under British protection, 1838.

BAICULL (Madras Presidency) came into possession of the H.E.I.C., 1799.

BAILLIE, Colonel, defeated by Hyder Ali and taken prisoner, September 9, 1780.

BAIRD, Major-General, commanded the assault on Seringapatam, May 4, 1799.

Baird, Major-General, appointed to command the expedition to Egypt, 1801; died 1829.

Bairseah ceded to the Dhar State, 1819.

—— to the H.E.I.C., on yearly payment of one lac of rupees, 1821.

Baitool ceded to the British, 1818.

Bajee Rao Peishwa signed the Treaty of Bassein, December 31, 1802.

—— signed the Treaty of Poona on June 13, 1817.

—— broke the Treaty and fled from his capital, November 17, 1817.

—— attacked British detachment under Captain Staunton and was defeated, January 1, 1818.

—— his dominions annexed by British Government 1818.

—— surrendered to the English, 1818.

Baker, Mr, Chairman of the Court of Directors in 1749, and from 1752 to 1756.

Balaghat Districts came under British rule, part in 1800 and the rest in 1841.

Balasinore came partially under British control during the minority of the Nawab in 1818.

—— was restored to him in 1846.

Balasore yielded by the Dutch to the English, 1846.

Banasa, on the Jumna, nearly destroyed by the fall of a precipice, 1816.

Bancoorah, the northern part of this district was ceded to the English by Meer Cossim, 1760.

—— the southern division by Shah Allum in 1765.

Bancoot Island attacked and conquered by Commodore James, 1755.

Banda came under British rule, 1802.

Bandsa placed under British superintendence, 1802.

Bangalore, siege of, began March 11, 1791.

—— taken, March 20, 1791.

Bank of Bombay incorporated by Act 3 of Government, February 17, 1840.

Baonee, H.E.I.C. obtained possession of, 1802.

Barabuttee captured by the British under Colonel Harcourt, October 14, 1803.

BARAMAHAL ceded to the British by Tippoo Sultan, 1792.

BAREE, granted by treaty to the Rana of Dholpore in 1805.

BAREILLY, Mohammedan outbreak in 1815; near this place was also fought the battle of Futtygunge between the English and Rohillas in 1774.

—— came under the British Government in 1801.

—— taken by rebels, June 1, 1857.

—— recaptured by Sir Colin Campbell, May 5, 1858.

BARING, F., Chairman of the Court of Directors, 1792.

BARKER, Sir R., assisted Clive in putting down a mutiny among the European officers of the Bengal Army, 1765.

BARLOW, Sir GEORGE HILARS, Bart., Governor-General from October 10, 1805, to July 31, 1807; Governor of Madras from December 24, 1807, to May 21, 1813.

BARNARD, General, commanded besieging army before Delhi, 1857.

—— died, September 20, 1857.

BARODA TOWN besieged for ten days, 1802.

—— treaty signed between the British Government and the Guicowar, April 21, 1805.

—— rite of Suttee abolished in, February 12, 1840.

BARRACKPORE, portion of the Bengal Native Army mutinied at, 1824.

—— and again in 1857.

BARREEAL, treaty between the British and the Bheels, 1803; latter consent to pay tribute, 1824.

BASSEIN, surrendered to General Goddard on December 11, 1780.

—— treaty of, signed December 31, 1802.

—— (Pegu) taken by the English, May 19, 1852.

BATHURST, Mr, President of the Board of Control, January 12, 1821, to February 5, 1822.

BATTLE of Agra, July 5, 1857; and October 10, 1857.

—— Almorah, April 17, 1858.

—— Aliwal, January 28, 1846.

—— Allyghur, October 5, 1857.

—— Alumbagh, February 21, 1858.

BATTLE of Areeng or Aurung, October 7, 1804.
—— Argaum, November 28, 1803.
—— Ashtee, February 19, 1818.
—— Assaye, September 23, 1803.
—— Bameean, September 18, 1840.
—— Banda, April 19, 1858.
—— Bangalore, December 6, 1791.
—— Bareilly, May 5, 1858.
—— Barodia, January 31, 1858.
—— Bednore, May 3, 1783.
—— Beejapoor, September 5, 1858.
—— Betwa, April 17, 1858.
—— Bithoor, August 16, 1857.
—— Bolundshuhur, September 27, 1857.
—— Budlee-ke-serai, June 9, 1857.
—— Bunkegaon, October 8, 1858.
—— Bushemtgunge, August 5, 1857.
—— Buxar, October 22, 1764.
—— Calpee, May 22, 1858.
—— Candahar, May 22, 1842.
—— Canouj, October 23, 1857.
—— Cawnpore, July 17, 1857.
—— Chanda, October 30, 1857; and February 19, 1858.
—— Chillianwallah, January 13, 1849.
—— Coel, August 28, 1803.
—— Corygaum, January 1, 1818.
—— Deeg, November 13, 1804.
—— Delhi, September 8, 1803.
—— Dhoondea Khera, December 24, 1857.
—— Dilkoosha, November 15, 1857; and March 3, 1858.
—— Dubba, March 24, 1843.
—— Ferozeshuhr, December 21, 22, 1845.
—— Furruckabad, November 17, 1804.
—— Futtegunge, April 23, 1774.
—— Futtehpore, July 13, 1857.
—— Geriah, August 2, 1763.
—— Ghazee-ood-deen Nuggur, May 30, 1851.
—— Gondah, February 4, 1858; and April 13, 1859.
—— Goojerat, February 21, 1849.

BATTLE of Goomtee, passage of the, December 21, 1858.
—— Goruckpore, January 6, 1858.
—— Goura-Alipore, June 21, 1858.
—— Gungeree, December 14, 1857.
—— Gwalior, June 17, 1858.
—— Heoree, September 15, 1858.
—— Huldwanee, February 11, 1858.
—— Hurchundpore, December 8, 1858.
—— Indose, October 14, 1801.
—— Jellalabad, April 6, 1842.
—— Jhansi, April 1, 1858.
—— Jheegun, April 10, 1858.
—— Jhelum, the, January 13, 1849.
—— Jugdespore, May 29, 1858.
—— Kalla Nuddee, January 2, 1858.
—— Kankar, April 6, 1858.
—— Khoord Cabul Pass (forced), January 8, 1841.
—— Kooshab, February 8, 1857.
—— Khyber Pass (forced), April 5, 1842.
—— Khudjnia, November 1, 1857.
—— Kineyree, May 20, 1848.
—— Kirkee, November 5, 1817.
—— Kirwee, August 13, 1858.
—— Koonch, May 7, 1858.
—— Koondye, November 14, 1858.
—— Kundoo, March 5, 1858.
—— Kutchla Ghaut, March 11, 1858.
—— Laswarree, November 1, 1803.
—— Maharajpore, December 29, 1843.
—— Mahidpore, December 21, 1817.
—— Malavelly, March 27, 1757.
—— Meeanee, February 17, 1843.
—— Meeangunge, October 5, 1857.
—— Meergunge, May 5, 1858.
—— Mohammerah, March 26, 1857.
—— Moodkee, December 18, 1845.
—— Mundesore, November 22, 24, 1857.
—— Mungarwar, September 21, 1857.

BATTLE of Mungrowlie, October 9, 1858.
—— Mynpoorie, December 27, 1857.
—— Nagpore, November 16, 1817.
—— Nanparah, December 31, 1858.
—— Nawabgunge, June 13, 1858.
—— Nuggur, April 30, 1858.
—— Nujuffghur, August 25, 1857.
—— Oodeypore (Chota), December 1, 1858.
—— Oonao, July 29, 1857.
—— Pagham Mew, February 9, 1826.
—— Panniput, 1526 and 1761.
—— Plassey, June 23, 1757.
—— Poona, November 16, 1817.
—— Porto Novo (or Cuddalore), July 1, 1781.
—— Prome, December 2, 1825; and October 9, 1852.
—— Pundoo Nuddee, July 15, 1757.
—— Punniar, December 29, 1843.
—— Puttialee, December 17, 1857.
—— Rajghur, September 15, 1858.
—— Rajpoor, November 14, 1858.
—— Ramnuggur, November 22, 1842.
—— Rangoon, December 7, 1824, and 1852.
—— Ranode, December 17, 1858.
—— Saunpore, December 26, 1857.
—— Selimpore, September 23, 1858.
—— Sobraon, February 10, 1846.
—— Soodalalpore, December 4, 1848.
—— Sundeela, October 7, 1858.
—— Trincomalee, September 26, 1767.
—— Wandewash, January 20, 1760.

BAYLEY, Hon. W. B., acted as Governor-General from March 13 to July 4, 1828.

BAYLEY, Mr, Chairman of the Court of Directors, 1840.

BEBB, Mr, Chairman of the Court of Directors, 1817.

BECKWITH, Sir T. S., K.C.B., Commander-in-Chief of Bombay from December 3, 1829, to June 31, 1832.

BEDNORE taken and pillaged by Hyder Ali in 1763.
—— occupied by General Matthews, 1783.

Bednore surrendered to Tippoo Sultan, May 3, 1783.

Beekaneer, Rajah of, entered into treaty with H.E.I.C., 1818.

—— invaded by George Thomas, 1799.

Beejapoor taken and destroyed by Aurungzebe, 1686.

Beerbhoom granted by Shah Allum to the H.E.I.C., 1765.

—— came under British rule, 1818.

Behar came under British rule, 1765.

Behree granted by H.E.I.C. to a Bhoondela Rajpoot feudatory, 1811.

Behut (Bundelcund) taken by the English in 1812.

—— granted by them as a jaghire to its former possessors, the Brahmins, 1817.

Beja, Ghoorkas expelled from, 1815.

Belgaum (Bombay Presidency) Fort taken by Sir T. Munro, 1818.

Bellary ceded by treaty with the Nizam to the H.E.I.C. in 1800.

—— inhabitants removed to native town, 1816.

Benares ceded by the Nabob of Oude to the English, 1775.

—— insurrection against Warren Hastings in, 1781.

—— Sanscrit College instituted, 1792.

Bencoolen, settlement made in, by the H.E.I.C., 1682.

—— York Fort erected, 1690.

—— Marlborough Fort in 1714.

—— settlement destroyed by the French, 1760.

—— came under Governor of Bengal in 1801.

—— ceded to the Netherlands, 1825.

Bengal conquered by the slave-kings of Delhi, 1206.

—— subdued by Baber, 1529.

—— first British factory established in, 1656.

—— taken by Sooraj-oo-Dowlah, 1756.

—— recovered from him by Clive, 1757.

—— conferred by the Emperor of Delhi on the H.E.I.C. by treaty of Allahabad, August 12, 1765.

—— great famine in, 1770, 1771.

—— finally ceded by the Nawab of Oude, 1801.

Bentinck, Lord W., born September 14, 1774.

BENTINCK, Lord W., Governor of Madras, August 30, 1803.
—— ordered the troops of Madras to wear a new head-dress, which order was followed by the mutiny at Vellore, July 10, 1806.
—— recalled September 11, 1807.
—— Governor-General from July 4, 1828, to March 20, 1835.
—— abolished Suttee in the British Provinces in 1829.
—— abolished corporal punishment in the army, 1834.
—— left India, March 19, 1835.
—— died, June 17, 1839.

BENYON, RICHARD, Governor of Madras from 1735 to 1744.

BERNADOTTE, General, served in India as a sergeant, and was taken prisoner by the British, June 25, 1783.

BERUMBAH, became tributary to the British Government, 1803.

BHADINYA FORT, dismantled, 1836.

BHAGUL or BAGUL, Ghoorkas expelled from, and the Rajah restored by the British, 1815.

BHAUBEIR, came partially under British rule in 1819.
—— more directly in 1826.

BHAUGULPORE (Bengal), Cossim Ali defeated in, by the English, 1763.
—— ceded to the H.E.I.C. by Shah Allum, 1765.

BHEWANNEE or BOWANEE FORT, taken by the English in 1809.

BHOOJ (Cutch), earthquake in, 1819.

BHOONDEE (Rajpootana), acknowledged the supremacy of the British Government, and promised to act in co-operation with it, 1818.

BHOONG BARA (Scinde), conferred by the H.E.I.C. on Bhawul Khan in acknowledgment of his tried friendship, 1843.

BHOPAL STATE, assisted the English army under General Goddard, 1778.
—— Nawab of, petitioned, but without success, for British protection, 1809.
—— siege of, by Scindia's army, 1813.

BHOPAL STATE; treaty with the British Government signed, and promise of protection given, 1818.

BHOTAN, treaty of peace signed between the British Government and Rajah of, 1774.

BHURTPORE besieged by the British troops, and assaulted four times without success, January 3, 1805.

—— Rajah makes peace with General Lake, April 10, 1805.

—— finally taken by Lord Combermere, January 18, 1826.

BHUTNEER taken by George Thomas, 1800.

BHUTTIANA brought into connection with the British Government, 1803.

—— invaded by Colonel Adams in consequence of the lawless state of the country, 1810.

—— North-western portion granted to the British, 1844.

BIDJEYGHUR surrendered to Major Popham, 1781.

BIE, Colonel, Danish Governor of Serampore, died May 18, 1805.

BIJAWAR, grant of, made by H.E.I.C. to the Rajah of Bundelcund, 1811.

—— confirmed to his nephew in 1833.

BIJNA, its obligation to pay tribute to Jhansi cancelled, 1821.

BIJNOOR, Rohilla power over this territory destroyed by the British, and the country subjected to the Government of Oude, 1774.

—— ceded to H.E.I.C., 1802.

BINDRABAN sacked by the Affghans, 1757.

BITHOOR lapsed to the British, 1851.

—— Nana Sahib defeated at, and the place burnt, July 1857.

BLACK HOLE, Calcutta, a hundred and forty-six British confined in, June 20, 1756.

BOAD (Cuttack) subject to the British Government, 1804.

BOARD OF COMMISSIONERS for the Affairs of India, Presidents of:

—— Viscount Sydney, from August 12, 1784, to 1790.

—— Mr W. W. Granville, from 1790 to 1792.

—— Right Hon. Henry Dundas, from 1792 to 1801.

—— Viscount Lewisham, from April 1801 to July 1802.

BOARD OF COMMISSIONERS for the Affairs of India, Presidents of—*continued.*

—— Viscount Castlereagh, from July 1802 to February 1806.

—— Earl of Minto, February 1806 to July 1806.

—— Right Hon. Thomas Grenville, July 1806 to September 30, 1806.

—— Right Hon. George Tierney, from September 1806 to April 1807.

—— Right Hon. D. Sunds, from April 1807 to July 1809.

—— Lord Harrowby, from July 1809 to November 1809.

—— Right Hon. Robert Dundas, from November 1809 to April 1812.

—— Earl of Buckinghamshire, from April 1812 to June 1816.

—— Right Hon. George Canning, from June 1816 to January 1821.

—— Right Hon. Charles Bathurst, from January 1821 to February 1822.

—— Right Hon. C. W. W. Wynn, from February 1822 to February 1828.

—— Viscount Melville, from February 1828 to September 1828.

—— Lord Ellenborough, from September 24, 1828, to 1830.

—— Right Hon. Charles Grant, from December 6, 1830, to December 20, 1834.

—— Lord Ellenborough, December 20, 1834, to 1835.

—— Sir J. C. Hobhouse, Bart., April 29, 1835.

—— Lord Ellenborough, September 9, 1841, to October 28, 1841.

—— Lord W. V. Fitzgerald de Vesey, October 28, 1841, to May 23, 1843.

—— Lord Ripon, May 23, 1843, to July 10, 1846.

—— Right Hon. Sir J. C. Hobhouse, July 10, 1846, to February 3, 1852.

—— Right Hon. Fox Maule, February 3, 1852, to March 1852.

Board of Commissioners for the Affairs of India, Presidents of—*continued.*

—— Right Hon. J. C. Herries, March 1852 to December 1852.

—— Right Hon. Sir Charles Wood, December 1852 to February 22, 1855.

—— Right Hon. Vernon Smith, February 22, 1855, to February 22, 1858.

—— Lord Ellenborough, February 22, 1858, to May 11, 1858.

—— Lord Stanley, last President of the Board, May 12, 1858, to August 1, 1858.

Bodham, Rawson Horn, first Governor of Bombay, from 1784 to January 9, 1788.

Bogoorah or Bograh granted to H. E. I. C. by Shah Allum, 1765.

Bolan Pass, army of the Indus marched through, 1839.

Bolarum, mutiny of Hydrabad force under Brigadier C. Mackenzie, September 21, 1855.

Bolundshuhur ceded to the H.E.I.C. by the treaty of Serjee Angengaum, December 30, 1803.

Bombay ceded to Charles II. by the King of Portugal, 1661.

—— granted to the E.I.C., 1669.

—— declared the chief seat of the British Government in India, 1683.

—— Captain Keigwin, Commander of the Company's troops, revolted and proclaimed the authority of the Crown, 1683.

—— restored to the H.E.I.C., 1684.

—— seat of Government removed from Surat to, 1685.

—— declared a Presidency subject to Bengal, 1773.

—— formed into a government, 1784.

Bombay, Governors of:

—— Sir G. Oxenden, from 1665 to 1667.

—— Mr Gerald Aungier, 1667.

—— Thomas Rolt, from 1667 to 1680.

—— Sir J. Child, Bart., from 1680 to 1690.

—— Mr John Vaux, 1690.

—— Bart Harris, from 1690 to 1692.

BOMBAY, Governors of—*continued.*
—— Annesley, from 1692 to 1698.
—— Sir J. Gayer, from 1698 to 1702.
—— Sir Nicholas White, from 1702 to 1707.
—— Sir H. Oxenden, Bart., from 1707 to 1709.
—— Mr William Aislabie, from 1709 to 1724.
—— Charles Boone, from 1724 to 1731.
—— William Phipps, from 1731 to 1734.
—— Robert Cowan, 1734.
—— John Horne, from 1734 to 1739.
—— Stephen Law, from 1739 to 1742.
—— William Wake, 1742.
—— John Geekie, from 1742 to 1750.
—— Richard Bouchier, from 1750 to 1760.
—— Charles Crommelin, from 1760 to 1767.
—— Thomas Hodges, from 1767 to 1776.
—— William Hornby, from 1776 to 1784.
—— R. H. Boddam, from 1784 to January 9, 1788.
—— Andrew Ramsay, from January 9, 1788, to September 6, 1788.
—— Sir W. Medows, K.B., from September 6, 1788, to January 21, 1790.
—— Sir R. Abercrombie, K.B., from January 21, 1790, to November 26, 1792.
—— George Dick, from November 26, 1792, to November 9, 1795.
—— John Griffith, from November 9, 1795, to December 27, 1795.
—— Jonathan Duncan, from December 27, 1795, to August 11, 1811.
—— George Brown, from August 11, 1811, to August 12, 1812.
—— Sir Evan Nepean, Bart., from August 12, 1812, to November 1, 1819.
—— Honourable Mountstuart Elphinstone, from November 1, 1819, to 1827.
—— Sir John Malcolm, K.C.B., from November 1, 1827, to 1830.
—— Sir T. S. Beckwith, K.C.B., from 1830 to 1831.

Bombay, Governors of—*continued.*

—— John Romer, 1831.

—— Earl of Clare, from March 2, 1831, to 1835.

—— Sir Robert Grant, G.C.H., from March 17, 1835, to 1838.

—— James Farish, from July 11, 1838, to 1839.

—— Sir J. Rivett Carnac, Bart., from 1839 to 1841.

—— Sir W. H. Macnaghten, Bart., 1841.

—— Honourable G. W. Anderson, from April 27, 1841, to 1842.

—— Sir George Arthur, Bart., from June 9, 1842, to 1846.

—— Honourable L. R. Reid, August 6, 1846.

—— Mr G. R. Clerk, from January 23, 1847, to 1848.

—— Viscount Falkland, from May 1, 1848, to 1853.

—— Lord Elphinstone, 1853 to May 11, 1860.

—— Sir G. R. Clerk, May 11, 1860.

Boodawul (Candeish) lapsed to the British, 1855.

Boondee, Rajah of, aided the English against Holkar, 1804, and again in 1817.

—— treaty between the Rajah of Boondee and the English, 1818; by the treaty of Gwalior in 1844 a portion of the state was ceded to the H.E.I.C.

Boone, Charles, Governor of Bombay from 1724 to 1731.

Boorhanpoor (Gwalior) occupied by the English, 1803.

—— restored to Scindia, 1803.

Bosanquet, Chairman of the Court of Directors, 1798, 1803, and 1811.

Boscawen, Admiral, made an unsuccessful attack on Pondicherry in 1748.

—— took possession of St Thomé in 1749.

Boscawen, Captain, defeated the Bareilly insurgents, April 25, 1816.

Boucher, Charles, Governor of Madras from 1767 to 1770.

Bouchier, Richard, Governor of Bombay, 1750 to 1760.

Boulton, Mr, Chairman of the Court of Directors, 1765, 1766, 1768, and 1773.

Bourquin, Louis, defeated by General Lake, when the former was in Scindia's service, September 11, 1803.

BRADSHAW, Colonel, intrusted to carry forward political arrangements at Katmandoo, 1814.

—— entered into a treaty on behalf of the British Government with the Nepaulese, 1815.

BRERETON, Major, took Conjeveram, 1759.

—— captured Wandewash in 1759.

—— fell at the battle of Wandewash, 1760.

BROACH (Bombay Presidency), taken by Akbar, 1583.

—— by the Mahrattas, 1685.

—— by the English 1772.

—— ceded by them to Scindia, 1783.

—— lastly, ceded by Scindia to the English, 1803.

BROWN, GEORGE, Governor of Bombay from August 11, 1811, to August 12, 1812.

BUCHANAN, Rev. C., D.D., Vice-Provost of the College of Fort William, 1800.

BUCKINGHAMSHIRE, Earl of, President of Commissioners for the Affairs of India from April 4, 1812, to June 4, 1816.

BUDDHA, religion of, introduced into India, B.C. 956.

BUDGE BUDGE, occupied by the British in 1756.

BUKKUR FORTRESS temporarily ceded to the English in 1839.

—— finally came into possession of the H.E.I.C. at the annexation of Scinde in 1843.

BULDEO SINGH, succeeded his brother as Rajah of Bhurtpore, 1823.

—— died, January 26, 1825.

BULWUNT SINGH, established as Rajah of Bhurtpore in 1826.

BUNDELCUND divided, after 1734, into several independent chieftainships.

—— by the treaty of Bassein the H.E.I.C. obtained Humeerpore and Banda, 1802.

—— the Peishwa surrendered to the British his right over the territory in 1817.

—— Jhansi, &c., formally annexed, 1858.

BUNGANAPILLY, British agent sent to administer justice in, 1843; withdrawn, 1848.

BUNSWARRA, treaty of, between Mahrattas and British Government, 1818.
BURDA (Guzerat), granted to the E.I.C. for military purposes, 1809.
BURDWAN under British control, 1760.
BURGES, J. S., Chairman of the Court of Directors, 1791.
BURHAMPOOR (Central India), yielded to the force of British arms, October 16, 1803.
BURMAH; the Burmese invaded British territory, 1794.
—— demanded the withdrawal of British troops from the island of Shapooree, January 1823.
—— war declared, 1824.
—— peace concluded by the treaty of Yandaboo, January 26, 1826.
—— second Burmese war began, 1852.
—— Burmese refused terms of peace, May 7, 1853.
—— yield to the British and hostilities ceased, without treaty, June 30, 1853.
—— send an ambassador to Calcutta, 1854.
—— receive British embassy in Ava, 1855.
BURN, Colonel, defended Delhi against Holkar in 1804.
BURN, Colonel H. R., Military Governor of Delhi, September 1857.
BUSSAHIR, tributary to the British since 1815.
BUXAR, battle of, October 23, 1764.

C

CABUL under British influence, 1839.
—— insurrection in, November 2, 1841.
—— recovered by General Pollock, September 16, 1842.
CACHAR lapsed to the British, 1830.
CADAVAUD or CARWAR (Madras Presidency), the English established a factory in, 1663.
CALCUTTA given to the H.E.I.C. in 1700.
—— taken by Sooraj-oo-Dowlah, June 1756.
—— Supreme Court of Judicature established, 1774.
—— Government House erected, 1804.

CALCUTTA Cathedral erected in 1840.
—— Town-Hall, about 1806.
—— Madrussah, by Warren Hastings, 1781.
—— first lighted with gas in 1858.

CALICUT, first place in India visited by any European (Vasco di Gama), 1498.
—— the H.E.I.C. established a factory in, 1616.
—— conquered by Hyder Ali, 1766.
—— inhabitants threw off his yoke, 1773.
—— retaken by Tippoo Sultan, 1789.
—— Tippoo Sultan defeated near Calicut by Colonel Hartley, 1790.
—— ceded by treaty to the British, 1792.

CALLIAUD, Captain, relieved Trichinopoly, when besieged by the French, by an extraordinary march, 1757.

CAMAC, Colonel, defeated Scindia, 1780.

CAMBAY became tributary to E.I.C., 1802.

CAMPBELL, Sir ALEX., K.B., Governor of Madras from April 6, 1786, to February 7, 1789.

CAMPBELL, Sir ARCHIBALD, appointed to command expedition against Ava, 1824.
—— concluded a treaty with the Burmese Emperor, 1826.

CAMPBELL, Colonel, defended Mangalore against Tippoo Sultan, 1783.
—— surrendered the town in January 1784.
—— died March 23, 1784.

CAMPBELL, Mr, was Chairman of the Court of Directors in 1831.

CAMPBELL, Sir COLIN, commanded the Peshawur district in 1851 and 1852; was Commander-in-Chief of the British army in India, July 1857 to June 4, 1860.

CANARA came under British rule, 1799.

CANDAHAR occupied by the English, 1839.

CANDEISH, famine in, 1803.
—— annexed by the British Government, 1818.
—— Bheel corps formed in, 1825.
—— formed into a distinct Zillah, 1849.

CANNANORE (Madras Presidency) garrisoned by the English, 1784, but subsequently returned to its former possessors; having, however, become the property of Tippoo, it was besieged and taken by General Abercromby, 1791.

CANNING, Earl, Governor-General from March 1856 to 1861.

CANNING, Mr, President of Board of Control from June 4, 1818, to January 12, 1821.

CARANGOLY taken by the English, 1780.

CARANJA ISLAND ceded to Great Britain by the Portuguese, 1661.

—— but returned to them until 1683.

—— when it fell into the hands of the Mahrattas, was taken by the English in 1774, and ceded to them by the Mahrattas in 1775 and 1776.

CAREY, Dr WILLIAM, born August 17, 1761.

—— landed in India, November 11, 1793.

—— died, June 9, 1834.

CARNAC, Sir J. R., Bart., Governor of Bombay from 1839 to 1841.

—— Chairman of the Court of Directors, 1836 and 1837.

CARNATIC, Meer Cossim Mohamud Ali assigned all his revenues to the H.E.I.C. in 1781.

—— title became nominal, 1801.

—— last Nabob of, died 1855.

CARTRIDGE disturbances began at Dum-Dum, Jan. 22, 1857.

—— proclamation, March 27, 1857.

CASHMERE conquered by Akbar, 1586.

—— by the Affghans, 1752.

—— by the Sikhs, 1819.

—— ceded to the British, 1845.

—— granted by them, on certain conditions, to Gholab Singh, 1845.

—— earthquake in, 1828.

—— famine, 1833.

CARRICAL surrendered to English, April 5, 1760.

—— restored to the French in 1814.

CAWNPORE, town of, constituted a military cantonment, 1775.

—— came under British rule, 1801.

—— massacre (boat), June 27, 1857.

Cawnpore, second massacre, in the town, July 15, 1857.
Champaneer, sustained twelve years' siege, from 1472 to 1484.
—— taken by the English, September 17, 1802.
—— restored to Scindia, 1803.
Champion, Major, defeated the Rohillas in Rohilcund, April 23, 1774.
Chanda, in Nagpore, was captured on the 20th April 1818 by Colonel Adams.
Chandernagore occupied by the French, about 1700.
—— taken by Clive, 1757.
—— restored to France, 1763.
—— retaken by the English, 1793.
—— again restored to the French, 1816.
Chandhairee Fort taken by the Mahrattas, 1816.
—— assigned by treaty for the use of the Gwalior contingent, 1844.
—— captured by Brigadier Stuart, March 17, 1858.
Chandore Fort surrendered to British, 1804.
—— subsequently restored to Holkar, it was again ceded by him to the English at the treaty of Mundisore, 1818.
Charnock, Job, formed an English settlement in Calcutta, 1690.
—— died, January 10, 1692.
Charshut in connection with British Government, 1819.
Charter, first East Indian, granted, December 31, 1600.
Chattwye or Chetwa (Madras Presidency) taken by Hyder Ali from the Dutch, 1776.
—— ceded to the British, 1792.
Cheduba (Arracan) occupied by the English, 1824.
Cheetoo, last of Pindarrees killed, February 1819.
Chellumbarm taken by the English, 1760.
—— attacked unsuccessfully, 1781.
Cheyt Singh deprived of his Zemindarry, 1781.
Child, Sir John, Bart., Governor of Bombay, 1680.
Chillianwallah, battle of, January 13, 1849.
Chinalgarh, East India Company's soldiers defeated by the Ghoorkas, 1814.
Chinsurah, Dutch defeated at, 1759.

CHINSURAH, ceded by the King of the Netherlands to the English, 1824.

CHIRGONG (Bundelcund) Fort attacked by the English; abandoned by the enemy, and consequent surrender of the town, April 1841.

CHIRKAREE (Bundelcund) ceded by the Peishwa to East India Company, 1803.

CHITTAGONG, granted by the Nabob of Bengal to the East India Company, 1760, confirmed by Shah Allum in 1765.

CHITTLEDROOG, mutiny of British troops, 1809.

CHOLERA first appeared in India, 1817.

CHONDA taken from the Mahrattas by the English, December 29, 1843.

CHONRAR partially under British control in 1819, and more immediately, 1826.

CHONSA, battle of, between Humaiyoon and Sheer Shah, 1539.

CHOOARS, rising of, 1832-33.

CHOTA NAGPORE, serious disturbances in, 1832.

CHOWREGURH ceded to the English, 1818.

—— besieged by 2000 Gonds, and held by 30 men, 1818.

CHUNAR FORT besieged, 1764, in possession of E.I.C., 1768.

CHUPATTIES sent over the North-west, Feb. 25, 1857.

CHUPPRA granted by treaty to Ameer Khan, 1818.

CHURCH, first built in Calcutta, about 1715.

—— destroyed, 1756.

CHUTTANUTTEE given to the E.I.C., 1700.

CIRCARS, the five northern, were obtained by the French in 1753, and remained in their possession till 1759, when they were seized by Clive.

—— secured by treaty, 1766.

CLARE, Earl of, Governor of Bombay from March 21, 1831, to March 17, 1835.

CLARKE, Sir ALURED, exercised the chief functions of Government in Calcutta during the absence of Lord Mornington, from 1798 to 1801.

—— Commander-in-Chief in Madras, 1796.

—— Chairman of the E.I.C. in 1835.

CLAVERING, General, appointed member of Council, Bengal, 1774.
—— Commander-in-Chief of the army in India, October 27 to August 30, 1777.
—— presided at the examination of Nuncomar, 1775.
—— assumed the office of Governor-General, 1776.
—— died, August 30, 1777.

CLERK, Sir G. R., Governor of Bombay from January 23, 1847, to May 1, 1848.
—— reappointed, May 11, 1860.

CLIVE, Lord ROBERT, born September 29, 1725.
—— arrived at Madras as writer in the E.I.C. service in 1744.
—— obtained an ensign's commission, 1747.
—— captured Arcot, August 30, 1751.
—— took Conjeveram, 1751.
—— defeated the French at Covespah, 1751.
—— captured Covelong and Chingleput, 1752.
—— returned to England, 1752.
—— returned to India and entered on his duties of Governor of Fort St David, 1755.
—— retook Calcutta, January 2, 1757.
—— conquered Sooraj-oo-Dowlah at the battle of Plassey, June 23, 1757.
—— defeated the Dutch at Chinsurah, 1759.
—— again left India for England, February 1760.
—— returned to India as Irish Viscount and head of the Government of Bengal, 1764.
—— obtained from the Emperor Shah Allum the Dewanny of Bengal, Behar and Orissa in April 1765.
—— founded the military fund, and suppressed a conspiracy among the officers of the army, 1766.
—— abolished the system of private trade, January 1767.
—— quitted India, January 1767.
—— his proceedings attacked, 1772.
—— a committee formed to examine the charges against him, 1773.
—— committed suicide, November 2, 1774.

CLIVE, Lord POWIS, Governor of Madras, from September 5, 1799, to August 30, 1803.

CLOSE, Captain, negotiated a treaty with Scindia in 1817.

CLOSE, Colonel, concluded the treaty of Bassein with the Peishwa, December 31, 1802.

—— assumed the command of the army of the Deccan, 1805.

COCHIN, conquered by Hyder Ali, and transferred by his son to the British, to whom it became tributary, 1792.

—— transit duties abolished in, 1836.

—— British resident appointed, 1839.

—— Town taken by the British, 1796.

COEL, a town in the British district of Allygurh, taken possession of by the English in 1803.

COIMBATORE FORT, surrendered by Lieutenant Chalmers to Kummeroodeen, a General of Tippoo Sultan, November 3, 1791.

COLEBROOKE, Chairman of the E.I.C., 1769, 1770, and 1772.

COLES, rising of, January 1858.

COLLEGE, FORT WILLIAM, established, 1800.

—— abolished, 1854.

COLLETT, JOSEPH, Governor of Madras from 1717 to 1720.

COLONY IN CHINGLEPUT, acquired by the French Imperial East India Company of Ostend in 1750. The town was captured by Clive in 1752.

COLVIN, J. R., Lieutenant-Governor North-west Provinces, died, September 9, 1857.

COMBERMERE, first Viscount, was born 1773.

—— entered the army, 1791.

—— assumed the chief command of the army in India, October 7, 1825.

—— captured Bhurtpore, December 18, 1826.

COMPANY, EAST INDIA, first Charter granted, December 31, 1600.

—— abolished, August 1, 1858.

—— last meeting as governing body, August 30, 1858.

CONCAN, came under British rule on the fall of the Peishwa in 1818.

CONFLANS, M., defeated by Colonel Forde, and yielded Masulipatam to the same officer soon after, April 1759.

CONJEVERAM, taken by Clive in 1751.

CONJEVERAM, abandoned by the English and burnt by the French, 1757.

—— retaken from the French by Major Brereton, 1759.

—— plundered by Hyder Ali, 1780.

CONTROL, BOARD OF, established, August 1784.

—— abolished, August 1858.

CONTROL, BOARD OF, Presidents of :

—— Mr Canning, from June 4, 1816, to January 21, 1821.

—— Charles Bathurst, from January 12, 1821, to February 5, 1822.

—— C. W. W. Wynne, from February 5, 1822, to February 4, 1828.

—— Viscount Melville, from February 4, 1828, to September 17, 1828.

—— Lord Ellenborough, from September 17, 1828, to November 22, 1830.

—— Charles Grant, from November 22, 1830, to November 1834.

—— Lord Ellenborough, from December 20, 1834, to April 29, 1835.

—— Sir J. C. Hobhouse, from April 29, 1835, to September 9, 1841.

—— Lord Ellenborough, from September 9, 1841, to October 28, 1841.

—— Lord W. V. Fitzgerald de Vesey, from October 28, 1841, to May 23, 1843.

—— Lord Ripon, from May 23, 1843, to July 10, 1846.

—— Sir J. C. Hobhouse, from July 10, 1846, to February 3, 1852.

—— Right Hon. Fox Maule, from February 3, 1852, to March 1852.

—— J. C. Herries, from March 1852, to December 1852.

—— Sir Charles Wood, from December 1852, to February 22, 1855.

—— Vernon Smith, from February 22, 1855, to February 22, 1858.

Control, Board of, Presidents of—*continued.*
—— Lord Ellenborough, from February 22, 1858, to May 11, 1858.
—— Lord Stanley, from May 11, 1858, to August 1, 1858.
Conway, Captain, murdered by Vizier Ali in 1799.
Coondapoor conquered by Hyder Ali in 1763, and by the British in 1799.
Coorg annexed to the British possessions in 1832.
Coote, Sir Eyre, captured Hooghly in 1757.
—— captured Arcot in 1760.
—— took Pondicherry from the French, 1761.
—— appointed Commander-in-Chief of the Bengal army, March 25, 1779, to April 26, 1783.
—— defeated Hyder Ali, July 1, 1781.
—— died, April 26, 1783.
Copool surrendered to General Medows in 1791.
Coringa, severe deluge in, 1787 and 1832.
Cornwallis, Marquis of, born December 31, 1738.
—— Governor-General from September 12, 1786, to October 28, 1793.
—— and from July 30 to October 5, 1805.
—— proclaimed war against Tippoo Sultan in 1790.
—— captured Bangalore, March 20, 1791.
—— took Hooliordroog, June 18, 1791.
—— besieged Seringapatam, February 5, 1792.
—— signed a treaty with Tippoo Sultan on March 18, 1792.
—— made decennial settlement perpetual in Bengal, March 22, 1793.
—— quitted India, October 28, 1793.
—— died at Ghazeepoor, October 5, 1805.
Corrie, Daniel, arrived in India, 1806.
—— first Bishop of Madras, 1835.
—— died, February 5, 1837.
Corygaum, battle of, January 1, 1818.
Cossimbazar, English factory taken by the Nawab of Bengal, 1756.
Cossinaut Baboo, commenced actions in the Supreme Court against Warren Hastings and other persons, November 1779; withdrew them in January 1780.

Court, Captain J., commanded land force attacking Amboyna, February 16, 1810.

Court of Directors elected in October 1600, and direct the engagement of a fleet to trade to the East Indies.

—— On the 31st December 1600 they obtain a charter from Queen Elizabeth.

—— On the 31st May 1609 they obtain a charter from King James.

—— In 1612-13 they form the first joint-stock, and the second joint-stock in 1617-18.

—— 1618-19. They answer the memorial of the Dutch East India Company, who complain of their interference with the natives of India.

—— 1624-25. They petition the king for power to try their servants by common and martial law.

—— 1627-28. They petition the king for his interposition with the States-General.

—— 1628-29. They petition the House of Commons for redress from the Dutch.

—— 1631-32. They establish the third joint-stock.

—— 1635-36. They petition the king against the licence granted to Sir William Courten.

—— 1636-37. They disapprove of the convention made with the Portuguese, and petition the king for redress for the depredations of Courten's ships.

—— 1639-40. They procure the revocation of Courten's licence, and project a fourth joint-stock.

—— 1640-41. They fail to procure a fourth joint-stock.

—— 1641-42. They apply to Lord Cottington and the House of Commons for payment of the bonds granted by the king as security for the pepper debt.

—— 1649-50. They project a fourth joint-stock, and make application to the Council of State for the renewal of their privileges.

—— 1650-51. They petition Parliament, and are referred to the Council of State.

—— 1652-53. They petition against the Dutch, and are encouraged by the Council of State.

COURT OF DIRECTORS—*continued.*

—— 1653-54. They petition Cromwell to be allowed to make reprisals on the Dutch.

—— 1654-55. They petition Cromwell for the cession of Bombay and Bassein.

—— 1655-56. They lend Cromwell £50,000, and have their rights acknowledged.

—— 1656-57. The Protector promises a new charter.

—— 1657-58. They unite with the "merchant adventurers" and form a new joint-stock.

—— 1660-61. They petition King Charles the Second to restore their charter and grant exclusive privileges.

—— 1661. Charter granted April 3.

—— 1662-63. Gave instructions to Sir George Oxenden to assist the Earl of Marlborough in taking possession of Bombay, and entered into an agreement with the Royal African Company.

—— 1666-67. The Court address the king to issue a proclamation against Sir Edward Winter.

—— 1667-68. They receive from King Charles the Island of Bombay.

—— 1668-69. They memorialise the Privy Council on the treaty of Breda.

—— 1669-70. They new-model their system of administration at Surat, and despatch ships to renew the trade at Bantam.

—— 1671-72. They draw up regulations for Bombay and St Helena, and attempt to trade with China, Tonquin, Tywan, and Japan.

——1672-73. They memorialise the king, praying that their affairs may be taken into consideration in the event of any treaty with the Dutch.

—— 1673-74. They prohibit the Bombay Government from making any treaty with the Portuguese.

—— 1674-75. They give instructions to Surat and Fort St George for their conduct towards the native powers, Dutch and Portuguese, and prohibit seamen from settling at Bombay as colonists.

COURT OF DIRECTORS—*continued.*

—— 1675-76. They form a new plan of administration for Surat and Bombay.

—— 1676-77. They obtain a charter from the King to establish a mint at Bombay.

—— 1678-79. They reduce the Presidency of Surat to an agency, and attempt to trade at Canton.

—— 1680-81. They form a new plan for the government of Fort St George and for Bantam.

—— 1681-82. They restore Surat to the rank of a Presidency.

—— 1682-83. They dispute with the Levant Company; attempt to cultivate flax in Bengal; and recommend a bank to be established at Madras.

—— 1683-84. They send two fleets to recover the Persian and Bantam trade.

—— 1684. They attempt to check interlopers, and appoint a secret committee to report to the King on the Bombay revolts. They also determine to make Acheen the centre of the southern trade.

—— 1685-86. They resolve to prosecute interlopers in England. They order seat of government to be transferred from Surat to Bombay. They censure their agents in Bengal for timidity, and order that hostilities shall be commenced against the Mogul and Nabob of Dacca in order to obtain possession of Chittagong. They also plan to make war in Siam, and attempt the conquest of Salsette.

—— 1686-87. They determine to establish a factory at Mergee and a mint at Madras, the last by the permission of the King. They establish a settlement at Bencoolen in Sumatra.

—— 1687-88. They determine to constitute Bombay a regency, and obtain a charter for erecting Madras into a corporation.

—— 1688-89. They determine to rule at Bombay and reduce Surat to an agency. They encourage the Armenians in Persia, and the settlers at St Helena are advised to remove to Bombay.

Court of Directors—*continued.*

—— 1689-90. They oppose the scheme for the creation of a new East India Company.

—— 1693-94. They obtain a new charter on the 7th October 1693, and enter into an obligation to export £150,000 of British manufactures. They obtain an additional charter on November 11, 1693, for augmenting their stock.

—— 1694-95. They obtain an additional charter, and establish at Madras a post office and insurance office. They fixed on Chutanutty as the Company's chief residence in Bengal.

—— 1696-97. They memoralise the Lords Justices on the piratical depredations in the Indian seas.

—— 1697-98. They apply to the King for authority to extirpate the pirates.

—— 1698-99. They (the London Company) are opposed by a rival company under the name of the English East India Company. They refuse to coalesce with the English Company. The Court of Directors of the English Company copy the constitution of the London East India Company.

—— 1699-1702. Ignoble rivalry of the two companies.

—— 1702-1703. The London Company and the English Company come to terms, but their coalition not effected till 1707-8.

—— In 1717 they send an embassy to Furacksere to solicit an extension and conformation of the Company's privileges.

—— In 1722 they oppose and overthrow the company known as the Ostend Company.

—— In 1730 they consent to reduce the interest on the debt due to them by the public from five per cent to four per cent, and advance £200,000. Their charter was therefore again renewed.

—— In 1732 they reduce their dividend from 8 to 7 per cent.

—— In 1743 they propose to lend Government £1,000,000

COURT OF DIRECTORS—*continued.*
at three per cent, provided their charter is extended to 1780. The Government consent.

—— In 1767 they offer to pay Government £400,000 a-year for two years, and in 1769 this agreement was extended for two years more.

—— In 1772 they apply to the Treasury for a loan. The dividend is restricted to six per cent until the money advanced to the Company is repaid. The Court of Directors were to be elected for four years only—six members annually. In same year they disapprove of the conquest of Tanjore.

—— In 1783 they petition Parliament to be excused from paying £400,000 a-year to the public, and beg a loan of £900,000. They are placed under the Board of Control. A secret Committee of the Directors is formed.

—— 1793. The Court of Directors obtain an extension of the charter till March 1, 1814. They advise Lord Cornwallis to inquire into the rights and interests of the Zemindars.

—— In 1795 they are authorised to add to the amount of their floating debt.

—— 1796. Authorised to add two millions to their capital stock, but the increase never effected.

—— In 1797 they issue additional bonds.

—— 1806. They recall Lord William Bentinck, the Governor of Madras. They appoint Sir George Barlow to the Governor-Generalship, but the appointment is vacated by royal authority. They refuse to appoint the Earl of Lauderdale Governor-General, and appoint Lord Minto.

—— 1813. Their charter is renewed for twenty years, but they are no longer permitted to have the exclusive right of trading to the East Indies.

—— 1833. Their charter renewed for twenty years, but they are prohibited from trading.

—— 1853. They obtain a renewal of their charter.

—— 1855. The Civil Service thrown open to competition.

—— 1858. They cease to exist.

Court of Directors, Chairmen of:

Chauncy, 1748.
Baker, 1749.
Chauncy, 1750.
Drake, 1751.
Baker, from 1752 to 1756.
Godfrey, 1756.
Payne, 1757.
Sulivan, 1758.
Godfrey, 1759.
Sulivan, 1760 and 1761.
Rous, 1762.
Dorrien, 1763.
Rous, 1764.
Boulton, 1765 and 1766.
Rous, 1767.
Boulton, 1768.
Colebrooke, 1769 and 1770.
Purling, 1771.
Colebrooke, 1772.
Boulton, 1773.
Wheler, from October 1773 to 1775.
Harrison, 1775.
Roberts, 1776.
Wombwell, 1777 and 1778.
James, 1779.
Devaynes, 1780.
Sulivan, 1781.
Gregory, 1782.
Fletcher, from July 31, 1782, to Nov. 1783.
Smith, from November 26, 1783, to 1785.
Devaynes, 1785.
Michel, 1786.
Motteux, 1787.
N. Smith, 1788, to Dec. 2.
Devaynes, 1789.
S. Lushington, 1790.
J. S. Burges, 1791.
F. Baring, 1792.
Devaynes, 1793 and 1794.
Lushington, 1795.
D. Scott, 1796.
H. Inglis, 1797.
Bosanquet, 1798.
Lushington, 1799.
Inglis, 1800.
Scott, 1801.
Mills, September 1801.
Robarts, 1802.
Bosanquet, 1803.
Elphinstone, 1804.
Grant, 1805.
Elphinstone, 1806.
Parry, 1807 and 1808.
Grant, 1809.
Astell, 1810.
Bosanquet, 1811.
Inglis, 1812.
A. Thornton, 1813.
Elphinstone, 1814.
Grant, 1815.
Reid, 1816.
Bebb, 1817.
Pattison, 1818.
Marjoribanks, 1819.
Robinson, 1820.
Reid, 1821.
Pattison, 1822.
Wigram, 1823.
Astell, 1824.
Marjoribanks, 1825.
Robinson, 1826.
Lindsay, 1827.
Astell, 1828.

Court of Directors, Chairmen of—*continued.*

Loch, 1829.
Astell, 1830.
Campbell, 1831.
Ravenshaw, 1832.
Marjoribanks, 1833.
Loch, 1834.
Tucker, 1835.
Clarke, 1836.
Carnac, 1837 and 1838.
Lushington, 1839.
Jenkins, 1840.
Bayley, 1841.
Lyall, 1842.
Lushington, 1843.
Cotton, 1844.
Shepherd, 1845.
Willock 1846.
Hogg, 1847.
Tucker, 1848.
Lushington, 1849.
Galloway, 1850.
Shepherd, 1851 and 1852.
Hogg, 1853 and 1854.
Oliphant, 1855.
Macnaghten, 1856.
Sikes, 1857.
Mangles, 1858.

Cowan, Robert, Governor of Bombay, 1734.

Cradock, Sir John, Commander-in-Chief of Madras army, October 17, 1804.
—— recalled September 17, 1807.

Crillon, M., captured on November 20, 1759, the island of Seringham.

Crommelni, Charles, Governor of Bombay from 1760 to 1767.

Cuddalore, in the southern division of Arcot, occupied by the French in 1758. It came into the possession of the English in 1760.

Cuddapah came into possession of the E.I.C. in 1800.
—— disturbances about landed property, 1846.
—— jail erected, 1813.

Culna, great fire at, lasting three days, December 24, 1838.

Culpee taken by the British from the Mahrattas, but again restored to them, 1778.
—— transferred to E.I.C., 1802.
—— successfully besieged by Nana Govind Rao, 1803.
—— restored to E.I.C., 1806.
—— taken by rebels, 1857.
—— recaptured by Sir H. Rose, May 23, 1858.

Cumoona surrendered to English, 1807.

Cutch, earthquake in, 1819.

CUTCH, 1st treaty with E.I.C., 1809.
—— 2d do. do., 1816.
—— 3d do. do., 1819.
—— 4th do. do., 1822.
—— slave trade declared illegal, 1835.

CUTTACK became tributary to the Rajah of Nagpore, 1750.
—— subject to the Mahrattas (directly), 1756.
—— occupied by the British under Col. Harcourt, 1803.
—— great inundation in, 1831.

D

DACCA was conferred on the British by Shah Allum, 1765.
—— commercial residency in, discontinued, 1817.
—— was demanded by the Burmese, 1823.
—— 73d N.I. mutinied in, 1857.

DALHOUSIE, ninth Earl of, Commander-in-Chief, 1829.

DALHOUSIE, tenth Earl of, born, 1812.
—— arrived as Governor-General, January 19, 1848.
—— annexed the Punjab, March 29, 1849.
—— created Marquis, 1849.
—— annexed Sattara, 1849.
—— annexed Pegu, December 20, 1852.
—— annexed Nagpore, February 1855.
—— annexed Oude, February 7, 1856.
—— left India, March 6, 1856.

DALTON, Captain, took possession of Seringham, June 3, 1752.

DALZELL, General, commanded at Barrackpore in the mutiny of 1824.

DAMAN sacked by the Portuguese, 1531.
—— rebuilt, 1558.

DANCE, Captain, defeated, with a fleet of E.I. merchantmen, a French squadron, February 15, 1804.

DARAPORAM, in Coimbatore, surrendered to Colonel Fullarton in July 1790.

DARJEELING ceded to the British, 1835.

DARWAR overrun by Hyder Ali, 1776.

—— incorporated in British dominions, 1818.

—— northern talooks transferred to Belgium, 1836.

—— American cotton successfully introduced into, 1842.

—— 25,000 acres sown with New Orleans seed, 1847.

DARWAR TOWN captured by Hyder Ali, 1778.

—— by a British force, 1791.

—— ceded to the E.I.C., 1818.

D'AUTUEIL, M., surrendered to Clive, 1752.

DAVIDSON, A., Governor of Madras from January 4, 1785, to April 6, 1786.

DAVIS, Captain, captured Carangoly, January 20, 1781.

DAVIS, magistrate of Benares, attacked by Vizier Ali's followers, 1799.

DE CAEN surrendered Mauritius to General Abercrombie, December 2, 1810.

DEEG, battle of, November 13, 1804.

—— Fort, in Bhurtpore, besieged by Lord Lake, December 16, 1804.

—— taken by Lord Lake, December 23, 1804.

—— taken by Lord Combermere, and dismantled, 1826.

DEHRA DHOON invaded by the Ghoorkas, 1803.

—— taken by the English, 1815.

—— grants of land to civilians in, 1837.

DEHRA, Ghazee Khan ceded, with rest of Punjab, 1849.

DELHI became seat of Mohammedan Government (Ghor dynasty), 1193.

—— burned by Tamalane, 1398.

—— occupied by Baker, 1526.

—— sacked by Nadir Shah, 1739.

—— taken by Mahrattas, 1758.

—— Shah Allum entered, December 25, 1771.

—— with its Emperor, taken by the British from the Mahrattas, September 12, 1803.

—— Mahrattas attacked unsuccessfully, October 1804.

—— last king of, ascended its throne, 1837.

DEHLI, last king of, massacred Europeans, May 1857.
—— taken, with king, September 20, 1857.
—— last king of, transported to Tounghov, December 3, 1858.
—— canal restored, 1820.
DEOGHAM, treaty of, signed December 17, 1803.
DEONELLY, birthplace of Tippoo Sultan, 1753.
DEONTUL ceded to British, April 1815.
DERBEND, scene of religious Sikh war, 1827.
DEVAYNES, Chairman of Court of Directors, 1780, 1785, 1789, 1793, and 1794.
DEVICOTTAH taken by the English, 1749.
—— taken by the French, June 1758.
—— recovered by the English, February 1760.
DHAMEE tributary to E.I.C., 1815.
DHAMONEE taken by General Marshall, 1818.
DHAR, first treaty between this state and the British Government signed, 1819; second, 1821.
—— confiscated by Lord Canning, October 1857.
—— restored to Rajah by order of Court of Directors, June 22, 1858.
DHARWAR, *see* DARWAR.
DHOLPORE, treaty between the Rana and E.I.C., 1779.
—— fort captured by Major Popham, 1780.
—— taken by Scindia, 1784.
—— restored to the Rana, 1805.
DHOONDIAH, robber-chief, defeated by Colonel Wellesley, at Conahgull, September 10, 1800.
DHULEEP SINGH born, 1833.
—— succeeds as Rajah, 1843.
—— deposed, 1849.
DHURRUMPOOR became tributary to the British, 1802.
DICK, GEORGE, Governor of Bombay, November 26, 1792, to November 9, 1795.
DINAGEPORE granted to E.I.C. by Shah Allum, 1765.
DIRECTORS' COURT, *see* COURT OF DIRECTORS.
DOBBILI FORT stormed by the French, 1758.
DON, Lieutenant-Colonel, captured Tonk Rampoora, May 15, 1804.

Donabue unsuccessfully attacked by General Cotton, March 8, 1825.

—— taken by Sir A. Campbell, April 2, 1825.

—— English seamen and marines under Captain Lock repulsed, February 4, 1853.

Dongurpoor, treaty between the Mahrattas and English, 1818.

Dooblana, battle of, 1744.

Doveton, General, served in the war against Tippoo Sultan and Bajee Rao, the Peishwa; captured Asseergurh, April 9, 1819.

Dowlutpoor granted by the English to Mahomed Bhawul Khan, 1843.

Drake, Chairman of Court of Directors, 1751.

Drake, Mr, Governor of Calcutta, which he abandoned on the approach of Sooraj-oo-Dowlah, June 19, 1756.

—— received 240,000 rupees from Meer Jaffier in 1757.

Duncan, Jonathan, Governor of Bombay, December 27, 1795, to August 11, 1812.

Dupleix, Governor of Pondicherry, 1744.

—— appointed by Mozuffar Jung, Governor of all the provinces south of the Kistna, 1750.

—— planned the erection of a new town, 1751.

—— superseded, and left India, October 14, 1754.

Dupre, Mr, negotiated a treaty with Hyder Ali in 1769. The treaty signed by the Governor and Council of Madras, April 3; and by Hyder Ali, April 4.

Dupre, Josias, Governor of Madras from 1770 to 1773.

Durba Canal constructed, 1825.

Dutch East India Company formed in 1602.

—— Amboyna, Tidore, Ceylon, taken from the Portuguese in 1605; the Moluccas in 1603.

—— in 1759 they concluded a treaty with Meer Jaffier, and were defeated by Colonel Forde and Commodore Wilson, November 23, 1759.

—— in 1772, purchased the town Nagore from the Rajah of Tanjore; town surrendered in the same year. In

1789 sold the forts of Cranganore and Ayacottah to the Rajah of Travancore.

DUWARKA stormed by Colonel Faithfull, 1812.

—— evacuated, 1838.

—— recovered from the Waghers, November 1, 1859.

E

EARTHQUAKE, Calcutta, 1737.

EAST, Colonel, captured the fort of Anjar in 1815.

ECHAWUR (Malwa), ceded by the Peishwa to the English, and granted by them to the Nawab of Bhopal, 1818.

EDUR, treaty with the English, 1820.

EDWARDES, Lieutenant-Colonel H., born January 1820.

—— landed in Calcutta, January 1841.

—— subjugated the valley of Bunnoo, 1848.

—— defeated Moolraj before Mooltan, May 1848.

—— held down mutinous Sepoys in Peshawur, 1857.

EGYPT, an expedition left India for this country, under the command of General Baird, in 1801.

ELECTRIC TELEGRAPH commenced in India, 1852.

—— opened March 24, 1854.

—— between Sardinia and Malta, first used for accelerating news to India, November 24, 1857.

—— submarine cable laid between India and Ceylon, September 14, 1858; finished, October 12, 1858.

—— between Kurrachee and Aden, 1860.

ELLENBOROUGH, Lord EDWARD LAW, born 1790.

—— President of the Board of Control, from September 17, 1828, to November 22, 1830; from December 20, 1834, to April 29, 1835; from September 9, 1841, to October 28, 1841; and from February 22, 1858, to May 11, 1858.

—— Governor-General of India, from February 28, 1842, to June 15, 1844.

—— issued famous Somnauth proclamation, November 16, 1842.

—— took possession of the Gwalior Fort, January 4, 1844.

ELLENBOROUGH, Lord EDWARD LAW, recalled by the Court of Directors, May 6, 1844.

—— left India, August 1, 1844.

ELLIOT, Right Honourable HUGH, Governor of Madras from September 16, 1814, to January 10, 1820.

ELLORA ceded to the British, 1818.

—— granted by them to the Nizam, 1822.

ELPHINSTONE, Honourable W. F., Chairman of the Court of Directors, 1804, 1806, and 1814.

ELPHINSTONE, Honourable MOUNTSTUART, sent as ambassador to Cabul, 1809.

—— Resident at Poona, 1815.

—— Governor of Bombay from November 1, 1819, to November 1, 1827.

—— died, November 20, 1859.

ELPHINSTONE, Lord JOHN, Governor of Madras from March 1837 to September 24, 1842.

—— Governor of Bombay from June 1853 to May 11, 1860.

—— died, July 19, 1860.

ELWICK, NATHANIEL, Governor of Madras from 1721 to 1725.

ENORORE, battle of, 1760.

ERICK, came into the possession of the E.I.C., 1843.

EXHIBITION, Calcutta, January 1855.

F

FACTORY, English, established in Calcutta, 1686.

—— first, in Bengal, at Hooghly, 1656.

FALKLAND, Viscount, Governor of Bombay from April 27, 1848, to June 1853.

FAMINE, North-Western Provinces, 1838-39.

—— (great), Bengal, 1770-71.

FANCOURT, Colonel, murdered at Vellore, July 10, 1806.

FARISH, JAMES, Governor of Bombay, from July 11, 1838, to April 27, 1841.

FEROZESHUHR, battle of, December 21, 1845.

FEROZPOOR (Cis-Sutlej), lapsed to English, 1835.

Ferozpoor; interview between Runjeet Singh and Lord Auckland, November 1838.

Filor Fort, built by Runjeet Singh, 1809.

Fletcher, Sir Robert, took an active part in the mutinous proceedings of the European officers of the Bengal army in 1766.

—— he was brought to court-martial and cashiered, but afterwards restored; and in 1771 possessed the chief military command at Madras and a seat in Council.

—— returned to England in 1771, but again succeeded to the command in 1775.

—— Chairman of the Court of Directors from July 31, 1782, to November 26, 1783.

Flint, Lieutenant, saved Wandewash in 1781.

Flogging abolished in native army by Lord W. Bentinck, March 1834.

Forde, Colonel, gained the battle of Peddapore in 1759.

—— captured Masulipatam in the same year, and defeated the Dutch near Chinsura, in two engagements, on October 23 and 24, 1759.

Fort St David was purchased by the E.I.C. from a native prince in 1691. On the capture of Madras by the French in 1746, the Company's agent at this station assumed the control of all the Company's possessions in Southern India. In 1758 it was invested by sea and land by the French, and, after a short siege, surrendered on June 2.

Fort St George was built by Mr Francis Day on a piece of land granted by a native prince in 1639.

Fort William, *see* Calcutta.

Fort William College, established by Lord Wellesley, 1805.

—— abolished by order of the Court of Directors, 1854.

Francis, Mr Philip, was in 1774 nominated a member of Council in Bengal.

—— in 1780 he fought a duel with Warren Hastings and was wounded; he left India in December of the same year.

Fraser, Colonel Hastings, aided by Colonel Drummond, obtained the surrender of the island of Bourbon in

1810. He was shot before Asseerghur, at the siege of which place he commanded a column of attack, on March 24, 1819.

Fraser, William, Governor of Madras from 1709 to 1711.

Fraser, General, mortally wounded at Deeg in attack on Holkar's infantry and guns, November 13, 1804.

Fraser, Colonel **Frederick**, assaulted Dharwar in 1791; was repulsed, and died of disappointment.

Fraser, Commissioner, at Delhi, assassinated March 1835.

French East India Company, established 1664.

—— besiege and take Fort St George, September 10, 1746.

—— send out an expedition under Count Lally to extend their power in India; he arrives at Pondicherry April 28, 1758; and unsuccessfully attacks Madras, February 1759. Returns to France, January 1761; beheaded, May 6, 1766.

Fureedpoor granted to E.I.C. by Shah Allum, 1765.

Furruckabad taken by Ahmed Shah in 1749.

—— afterwards reverted to the Vizier of Oude, who transferred his claims to the H.E.I.C. in 1801.

—— invaded by Holkar, 1804.

—— town occupied by the British, 1802, in consequence of a treaty with the Vizier of Oude.

—— European residents of, massacred at Bhitoor, June 1857.

—— town retaken by Sir C. Campbell, January 3, 1858.

—— battle of, gained by Lord Lake over Holkar, November 17, 1804.

Futteghur, cantonment first established, 1777.

—— town attacked by Holkar, 1804.

—— 10th Bengal Native Infantry revolted at, June 18, 1857.

—— European refugees from, massacred at Cawnpore on June 27, 1857.

—— battle of, gained by Brigadier A. Hope, January 27, 1858.

Futtehpoor, a town and district between Allahabad and Cawnpore. Shuja-oo-Dowlah, Nawab of Oude, assigned this district to Shah Allum, emperor of Delhi, August 16, 1765.

FUTTEHPOOR; Shah Allum surrendered his right to the Mahrattas in 1772.

—— the H.E.I.C. and the Oude Nawab considered this as an infraction of the former treaty, and the country was accordingly retransferred to the Nawab on November 10, 1801.

—— the Oude Nawab conveyed the territory to the Company. The town was occupied by the rebels in 1857; but they were thence expelled by General Havelock on July 13, 1857.

FUTTYGUNGE, battle of, gained by Colonel Champion, April 23, 1774.

—— Rohilla Patans defeated at this place by the British troops under Sir Robert Abercromby, 1796.

FYZABAD; on June 8, 1857, the Native troops revolted, and the district and town were saved by Maun Singh.

—— the town was reoccupied by General Sir H. Grant, July 29, 1858.

FYZOOLA KHAN, Rohilla chief, guaranteed, in 1781, to furnish from 2000 to 3000 troops to assist the Oude Vizier. He was required shortly afterwards to furnish more troops than the treaty stipulated for, and having declined to do so, was declared in consequence to have forfeited the British protection. He died in 1795.

G

GANJAM obtained by the French, with the rest of the Five Circars, 1753.

—— ceded by Emperor of Delhi to E.I.C., 1765.

—— town of, epidemic in, 1815.

GARAKOTA surrendered to the British, 1818.

GAWILGHUR, a fort in Hydrabad; it was taken by storm by Colonel Stevenson and General Wellesley on December 15, 1803.

GAYER, Sir JOHN, Governor of Bombay from 1693 to 1704.

GEEKEI, JOHN, Governor of Bombay from 1742 to 1750.

GEORGEGURH; here its builder, George Thomas, was attacked by the Mahrattas, 1801.

GERIAH, the battle of, between Meer Cossim and the English, occurred on August 2, 1763. Meer Cossim was defeated.

GHAZEEPORE, granted to the E.I.C., 1764.

—— granted by the English to the Nawab Vizier of Oude, 1765; and again ceded by him to the E.I.C., 1775.

GHERIAH, a fortress on the Malabar coast, taken by the English in 1756, was given up in the same year to the Peishwa; and again acquired by the English, 1818.

GHUZNY, storm of, July 23, 1839.

GIBBS, Colonel, obtained a victory over General Janssens in Java on September 16, 1811.

GIFFORD, JOHN, first President of Madras, from 1683 to 1686.

GILLESPIE, Colonel, suppressed the mutiny at Vellore on July 10, 1806.

—— commanded a division of the army against Nepaul, and was mortally wounded at Kolunga on October 31, 1814.

GINGEE, a town in South Arcot, taken by the French in 1750.

—— the French yielded the town and fortress to Captain Stephen Smith in 1761.

GOA, the former capital of the Portuguese possessions in India. The town was seized by them February 25, 1510. It has ever since remained a Portuguese possession.

GOALPARA granted to E.I.C., 1765.

—— great fire in, 1838.

GODAVERY ANICUT, begun December 1846.

GODFREY, Chairman of the Court of Directors, 1756 and 1759.

GOHUD, in the territory of Gwalior. The Rana of the district made an alliance with the British Government, 1779. He was besieged there by Scindia in 1784, and compelled to surrender. Gohud also was seized by Scindia. A new treaty was made with the Rana by the Honourable East India Company in 1803; but subsequently Gohud was transferred to Scindia by Lord Cornwallis in 1805.

GOLDEN ROCK. This British post was attacked and carried by M. Artruc in 1753, but subsequently retaken by Major Lawrence.

GOLDSBOROUGH, Sir J., Governor of Madras, November 23, 1692, to 1693.

GOMM, Sir WILLIAM, Commander-in-Chief, December 6, 1851; born 1782. Left India, January 1856.

GOOMSOOR, having been tributary to the British, came at length under their rule, 1835.

GOORGAON district, chiefly ceded to E.I.C. on December 30, 1803; and the remaining portion lapsed to them, 1836.

GOORKHA TRIBE, established themselves in Nepal in 1768. In 1790 they invaded Thibet, but were driven out by the Chinese. A treaty of commerce was concluded with the Honourable East India Company, March 1, 1792, and a political alliance was entered upon between their government and the Thibet in October 1801. The alliance was formally dissolved in 1804. From that time they encroached upon British territory, but were compelled to sign a new treaty, and cede certain usurped territory, March 1816. In May 1857 Jung Bahadoor, the Prime Minister, at the instigation of Major Ramsay, volunteered to march to the relief of Lucknow and Cawnpore, then besieged by the rebels; his offer was declined by the Governor-General, and Cawnpore fell. Subsequently Lord Canning asked the King of Nepal for help, and Jung Bahadoor marched twenty regiments through Goruckpore and Oude to Lucknow. He had an interview with the Governor-General at Allahabad in April 1858, and finally returned to Nepal.

GORIHAR held in the Jaghire of the E.I.C. since 1807.

GORUCKPORE granted to the E.I.C. by the Government of Oude, November 10, 1801.

GORUCKPORE retaken by English, January 6, 1858.

GOUGH, Viscount HUGH, G.C.B., born 1779.

—— in command of a division of the Indian army, 1837.

—— Commander-in-Chief of British troops in China, 1841.

—— Commander-in-Chief of British army in India, August 11, 1843.

—— defeated the Mahrattas at the battle of Maharajpoor, December 29, 1843.

—— in conjunction with Lord Hardinge, defeated the Sikhs at Moodkee, December 18 ; Ferozeshah, December 21 and 22, 1845 ; and at Sobraon, February 22, 1846.

—— raised to the peerage as Baron Gough, April 1846.

—— subdued the Sikhs a second time at Gujerat, February 21, 1849.

—— created a Viscount, June 4, 1849.

—— succeeded by Sir C. J. Napier, May 7, 1849.

GOVERNORS-GENERAL :

—— Warren Hastings, from April 13, 1772, to February 1, 1785.

—— Mr Macpherson, February 1, 1785.

—— Earl Cornwallis, from September 22, 1786, to October 28, 1793.

—— Sir J. Shore (Lord Teignmouth), October 28, 1793, to March 12, 1798.

—— Sir A. Clarke, officiating from April 5, 1798, to May 17, 1798.

—— Earl of Mornington (Marquess Wellesley), from May 17, 1798, to July 30, 1805.

—— Marquess Cornwallis, from July 30 to October 5, 1805.

—— Sir G. H. Barlow, from October 10, 1805, to July 31, 1807.

—— Lord Minto, from July 31, 1807, to October 4, 1813.

—— Lord Moira (Marquess Hastings), from October 4, 1813, to January 9, 1823.

—— Hon. J. Adam, officiating from January 13 to August 1, 1813.

GOVERNORS-GENERAL—*continued.*

—— Lord Amherst, August 1, 1823, to March 10, 1828.

—— Hon. W. B. Bayley, officiating from March 13 to July 4, 1828.

—— Lord William Bentinck, July 4, 1828, to March 20, 1835.

—— Sir Charles Metcalfe, officiating from March 20, 1835, to March 4, 1836.

—— Lord Auckland, from March 4, 1836, to February 28, 1842.

—— Lord Ellenborough, February 28, 1842, to June 15, 1844.

—— W. W. Bird, officiating from June 15 to July 23, 1844.

—— Sir Henry Hardinge (afterwards Viscount), from July 23, 1844, to January 12, 1848.

—— Lord Dalhousie, January 12, 1848, to March 6, 1856.

—— Viscount Canning, March 6, 1856, to 1861.

GOVINDPORE, in Bengal, ceded to the H.E.I.C. in 1700, with the villages of Chuttanuttee and Calcutta, by Azim, grandson of Aurungzebe.

GRAEME, H. S., Governor of Madras from July 10, 1827, to October 18, 1827.

GRANT, Mr CHARLES, President of the Board of Commissioners for the Affairs of India from November 22, 1830, to November 1834.

—— Chairman of the Court of Directors in 1805, 1809, and 1815.

GRANT, Sir ROBERT, G.C.H., Governor of Bombay from March 17, 1835, to July 11, 1838.

GREGORY, Chairman of the Court of Directors in 1782.

GRENVILLE, Mr W. W., President of the Board of Commissioners for the Affairs of India from 1790 to 1792.

GRENVILLE, Mr THOMAS, President of the Board of Commissioners for the Affairs of India from July 15, 1806, to September 30, 1806.

GRIFFITH, JOHN, Governor of Bombay from November 9 to December 27, 1795.

Gujelhatti, a fort besieged and taken by the British, 1768; retaken by Hyder Ali, 1768.

Gujerat, battle of, February 21, 1849.

Gungadhur Shastry, chief minister of the Guicowar, selected to negotiate with the Peishwa in 1815.

—— murdered at Punderpore, July 14, 1815.

Gungeree, battle of, December 14, 1857.

Guntoor, a collectorate in Madras, ceded to the E.I.C. in 1765, by the Emperor of Delhi. The territory was not, however, acquired till 1788, when it was surrendered by the Nizam.

Guntoor, the principal place of the British district of the same name, rented of Basalut Jung in 1778. In 1788 surrendered to the British, in accordance with the firman of the King of Delhi in 1765.

Gurudwara, battle of, 1803.

Guzerat, sovereignty of, acquired in 1721 by Pelajee, Guicowar, commander of the Mahratta armies; he was murdered in 1732, and succeeded by his son Damajee, who renounced allegiance to the Peishwa. Syajee succeeded, but died without issue in 1792, when he was succeeded by his elder brother Govind Rao. In 1800, Annund Rao became Guicowar, but his illegitimate brother Canojee usurped the administration until expelled by Rawajee, who entered into relations with the Bombay Government; a convention signed between the Governments, March 15, 1802; a defensive alliance concluded April 21, 1805, the Guicowar agreeing to receive a permanent subsidiary force. The rite of suttee abolished by proclamation, February 12, 1840.

Gwalior, taken possession of by Madhajee Scindia in 1779.

—— the fort surprised by Captain Popham, August 3, 1780.

—— ceded to the Rana of Gohud in 1781.

—— captured by Scindia in 1784.

—— surrendered to the British in 1803 by the treaty of Serjee Anjengaum, and by them transferred to the Rana of Gohud.

Gwalior, in 1805 conferred on Dowlut Rao Scindia by Lord Cornwallis.
—— on the 4th January 1844 the fort was again occupied by the British; a contingent force, commanded by British officers, provided for by treaty of January 13, 1844.
—— present Maharajah ascended the musnud in 1853.
—— the contingent mutinied June 16, 1857, and massacred many Europeans.
—— the Maharajah fled to Agra, June 1, 1858.
—— reinstated by Sir Hugh Rose, June 20, 1858.

H

Hansi, rebuilt by George Thomas, 1798.
—— George Thomas besieged by the Mahrattas, and compelled to flee into British territory, 1801.
Hardinge, Sir H., born 1785.
—— Governor-General, July 23, 1844.
—— finally settled the purchase of the Danish settlements in India, February 22, 1845.
—— defeated the Sikhs at Ferozeshur, December 22, 1845, and at Sobraon, February 10, 1846.
—— created Viscount, May 4, 1846.
—— resigned government of India, 1847.
—— returned to England, January 12, 1848.
—— died, 1856.
Harland, Sir Robert, arrived at Madras, bearing a letter from the King to the Nabob of Arcot, August 1771.
Harris, Bartholomew, Governor of Bombay, 1690 to 1693.
Harris, Lord, Governor of Madras from 1853 to March 28, 1859.
Harris, General Lord, G.C.B., entered the artillery 1759.
—— made Lieutenant-Colonel, 1780.
—— accompanied Sir William Medows, as secretary and aide-de-camp, to Bareilly in 1788, and was with him during the campaigns of 1790, 1791, and 1792, particularly at the storming parties of the Pettah and fort-

ress of Bangalore, March 20, 1791; Savandroog, December 20, 1791; and Nundedroog, October 19, 1791.

HARRIS, General Lord, G.C.B., was engaged under Lord Cornwallis in the attack on the fortified camp of Tippoo at Seringapatam on February 6, 1792.

—— left Madras, and returned to England in August 1792.

—— he joined his regiment at Calcutta in October 1794, and was appointed to the command of Fort William.

—— he was made a lieutenant-general in 1797, and appointed to command the Madras army. He had also a seat in Council, and obtained the right of nominating officers to purely military appointments, previously held by the civil power.

—— appointed to take charge, until the arrival of Lord Clive, of the Civil Government of Bengal, from February 21, 1798, to September 5, 1799, in addition to his duties as Commander-in-Chief. In the same year he was appointed to the command of the expedition against Mysore, and took the fort of Seringapatam, May 4, 1799, which concluded the war with Tippoo Sultan. In June 1815 he was raised, through the good offices of Lord Liverpool, the Duke of York, and his own deserts, to the peerage, under the style and title of Lord Harris of Belmont, in Kent, and of Seringapatam and Mysore in the East Indies. He died on May 15, 1829.

HARRIS, Lieutenant-General Lord, K.C.H., was the eldest son of the first Lord Harris; he served at Seringapatam, in 1779, at the storming of which fort he was Lieutenant of H.M.'s 74th. He was sent home with Tippoo's captured standards.

HARRISON, E., Governor of Madras, 1711 to 1717.

HARRISON, Chairman of the Court of Directors, 1775.

HARROWBY, Lord, President of the Board of Commissioners for the Affairs of India from July 11, 1809, to November 7, 1809.

HASTINGS, WARREN, born in 1732.

—— sent to India as a writer, 1749.

—— returned to England about 1763.

HASTINGS, WARREN; while still in England, he was appointed to the second seat in the Council of Madras in 1769.

—— President of the Council of Bengal, 1772.

—— constituted first Governor-General, by Act of Parliament, 1773.

—— set sail for England, February 1785.

—— impeached on four heads, 1786-87.

—— trial commenced, February 13, 1788; prosecution lasted until June 1791; and his defence was not concluded until April 23, 1795, on which day he was acquitted of the charges brought against him.

—— annuity of £4000 granted to him by the Company for twenty-eight and a half years, 1796.

—— died, August 22, 1818.

HASTINGS, Marquess of (Lord Moira), Governor-General from October 4, 1813, to January 9, 1823.

—— Nepaul war, October 1814, to February 1816; Candy annexed, March 2, 1815; Pindarrees suppressed, 1819; Mahratta Confederacy dissolved, 1819.

HASTINGS, Mr F., Governor of Madras from 1720 to 1721.

HATTRASS TOWN stormed and taken by the British, February 23, 1817.

—— Fort, March 1, 1853.

HAVELOCK, HENRY, born April 5, 1795. Served in the first Burmese war, 1824 to 1826; in Affghanistan, 1838 to 1842; in first Punjab campaign, 1846.

—— second in command in Persia, 1856 and 1857.

—— received command of force assembled for the relief of Cawnpore garrison, July 9, 1857.

—— relieved Lucknow, September 25, 1857.

—— created a Baronet, November 26, 1857.

—— died, November 24, 1857.

HAWKINS, Captain, mission to Jehangire, 1609.

HAY, Mr, murdered by order of Meer Cossim, Oct. 3, 1763.

HAYLEYBURY COLLEGE established, 1805; abolished, 1857.

HAZAREERBAGH ceased to be a British cantonment, 1845.

HEBER, Bishop of Calcutta from 1824 to 1826. Born 1783; died, April 3, 1826.

HERRIES, Right Hon. J. C., President of the Board of Control from March to December 1852.

HIDGELLEE granted to E.I.C., 1765.

HIGGINSON, Mr NAT., Governor of Madras from 1692 to 1697.

HINDIA or HANDIYA, occupied by the British, 1820.

—— by treaty placed under their management, 1844.

HINDOOR held by a Rajah under E.I.C. since 1815.

HINGLAJGARH (Malwa), fort taken by the English under Major Sinclair, July 3, 1804.

—— restored to Holkar, 1805.

HISLOP, Sir THOMAS, Commander-in-Chief of the Madras army, was in 1817 intrusted with the military and political command in the Deccan. On December 21, 1817, he gained the battle of Mahidpore ; on February 27, 1818, captured the fort of Tabneir on the Taptee, and hanged the Killadar.

HOBART, Right Hon. Lord, Governor of Madras from September 7, 1794, to February 21, 1798.

HOBHOUSE, Sir J. C., President of the Board of Control from April 29, 1835, to September 9, 1841, and from July 10, 1846, to February 3, 1852.

HODGES, THOMAS, Governor of Bombay, 1767 to 1776.

HOLKAR, MULHAR RAO, rose to power as a general under the Peishwa Bajee Rao, about 1726.

—— received a grant of land in Malwa, 1731.

HOLLA HONOOR subjugated by the British, 1791.

HOLLOND, J., Governor of Madras from February 7, 1789, to February 13, 1790.

HOLLOND, Mr E. J., Governor of Madras from February 13, 1790, to February 20, 1790.

HOLWELL, Mr, assumed the command in Calcutta on the abandonment of his office by Mr Drake on June 19, 1756 ; confined in the Black Hole ; survived, and wrote a narrative of his sufferings. He was dismissed the service by the Court of Directors in 1761.

HONAHWAR taken by assault by the English, 1783.

—— ceded to Tippoo, 1784.

—— reverted to the E.I.C., 1798.

HOOBLEE FACTORY plundered by Sevajee, 1673.
—— town came into possession of E.I.C., 1818.

HOOGHLY, a British district in Bengal. The territory was ceded to the East India Company by Meer Cossim in 1760 ; and its cession was confirmed in 1765 by the Emperor Shah Allum.

HOOGHLY, the principal place of the district of the same name, was founded by the Portuguese in 1537.
—— in 1632 it was stormed by the troops of Shah Jehan and captured.
—— the English established a factory in 1676, which was fortified in 1681.
—— in 1756 it was taken by Sooraj-oo-Dowlah, and re-taken by Clive in 1757.
—— the church was built by the Jesuits in 1599, and the college was founded in 1836.

HOOLIORDROOG, in Mysore, was acquired in 1659 by Dud Deo Raj, ruler of Mysore ; it then passed into the possession of Hyder Ali, and was surrendered by Tippoo Sultan to the British under Lord Cornwallis in 1791. It having been dismantled and relinquished by Lord Cornwallis, Tippoo Sultan occupied the fort and town. It was again, before the close of the war, seized by the British ; it now belongs to Mysore.

HORNBY, WILLIAM, Governor of Bombay, 1776 to 1784.

HORNE, JOHN, Governor of Bombay, 1734 to 1739.

HOSHUNGABAD, ceded by the Rajah of Nagpore to the British, 1818.

HOSURU, after being subjected to rulers many and various, was finally occupied by the British, 1791.

HUGHES, Sir EDWARD, defeated French fleet under M. Suffrein in 1782, and captured six vessels.

HUMEERPOOR attacked by British troops, 1778.
—— granted to E.I.C. at the treaty of Bassein, 1802.

HURDA, granted for the use of the Gwalior Contingent, 1844.

HYDERABAD, the name of the territory of the Nizam. Nizam Ali ravaged the Carnatic in 1765 ; concluded a treaty with the H.E.I.C., 1766 ; a second treaty was concluded in 1768. Under the partition treaty of 1799 the Nizam received a large accession of territory. In 1804 the Nizam received other advantages. In 1817 certain exchanges of territory took place. Nizam Ali died in 1803, and was succeeded by Secunder Jah, who died in 1829, and was succeeded by the present sovereign.

HYDERABAD, the principal place in the territory of the Nizam. The British Residency, and the city and palace, are connected by a handsome stone bridge built in 1831.

HYDER ALI, born about 1700.

—— negotiates with the Council of Bombay, 1763.

—— meets the English in battle, September 26, 1767, and November 8.

—— Amboor besieged by Hyder, November 1767.

—— Zingra Cottah taken from Hyder on February 12, 1767; Salem on March 20; Kistonagherry on May 2; Vencatigherry on June 10; Muliavakeel on June 28; Oosoor on July 11; Amicalle, July 13; Mangalore, March 1, 1769; Onore on March 25.

—— advanced on Madras, March 29, 1769.

—— treaty signed with English, April 4, 1769.

—— repeatedly defeated in 1781 and in 1782.

—— died, December 7, 1782.

I

IMPEY, Sir ELIJAH, Chief Justice of Supreme Court of Calcutta, was made judge of the Sudder Dewanny Adawlut in 1780; accused by Burke in 1789 of having murdered Nuncomar.

INDIA, route to, *via* Cape of Good Hope, discovered by the Portuguese, Vasco de Gama, 1497.

—— Albuquerque seized and fortified Goa in 1510.

—— Captain Stephens, Sir F. Drake, and Mr Thomas Cavendish, followed by the same route in 1582 and 1586.

INDIA; first British East India Trading Company formed, and charter granted, December 31, 1600.

—— Dutch began to establish themselves and get power, 1594.

—— first expedition of the East India Company sailed, under Captain James Lancaster, February 1601.

—— they arrived at their destination, Acheen in Sumatra, on June 5, 1602.

—— Lancaster returned to the Downs on September 11, 1603.

—— Captain Best obtained a firman from the Emperor of Delhi to establish a trading factory at Surat in 1612.

—— massacre of Amboyna occurred February 27, 1623.

—— permission given to build Fort St George, 1640.

—— Madras raised to a Presidency, 1653. Cromwell renewed the Charter of the Company in 1657; and this renewal confirmed by Charles II., April 3, 1661. Charles II. gave Bombay to the Company, March 27, 1668. The French East India Company was formed in 1664; and the foundation of their settlement at Pondicherry was laid ten years afterwards. The East India Company obtained a renewal of their Charter in 1677, as also in 1693 and in 1702, when the old and new Companies united. The Charter was again renewed, in 1730, to 1766, and no very considerable alteration was made till 1783, when Mr Fox brought forward his India Bill. In 1793 the Company's Charter was prolonged till 1814; the propriety of granting the Charter was again discussed in 1813, and the Company ceased to monopolise the trade with India. In 1814 the Charter of the East India Company was renewed till April 10, 1831. In 1833 the Company was deprived of its commercial character, but continued to govern India till 1858, when the government was assumed by the Crown.

—— the Company acquired from Azim, the grandson of Aurungzebe, Calcutta and an adjoining village, in 1698.

—— war broke out between England and France in 1745. The French were defeated; and by a treaty, negotiated by Clive in 1765, the Company acquired Bengal, Behar, and Orissa.

INDIA; Company acquired all the territories of Tippoo Sultan, captured Delhi, &c., between 1797 and 1804.

—— Nepaulese war broke out, 1814; a treaty concluded in 1816.

—— Holkar, Scindia, and Appa Sahib defeated by Lord Lake, 1805. Treaty signed with Scindia, November 23, 1805.

—— war broke out with Burmah, 1824; which was concluded on February 24, 1826, by the treaty of Yandaboo, when the Tenasserim coast, with the province of Arracan and its dependencies, were ceded to Great Britain. The second war with Burmah commenced November 1852, and peace was made in June 1853.

—— Bencoolen, and the other British possessions in Sumatra, were given to the Dutch in 1825, in exchange for Malacca and Singapore, and the possessions of the Dutch on the continent of India.

—— Coorg was annexed in 1837.

—— the Affghan war commenced in 1839, and terminated in 1842; but a treaty of alliance was not finally entered into with the ruler of Cabul till March 30, 1855.

—— Scinde was conquered and annexed, March 12, 1843; and the Punjab on March 24, 1849.

—— war with Gwalior, 1843; which terminated on January 13, 1844, after the occupation of Gwalior, with the exception of the Burmese wars, and the annexation of Oude in 1856.

—— from 1850 to 1857 the dominions of the East India Company were undisturbed.

—— great mutiny of the Bengal army began May 9, 1857. Her Majesty's proclamation of peace issued November 1, 1858.

INDORE. The founder of the family of Holkar was Mulhar Rao, born in 1693. He served under the Peishwa, and obtained a jaghire, in 1728, north of the Nerbudda. His jaghire was increased in 1731, and

Indore was granted to him in 1733. He died in 1767. The most famous of his descendants was Jeswunt Rao Holkar, who, in October 1802, obtained victory over the Peishwa and Scindia; he was defeated at Furruckabad, November 17, 1804, by General Lake. Holkar made a treaty with the British in 1805, in which he relinquished all claims in Tonk, Rampoora, Bhoondee, and places north of the Bhoondee hills. Jeswunt Rao Holkar died in 1811, and was succeeded by Mulhar Rao in 1817. The Regency commenced hostilities with the British, but were defeated, on December 21, 1817, at Mahidpore. A treaty was concluded with the British Government on January 18, 1818. Mulhar Rao Holkar died in 1833, and was succeeded by his adopted son, Martund Rao Holkar. He was shortly afterwards dispossessed by Hurree Rao Holkar, who was succeeded by Kumdee Rao Holkar. The country was then governed by a Regency, until, in February 1852, the nominee of the British Government, Mulkerjee, ascended the guddee.

INDORE, the principal place of the territory of the same name, was built by the widow of Mulhar Rao Holkar in 1767. It was occupied by a British force, 1804, but restored in 1805. In the year 1857 there was an outbreak amongst the native troops; many Europeans were murdered, and the resident, Colonel Durand, fled. Order was eventually restored, and the murderers were punished, December 1857, by Sir Robert Hamilton and Sir Hugh Rose.

INGLIS, H., Chairman of the Court of Directors, 1797, 1800, and 1812.

INQUISITION introduced, 1526.

ISTALIFF taken by General M'Caskill, September 29, 1842.

J

JACOB, General JOHN, arrived in India, 1828.

—— appointed to the command of the Scinde Horse, 1842.

JACOB, General JOHN, commanded the cavalry in the last war with Persia.

—— created a Brigadier-General, 1857.

—— died, December 5, 1858.

JALNA (Bombay Presidency), occupied by the British in 1804; but having been restored to Holkar, it was by him ceded to the English, 1818.

JALOUN granted to E.I.C., 1802-3; subsequently to Nana Govind Rao, 1817. Possession resumed by the Company, 1838; revenue settlement made, 1849.

JAMALLABAD attacked and taken by the British, 1799.

JAMES I., King of England, deputed Sir Thomas Roe Ambassador to the Great Mogul in 1614.

JAMES, Commodore, captured Severndroog and the island of Bancoot in 1755.

JAMES, Chairman of the Court of Directors in 1779.

JAMES, J. T., Bishop of Calcutta, born 1786.

—— Bishop of Calcutta, 1827.

—— died August 1828.

JAUNSAR subject to the British, 1815.

JEH-NUNGIE, Emperor of Delhi, 1605.

JEITPORE came into English possession, 1849.

JELLALABAD, earthquake in, February 19, 1842; siege raised by British garrison, and Akbar Khan's besieging army defeated, April 7, 1842.

JENKINS, Chairman of the Court of Directors, 1839.

JESSULMERE founded by a Bhatti prince, 1156.

JEYPOOR territory became tributary to the H.E.I.C. in April 1818.

—— after the death of the Ranee, the British Government assumed the protectorate of, 1831.

—— young Chief of, allowed to assume the reins of government, 1851.

JEYPOOR, the principal place of the territory of the same name, was built in the early part of the eighteenth century, by Sewaè Jai Singh, Rajah of Dhoondar.

—— slavery and child-stealing abolished in, 1847.

JHANSI, treaty between the Soubahdar and the British, 1804; second treaty, 1817.

JHANSI, Soubahdar made Rajah, 1832.
—— territory lapsed to British Government, 1854.
—— massacre in, of Europeans, June 8, 1857.
—— retaken by English troops, April 4, 1858.
JHELIM, battle of the, January 13, 1849.
JOOBUL RAJPOOT restored to power by the English, 1815.
JOUDPORE, treaty signed between the British Government and the native prince, 1818. This treaty was infringed, and Colonel Sutherland marched against the town, upon which the Rajah submitted, and the fortress was garrisoned by a British force, 1834.
—— part of the Joudpore contingent mutinied at Erinpoora, August 22, 1857.
JOUNPOOR, in 1764, granted to E.I.C., and by them to the Nawab Vizier of Oude, by whom it was again ceded to the E.I.C. in 1775.
JUGGERNAUT taken by the English, October 18, 1803.
—— shrine of, first connection with the British Government of India in April 1806.
JULINDER DOOAB (Punjab) ceded to the E.I.C., March 1846.
JYNTEEA annexed to British dominions, 1835.
JYTUK besieged and taken by the English, May 1815.

K

KAISERBAGH taken, March 14, 1858.
KAIRA, unsuccessful attempt to introduce American ploughs, 1843.
—— fort ceded to the British, May 3, 1803, and subsequently the whole district.
KALLEENJUR. This celebrated hill-fort has suffered many sieges.
—— was besieged by an officer of Mahomed Sultan in 1202.
—— by Humayoon, Emperor of Delhi, in 1532.
—— by Sher Shah, the Patan ruler, in 1543.
—— about 1790 it suffered a blockade of ten years by the Mahrattas; and was lastly taken by the British, February 28, 1812, by whom it was destroyed in 1854.

KALLEE NUDDEE, battle of, January 2, 1838.

KAMONAH fell into British hands, first in 1805, and again in 1807.

KAMPTEE, great hailstorm in, April 1830.

KARANJA taken by the Mahrattas from the Portuguese, 1683.

—— taken by the English, 1774.

—— formally ceded to them by treaty of Poorunder, 1775.

KATTARA, battle of, August 14, 1858.

KATTYWAR, famine produced by migratory rats, 1814.

KEANE, Lord JOHN, of Ghuznee, Affghanistan, born 1781.

—— Commander-in-Chief of the Bombay army from July 2, 1834, to February 14, 1840.

—— took the fortress of Ghuznee, July 12, 1839.

—— created Baron Keane of Ghuznee, December 1839.

—— died August 24, 1844.

KEIGWIN, Captain, Commander of the Company's troops at Bombay, revolted, and proclaimed the authority of the Crown, December 27, 1683.

KEONGPULA, in Arracan, unsuccessful attack upon, 1825.

KHOLES, war with, January 1832.

—— authority of English Government restored, April 1832.

KHUNNAH escheated to the British on the death of the Ranee, 1851.

KHYBER PASS forced by the British troops, April 7, 1842.

KINEYREE, battle of, May 18, 1848.

KISTNAGHERRY surrendered to Colonel Smith, May 2, 1768.

KOH-I-NOOR sent to England, April 1850.

KOLAPOOR, after sundry treaties, as often violated, the English assumed its government, 1844.

KOLOBAH (Bombay Presidency), fortified by the Mahrattas, 1662.

—— unsuccessfully attacked by British and Portuguese, 1722.

—— placed under British protection, 1822; annexed, 1840.

KOMULMAIR, Fortress and Pass, gained by E.I.C., 1818.
KOOCH BEHAR, Hindoo Raj, nominally restored, 1773.
KOOMBHER surrendered to British, 1826.
KOONYHAR conquered from the Ghoorkas, 1815.
KOOTCHEA, battle of, January 14, 1858.
KOSY taken by General Lake, 1804.
KOTAH, treaty concluded between this State and British Government, 1817.
—— agreed to pay for Kotah contingent, April 1838.
—— contingent mutinied, and murdered British officers, October 14, 1857.
—— town recovered by General Roberts, March 30, 1857.
KOTHKHAEE annexed to the British dominions, 1828.
KOTIE KE SERAI, battle of, June 16, 1858.
KUDDI (Bundelcund), lapsed to the British, 1850.
KUMAON acknowledged as part of the British dominions, 1815.
KUNNOUJ, engagement between Humayoon and the Affghans, the latter victorious, 1540.
KURNOOL (Madras), attacked and taken by the British, in consequence of the discovery of a Mohammedan conspiracy, 1838.
—— great storm destroyed much property, 1851.
KURRACHEE, first voyage direct from England to this port, 1852.
—— fort built, 1797 ; occupied by British troops, 1839.
—— arsenal blown up by accident, October 19, 1858.
—— submarine telegraph to Aden, 1860.
KUTUBO destroyed by the Mahrattas, October 29, 1803.
KYTHUL (Sirhind), lapsed to the British, 1843.

L

LAHORE taken by Baher, 1523.
—— by Ahmed Shah, 1748.
—— bestowed upon Runjeet Singh by Zeman Shah, 1799.
—— treaty signed between Shah Sojoah, Runjeet Singh, and the English, June 26, 1838.

Lahore taken by Sir H. Gough, 1846.
—— treaty of, signed March 9, 1846.
Lake, General Lord, born, March 1772.
—— won the battle of Laswaree, November 1, 1803.
—— took Agra and Delhi in 1803.
—— raised to the Peerage in 1804.
—— defeated Holkar at Furruckabad, November 17, 1804.
—— at Bhurtpore, April 3, 1805.
—— created a Viscount, November 4, 1807.
—— died, February 1808.
Langhorne, Sir W., Governor of Madras until 1678.
Laswaree, battle of, November 1, 1803.
Latoo, battle of, December 18, 1857.
Latter, Captain T., D. C. of Prome, murdered, December 3, 1853.
Law, Stephen, Governor of Bombay, 1739 to 1742.
Lawrence, Major Stringer, Governor of Madras for sixteen days, 1749.
Lawrence, Sir Henry, Political Agent of Affghanistan, 1842.
—— Resident at Ajmere, 1853.
—— Resident in Oude, 1857.
—— defeated at Chinhut, June 30, 1857.
—— died, July 4, 1857.
Lawrence, Sir John, arrived in India, 1830.
—— Chief Commissioner of Punjab, 1853.
—— made K.C.B. in 1856, G.C.B. in 1857, and Baronet in 1858.
—— Member of the Council of India, 1858, and of her Majesty's Privy Council, 1859.
Lewisham, Viscount, President of the Board of Commissioners for the Affairs of India from April 25, 1801, to July 1802.
Library, Calcutta Public, founded, 1835.
Loodiana, part lapsed to the English Government in 1836, and the remainder in 1846-47.
—— great hurricane, 1846.
—— Fort built, 1808.
Lotteries, State, abolished in India, 1844.

LUCKNOW, siege of Europeans in, began, July 1, 1857.
—— relieved by Outram and Havelock, September 25.
—— Outram and Havelock besieged in, September 27.
—— relieved by Sir C. Campbell, November 17.
—— British evacuate the city, November 23, 1857.
—— finally conquered by the English, March 21, 1858.
LUSHINGTON, Right Hon. S. R., Governor of Madras from October 18, 1827, to October 25, 1832.
—— Chairman of the Court of Directors in 1838, 1842, and 1848.
LUSHINGTON, J., Chairman of the Court of Directors, 1790, 1795, and 1799.
LUTTEEPORE, massacre by Cheyt Singh of E.I.C.'s troops, 1781.

M

MACARTNEY, Lord, born, May 14, 1737.
—— Governor of Madras, June 1781.
—— declines the offer of the Governor-Generalship, and returns to England, 1785.
—— died, 1806.
M'DOWALL, General HAY, in Madras, 1807.
—— resigned office and re-embarked for England, January 1809. Lost on the passage home.
MACKESON, Colonel, murdered, September 10, 1853.
MACNAGHTEN, Sir W., Bart., Governor of Bombay, 1841.
—— murdered, December 23, 1841.
MACPHERSON, Mr, Governor-General, February 1, 1785, to February 12, 1786.
MACRAE, JAMES, Esq., Governor of Madras, 1725 to 1730.
MADDOCK, Sir HERBERT, arrived in India, 1814.
—— appointed Resident to Lucknow, September 1829.
—— appointed Resident to Katmandoo, 1831.
—— Deputy-Governor of Bengal, October 1845.
—— left India, 1849.
MADRAS, first English settlement at, 1639.
—— Fort St George built, 1639.
—— made a presidency, 1684.

MADRAS taken by the French, 1746.
—— restored, 1749.
—— placed under separate governor, 1784.
—— mutiny of Madras troops, 1809.
—— great fire in, 1803.
—— besieged by Lally, December 14, 1758.
—— siege abandoned, 1759.
—— threatened by Hyder Ali, March 29, 1769.
—— great hurricane in, 1811.
MADRAS, Governors of :
—— Sir W. Langhorne, until 1678.
—— Streynsham Master, Esq., 1678 to 1684.
—— Wm. Gifford, Esq., 1684 to 1687.
—— Elihu Yale, Esq., 1687 to 1692.
—— Sir J. Goldsborough, 1692 to 1693.
—— Nathaniel Higginson, Esq., 1693 to 1698.
—— Thomas Pitt, Esq., 1698 to 1700.
—— Gulstom Addison, Esq., 1700 to 1709.
—— Edmund Montague, 1709.
—— William Fraser, 1709 to 1711.
—— E. Harrison, Esq., 1711 to 1717.
—— Joseph Collett, Esq., 1717 to 1720.
—— Francis Hastings, Esq., 1720 to 1721.
—— Nat. Elwick, Esq., 1721 to 1725.
—— James Macrae, Esq., 1725 to 1730.
—— G. M. Pitt, Esq., 1730 to 1735.
—— Richard Benyon, Esq., 1735 to 1744.
—— N. Morse, Esq., 1744 to 1749.
—— Major Stringer Lawrence, 1749.
—— N. Price, Esq., 1749 to 1750.
—— M. Starke, Esq. (Deputy), 1750 to 1752.
—— Thomas Saunders, Esq., 1752 to 1755.
—— George Pigott, Esq., 1755 to 1763.
—— Robert Palke, Esq., 1763 to 1767.
—— Charles Boucher, 1767 to 1770.
—— Josias An Pre, 1770 to 1773.
—— Alexander Wyach, Esq., 1773 to 1775.
—— Right Hon. Lord Pigott, 1775 to 1776.
—— George Straton, Esq., 1776 to 1777.

MADRAS, Governors of—*continued.*
—— John Whitehill, 1777 to 1778.
—— Thomas Rumbold, Esq., 1778 to 1780.
—— John Whitehill, Esq., 1780 to 1781.
—— Charles Smith, 1781.
—— Right Hon. Lord Macartney, 1781 to 1785.
—— Alexander Davidson, June 4, 1785, to April 6, 1786.
—— Sir Archibald Campbell, K.B., April 6, 1786, to February 7, 1789.
—— John Hollond, Esq., February 7, 1789, to February 13, 1790.
—— E. J. Holland, Esq., February 13, 1790, to February 20, 1790.
—— Major-General Wm. Medows, February 20, 1790, to August 1, 1792.
—— Sir Charles Oakeley, Bart., August 1, 1792, to September 7, 1794. (Acted as Governor in the absence of General Medows, from October 15, 1790, to December 21, 1791.)
—— Right Hon. Lord Hobart, September 7, 1794, to February 21, 1798.
—— Lieut.-General George Harris, February 21, 1798, to January 2, 1799.
—— Right Hon. Lord Clive, September 5, 1799, to August 30, 1803. (Governor-General Lord Mornington, acted as Governor from January 2 to September 5, 1799.)
—— Right Hon. Lord W. C. Bentinck, August 30, 1803, to September 11, 1807. (Recalled by the Court of Directors.)
—— Wm. Petrie, Esq., September 11, 1807, to December 24, 1807.
—— Sir G. H. Barlow, Bart., K.B., December 24, 1807, to May 21, 1813.
—— Lieut.-General Hon. J. Abercromby, May 21, 1813, to September 16, 1814.
—— Right Hon. Hugh Elliot, September 16, 1814, to June 10, 1820.
—— Major-General Sir T. Munro, Bart., K.C.B., June 10, 1820, to 1826.
—— H. S. Græme, Esq., June 10, 1827, to October 18, 1827.

MADRAS, Governors of—*continued.*
—— Right Hon. J. R. Lushington, October 18, 1827, to October 25, 1832.
—— Lieut.-General Sir F. Adams, K.C.B., October 25, 1832, to March 2, 1837.
—— G. E. Russell, Esq., 1837, two days.
—— Right Hon. John Lord Elphinstone, G.C.H., March 4, 1837, to September 24, 1842.
—— The Most Noble the Marquess of Tweeddale, September 24, 1842, to April 7, 1848.
—— Right Hon. Sir Henry Pottinger, Bart., April 7, 1848, to 1853.
—— Lord Harris, 1853, to March 28, 1859.
—— Sir Charles Trevelyan, March 28, 1859, to June 24, 1860.
—— Morehead, officiating from June 24 to July 5, 1860.
—— Sir Henry George Ward, Knt., G.C.M.G., July 5 to August 2, 1860.
—— Morehead, officiating from August 2, 1860, till the arrival of Sir William Denison.

MADRUSSAH instituted, 1771.

MAHABULESHWAR made a sanatorium by Sir John Malcolm, 1828.

MAHARAJPOOR, battle of, between Sir H. Gough and Mahrattas, December 29, 1843.

MAHE reduced by the English, 1779.
—— formal possession taken, 1793.
—— restored to the French, 1815.

MAHOBA (Bundelcund) ceded to E.I.C., 1817.

MAHRATTA, first war began January 1779 ; ended, October 13, 1781.
—— second began and ended in 1803.
—— third began December 1843, and ended January 1844.

MAHRATTA ditch made, 1742.

MAJORIBANKS, Chairman of the Court of Directors 1819, 1825, and 1833.

MALABAR, English came into possession, 1799.

MALACCA reduced by the Portuguese 1509, who were expelled by the Dutch in 1642.

MALACCA; Dutch supplanted by British, 1795.
—— restored to the Dutch, 1801.
—— fell again under British rule, 1807; was a second time restored to the Dutch, 1818; and lastly transferred to the British, 1824.
MALCOLM, Sir JOHN, G.C.B. and K.L.S., born 1769.
—— sent as Cadet to Madras, 1782.
—— as Envoy to Persia, 1799.
—— returned to India and appointed Private Secretary to the Governor-General, 1801.
—— Resident at Mysore, 1803.
—— a second time sent to Persia, 1808.
—— second in command at Mahidpoor, December 21, 1817.
—— Governor of Bombay from November 1, 1827, to March 31, 1831.
—— died, May 31, 1833.
MALDAH granted to the E.I.C. by Shah Allum, 1765.
MALOWN FORT, Goorkhas besieged in, and obliged to surrender to General Ochterlony, May 15, 1815.
MALWAN ceded to E.I.C. by Rajah of Colapore, 1812.
MANDAVEE (Bombay Presidency) lapsed to the British, 1840.
MANGALORE taken by the British, 1768.
—— retaken by Hyder Ali, 1768.
—— a second time surrendered to the English, 1783.
—— yielded to Tippoo Sultan, 1783.
—— finally in possession of E.I.C., 1798.
MANGOR, Mahrattas defeated at, December 29, 1843.
MARSHMAN, Dr JOSHUA, born April 20, 1768.
—— sent out to India as Baptist missionary, 1799.
—— arrived at Serampore, October 13, 1799.
—— died, December 5, 1837.
MARTABAN yielded to English arms, April 5, 1852.
MARTYN, Rev. H., born 1781; embarked for India, 1805; died, 1812.
MASSACRE at Allahabad, June 6, 1857.
—— Amboyna, February 17, 1623.
—— Bareilly, June 2, 1857.

MASSACRE of Delhi, May 10.
—— boat, Cawnpore, June 27, 1857.
—— Cawnpore, July 15, 1857.
—— Jhansi, June 8, 1857.
—— Meerut, May 10, 1857.
—— Shajehanpore, May 31, 1857.
MASTER, STREYNSHAM, Governor of Madras, 1678 to 1684.
MASULIPATAM taken by the French, 1753; by Clive, 1759.
—— ceded to the E.I.C. by the Emperor of Delhi, 1765.
MAYOR'S COURT established in Calcutta, 1726.
—— in Madras, 1726.
MEDOWS, Major-General Sir WILLIAM, K.C.B., Governor of Madras, February 20, 1790, to August 1, 1792.
—— Governor of Bombay from September 6, 1788, to January 21, 1790.
MEEANEE, battle of, February 17, 1843.
MEEANGUNGE taken by English troops, February 23, 1858.
MEERUT lapsed to British Government, 1836.
—— sepoys revolted at, May 10, 1857.
MEHIDPOOR; opposite this town Holkar was defeated by Sir Thomas Hislop, December 21, 1817.
MELOWN (Burmah), town attacked and taken, 1826.
MELVILLE, Viscount, President of the Board of Commissioners for the Affairs of India from February 4, 1828, to September 17, 1828.
MERGUI formally placed under British rule, February 1826.
MERKARA FORT built by Hyder Ali, 1773; occupied by British, 1834.
METCALFE, Sir CHARLES (Lord M.), came to India, 1801.
—— sent on mission to Runjeet Singh, 1809.
—— Resident at Scindia Court, 1810.
—— Resident at Delhi, 1811.
—— Governor-General from March 20, 1835, to March 4, 1836.
—— Lieutenant-Governor of the North-Western Provinces, May 1836.
—— left India, February 15, 1838.

METCALFE, Sir CHARLES (Lord M.), died, September 5, 1846.
MIDDLETON, Bishop of Calcutta, November 1814.
—— died, July 8, 1822.
MIDNAPORE, obtained by the E.I.C. from Cossim Ali Khan, 1760.
MINTO, Lord, Governor-General from July 31, 1807, to October 4, 1813.
—— President of Board of Commissioners for the Affairs of India from February 11, 1806, to July 15, 1806.
—— died, June 21, 1814.
MIRZAPORE ceded to the E.I.C., partly in 1775, and the remaining portion in 1801.
MOGUL power established by Baber, 1526.
MOHAMMED, DOST, ruler of Affghanistan from 1826 to 1839.
—— surrendered himself a prisoner, 1840.
—— restored to the throne, 1842.
MOIRA, Lord (Marquess Hastings), Governor-General from October 4, 1813, to January 9, 1823.
MONGHYR granted by Shah Allum to E.I.C., 1765.
MONTAGUE, EDMUND, provisional Governor of Madras, 1709.
MOODKEE, battle of, between British army and Sikhs, December 18, 1845.
MOOLRAJ DEWAN tried and condemned, 1849.
MOOLTAN, captured after a long siege by Runjeet Singh, 1818.
—— two British officers assassinated, 1848.
—— captured by General Whish, January 2, 1849; fort, January 22.
—— fortress destroyed by flood, August 28, 1849.
MOORSHEDABAD, granted by Shah Allum to E.I.C., 1765.
MORADABAD ceded to E.I.C. by Nawab of Oude, 1801.
MORNINGTON, Earl of (Marquess Wellesley), Governor-General from May 17, 1798, to July 30, 1805.
MORSE, NICHOLAS, Governor of Madras from 1744 to 1749.
MOTTEUX, Chairman of the Court of Directors, 1787.
MOZUFFURNUGGUR ceded by Scindia to E.I.C., 1803.
—— Jaghire of, lapsed to E.I.C., 1836.
MUNDESORE, treaty of, signed January 1818.
—— battle of, November, 21-24, 1857.

MUNDLAH, stormed by British force and ceded to E.I.C., 1818.

MUNRO, Colonel Sir HECTOR, took command of the British army in Bengal in May 1764; defeated the Nabob of Oude at the battle of Buxar, October 23, 1764; died, 1806.

MUNRO, Major-General Sir THOMAS, Governor of Madras from 1820 to 1826.

—— died, 1826.

MUNSEATA, battle of, January 5, 1858.

MUTINIES. Mutiny in English army in consequence of the reduction by Court of Directors of double batta, began at Monghir in January 1766; quelled by Lord Clive and the firmness of the Council, 1766.

—— at Patna, 1764.

—— of Vellore, July 10, 1806.

—— at Barrackpore, November 1824.

—— of six regiments at Ferozepore, 1844.

—— of Bengal army, 1857.

—— 34th B.N.I., March 30; disbanded, May 5.

—— 19th B.N.I. disbanded, March 31.

—— began at Meerut, May 10.

—— at Lucknow, May 30.

—— of 7th Oude Infantry, May 3; 11th and 20th B.N.I. and 3d B.N.C. marched from Meerut to Delhi, May 10.

—— of 38th, 54th, and 74th B.N.I. at Delhi, May 11.

—— of B.N. Sappers and Miners at Meerut, May 16.

—— of 55th B.N.I. at Murdan, May 25.

—— of 9th B.N.I. at Mynpoorie and Allygurh, May 23.

—— of 15th and 30th B.N.I., May. Miseerabad, May 29th.

—— of 13th, 48th, and 71st B.N.I. and 7th N.C. at Lucknow, May 31.

—— of 28th B.N.I. at Shahjehanpore, May 31.

—— of 17th B.N.I. at Azimghur, June 3.

—— of 41st B.N.I., 9th and 10th Oude Irreg. I., and 2d Oude Military Police, at Seetapore, June 3.

—— of 29th B.N.I. at Mooradabad, June 3.

Mutinies—*continued.*

—— of 72d B.N.I., and a portion of 1st B.N.C., at Neemuch, June 3.

—— of 37th B.N.I., 13th Irreg. C., and Loodianah Sikhs, at Benares, June 4.

—— of 12th B.N.I. and 14th Irreg. C. at Jhansi, June 4.

—— of 1st, 53d, and 56th B.N.I., and 2d B.N.C., at Cawnpore, June 6.

—— at Jounpoor, a portion of Loodianah Sikhs, June 5.

—— of 6th B.N.I. at Allahabad, June 6.

—— of Hurrianah battalion, and 4th Irreg. C., at Hansi and Hissar, May 29.

—— of Bhurtpore Levies, at Bhurtpore.

—— of 36th and 61st B.N.I. and 6th B.C. at Jullundur, June 8.

—— of 22d B.N.I. and 6th Oude I. at Fyzabad, June 8.

—— of 15th Irreg. C. at Sultanpore, June 6.

—— of 1st Oude Irreg. I. at Pershadeepore, June 10.

—— of a portion of 12th B.N.I., and 14th Irreg. C. at Nowgong, June 10.

—— of 60th B.N.I. at Rohtuk, June 11.

—— of 45th and 57th B.N.I. at Ferozpore, June 13.

—— of Gwalior Contingent, at Gwalior, June 14.

—— of 10th B.N.I. at Futteghur, June 18.

—— of 4th Irreg. C. at Mozuffernugger, June 30.

—— of 23d B.N.I. at Mhow, July 1.

—— of Kotah Contingent at Agra, July 2.

—— of 14th B.N.I. at Jelum, July 7.

—— of 42d B.N.I. and 3d Irreg. C. at Saugor, July 7.

—— of 46th B.N I. and 9th C. at Sealkote, July 9.

—— of 12th Irreg. C. at Legowlie, July 24.

—— of 7th, 8th, and 40th, B.N.I. at Dinapore, July 25.

—— of 26th B.N.I. at Lahore, July 29.

—— of 27th Bombay I. at Kolapore, August 1.

—— of 5th Irreg. C. at Berhampore, August 14.

—— of Jhodpore Legion at Erinpoora, August 22.

—— of 51st B.N.I. at Peshawur, August 28.

—— of 50th B.N.I. at Nagode, September 16.

—— of 52d B.N.I. at Jubbulpore, September 18.

MUTINIES—*continued.*
—— of 32d B.N.I. at Deoghur, October 9.
—— of troops belonging to Rajah of Kotah, October 15.
—— of portion of 34th B.N.I. at Chittagong, November 18.
—— of 73d B.N.I. at Dacca, November 20.
—— of 62d and 69th B.N.I. at Moultan, August 31.
—— Delhi retaken by British troops on September 20, 1857.
MUTTRA ceded to the E.I.C., 1803.
MYAPORE, battle of, January 10, 1858.
MYHEE CAUNTA, first political transactions with the E.I.C., 1820.
MYNPOORIE granted to the British Government, 1803.
—— battle of, December 27, 1857.
MYSORE, Hyder Ali ruler of, 1760.
—— partial destruction of the old city by Tippoo Sultan, 1787.
—— on the death of Tippoo, 1799, the territory was divided, and one-third came under British rule; and in 1832 a still further portion was appropriated by them, in consequence of the misrule of the Rajah.

N

NAGPORE besieged by the British; garrison surrendered, December 30, 1817.
—— annexed to the British dominions, December 1853.
NALAPANI or KALUNGA, a fort attacked and destroyed by the British, November 1814.
NALCHA placed under British protection, 1819.
NANUK, founder of the Sikhs, born, 1469.
—— died, 1539.
NAPIER, Sir CHARLES JAMES, G.C.B., born August 10, 1782.
—— appointed to the command of the army in Bengal, 1841.
—— defeated the Ameers of Scinde at Meeanee, February 17, 1843.
—— returned to England, September 20, 1847.

Napier, Sir Charles James, G.C.B., returned to India, May 6, 1849.
—— left India, December 6, 1850.
—— died, August 29, 1853.
Nariengaum Fort taken, January 7, 1853.
Narnool, battle of, November 16, 1851.
Nawabgunge, battle of, June 13, 1858.
Neemuch sold to the British, 1817.
—— mutiny at, June 3, 1857.
—— garrison relieved, November 23, 1857.
Neepanee lapsed to the British, 1840.
—— annexed, 1842.
Nellore ceded to E.I.C., 1801.
Nepaul conquered by the Goorkhas in 1768.
—— the East India Directors sent their first expedition, under Captain Kinloch and Mr Logan, to establish trade in, 1770.
—— first commercial treaty between the British Government and that of Nepaul signed in 1792.
—— a second treaty—political—in October 1801.
—— alliance between the two Governments dissolved, 1804.
—— war commenced, October 20, 1814.
—— a third treaty signed, March 3, 1816.
Nepean, Sir Evan, Bart., Governor of Bombay from August 12, 1812, to November 1, 1819.
Nujuffghur, battle of, August 26, 1857.
Nuncomar, Maha Rajah, tried for forgery, and sentenced to death and executed, August 5, 1775.
Nundydroog Fort taken by assault by British troops, October 20, 1791.

O

Oakeley, Sir C., Bart., Governor of Madras from August 1, 1792, to September 7, 1794.
Ochterlony, Sir David, defended Delhi against Holkar, October 1804.

OCHTERLONY, Sir DAVID, commanded in Nepaulese war, 1814-15.
—— died, July 15, 1825.
ODEYPOOR became tributary to the British Government in 1818.
OODWA NULLAH FORT taken from Meer Cossim Ali, September 1763.
ORISSA, chiefly acquired by the E.I.C. in 1765.
—— finally conquered and annexed, October 1803.
OUDE. The British army occupied Lucknow, 1765.
—— the Nawab of, ceded the fortress of Allahabad, 1798.
—— the Nawab ceded a portion of his territory, and the British renewed their defensive treaty, November 10, 1801.
—— the Nawab Vizier took the title of King of Oude, 1819.
—— the whole territory was annexed to the British dominions, February 7, 1856.
—— province revolted, 1857.
—— subdued, 1858.
—— Lord Canning's proclamation, March 3, 1858.
OVERLAND communication between England and India established with some regularity, 1787.
—— steam communication attempted, 1830.
—— established, 1836.
OXENDEN, Sir GEORGE, President of Surat from 1661 to 1668.
—— Governor of Bombay, 1668.
—— died, July 14, 1669.
OXENDEN, Sir H., Bart., Governor of Bombay from 1707 to 1709.

P

PACHETE granted to the British, 1765.
PAGAHM MEW, Burmese defeated at, February 9, 1826.
PAHLUNPORE under British superintendence and protection, 1813.
—— infanticide suppressed, 1853.

PALAMOW, insurrection in, 1832.

PALGHAT FORT built by Hyder Ali, 1757.

—— taken by the British under Colonel Fullarton, 1783.

—— restored to Tippoo Sultan, 1784.

—— surrendered to a British force under Colonel Stuart, September 21, 1790.

PALKE, ROBERT, Governor of Madras from 1763 to 1767.

PANEEPUT, battles of, 1526 and 1761.

PARRY, Chairman of the Court of Directors, 1807 and 1808.

PATCHMARREE (Nagpore), British power established, 1818.

PATEETA, fortified town stormed by Major Popham, 1781.

PATNA acquired by E.I.C., 1765.

—— was attacked by the Great Mogul and Nabob of Oude early in 1760, but relieved by Colonel Calliaud on the 22d of February.

—— English factory at, destroyed by Meer Cossim, June 24, 1763.

PATTISON, Chairman of the Court of Directors, 1818 and 1822.

PAYNE, Chairman of the Court of Directors, 1757.

PEGU, old city destroyed by Alompra, 1757.

—— town captured by the British, 1824.

—— a second time, June 4, 1852.

—— annexed to the British dominions, December 1852.

PEINT-HURSOOL came under British rule, 1842.

PEISHWA, title of, created, 1708.

—— abolished, 1817.

—— treaty signed between the British Government and, December 31, 1802.

—— second treaty signed, June 13, 1817.

PERIAPATAM occupied by a British army, 1791.

—— again by General Stuart in 1799.

PERMACOIL surrendered to English army under Colonel Coote, March 5, 1760.

PERSIAN language abolished in Judicial and Revenue departments, January 1, 1839.

PETRIE, WM., Governor of Madras from September 11, 1807, to December 24, 1807.

PHIPPS, WILLIAM, Governor of Bombay, 1731, 1734.
PIGOT, Right Hon. Lord, Governor of Madras from 1775 to 1776.
—— placed under arrest, August 24, 1776, and died shortly afterwards.
PINDARREES, war between English and, began November 4, 1817.
—— a great army sent against Cheetoo, 1817.
—— its progress retarded by cholera in November of the same year.
—— defeated at Mahidpore, December 21, 1817. Cheetoo killed by a tiger, February 1819.
PITT, THOMAS, Esq., Governor of Madras from 1697 to 1700.
PITT, G. M., Governor of Madras from 1730 to 1735.
PLASSEY, battle of, June 23, 1757.
PONDICHERRY taken from the French and destroyed by the English, first in 1761, and again taken in 1768.
—— restored to the French, 1802.
POONA, British power established in, 1803.
—— the Peishwa delivered up the sovereignty of the place to the British Government, 1818.
POPLAR HOSPITAL founded, 1627.
—— its regulations revised, 1681, 1768, and 1813.
PORTO NOVO burned by Hyder Ali, 1780.
—— battle of, Hyder Ali defeated at, 1781.
PORTUGUESE, under Vasco de Gama, landed in Hindostan, May 1498.
—— English allowed to trade with, 1635.
POSTAGE, uniform newspaper, one anna, January 1855.
POTTINGER, Right Hon. Sir H., Governor of Madras from April 7, 1848, to 1853.
PRESS, printing, first established in Calcutta, 1780.
—— censorship of, abolished, August 19, 1818.
—— law passed to restrict, 1823.
—— freedom of, given by Sir C. Metcalfe, September 15, 1835.
—— Gagging Act passed, June 13, 1857.
—— ceased to exist, June 13, 1858.

PRICE, N., Governor of Madras from December 1749 to March 1750.

PRINTING first accomplished in Bengalee, 1778.

PROCLAMATION, her Majesty's, declaring India henceforward to be under the Supreme Government, November 1, 1858.

PROME temporarily occupied by English, December 2, 1825.

—— finally, October 10, 1852.

—— great fire in, 1856.

PUNDOO NUDDEE, battle of, July 15, 1857.

PUNIAR, battle of, December 29, 1843.

PUNJAB, the; Runjeet Singh obtained a grant of Lahore, 1799; he stormed Mooltan, and took Peshawur, 1818.

—— first war, December 1845.

—— battle of Moodkee, December 18; Ferozeshah, December 21-22; Aliwal, January 28, 1846; Sobraon, February 10.

—— the fort of Kussoor taken, February 11.

—— British army enters Lahore, February 20.

—— annexed to the British dominions, March 30, 1849.

PUNNAH, partly ceded by the Peishwa to E.I.C. in 1802; wholly in 1817.

PURLING, Chairman of the Court of Directors, 1771.

PURNEAH acquired by E.I.C., 1765.

PURTABGHUR became tributary to E.I.C., 1818.

PUTPURGUNJ, Mahrattas under French generalship defeated by General Lake, 1803.

PUTTEEALA, battle of, December 17, 1857.

R

RADHUNPOOR tributary to E.I.C., 1819.

RAEEGURH invested and destroyed by the British troops, April 1818.

RAFFLES, Sir STAMFORD, Secretary to the Government of Prince of Wales Island, 1808.

RAFFLES, SIR STAMFORD, accompanied Governor-General to Malacca, 1811.
—— constituted Lieutenant-Governor, 1811.
RAGOBAH, E.I.C.'s treaty with, March 6, 1775.
RAILWAYS commenced, 1851.
—— Madras, opened, first in India, April 16, 1853.
—— Bombay to Tannah, April 16, 1853.
—— Bengal, first section, August 15, 1854; formally February 1855.
—— Malabar, June 16, 1858.
—— Calcutta to Rajmahal, October 17, 1860.
RAINGURH FORT; Goorkha garrison surrendered to the British, June 10, 1815.
RAIREE FORT, built by Sevajee, 1662.
—— taken by the English, 1765.
—— restored, 1766.
—— ceded by treaty to the British Government, 1819-20.
RAJAHMUNDRY occupied by the French, 1753.
—— transferred to British power, 1759.
—— ceded to them by treaty, 1765.
RAJESHAYE ceded to the E.I.C., 1765.
RAJGHUR, battle of, September 15, 1858.
RAJMAHAL occupied by British force, 1763.
—— ceded by Shah Allum, 1765.
RAJMAHAL HILLS, Santhal insurrection in, June 1855.
RAMAGIRI FORT surrendered to the British army, 1791.
RAMGURH or HAZAREEBAGH ceded by Shah Allum in 1765.
—— insurrection in, 1832.
RAMGURH (Hindoor) captured by British, February 1815.
RAMPOORA (Indore), Roshun Beg defeated by the British, January 1818.
RAMPOORA (Rajpootana) stormed by Col. Don, May 15, 1804.
—— restored to Holkar, 1805.
—— came into possession of British Government, 1818, and bestowed upon Ameer Khan.
RAMREE (Arracan), English obtained possession of, April 22, 1825.
RAMSAY, ANDREW, Governor of Bombay, January 9 to September 6, 1788.

RANGOON built by Alompra, 1753.
—— first occupied by the British, May 11, 1824.
—— given back by treaty of Yandaboo to Burmese, 1826.
—— destroyed by fire, 1850.
—— attacked, taken, and annexed by British, April 1852.
—— great fires, 1853 and 1855.

RATGHUR FORT taken by Sir Hugh Rose, January 29, 1858.

Regulations for the Year

1793.

REGULATION 1. For enacting into a Regulation some articles of a Proclamation, issued March 22, 1793, declaring the permanent settlement of Bengal, Behar, and Orissa. Passed May 1.
—— 2. For abolishing Revenue Courts, and transferring Suits from them to the Courts of Dewanny Adawlut; concerning conduct of Revenue Board, Collectors, &c. May 1.
—— 3. Defining and extending the jurisdiction of Zillah Courts of Judicature. May 1.
—— 4. Deciding Suits declared cognisable at first in the Courts of Dewanny Adawlut. May 1.
—— 5. Concerning Courts of Appeal, defining their relation to the Court of original jurisdiction. May 1.
—— 6. Concerning Sudder Dewanny Adawlut. May 1.
—— 7. Concerning appointment of Vakeels. May 1.
—— 8. Concerning decennial settlement of Revenue. May 1.
—— 9. Concerning apprehension of Criminals. May 1.
—— 10. Concerning disqualified Landholders. May 1.
—— 11. Concerning operation of Hindoo and Mohammedan Law. May 1.
—— 12. Appointment of Hindoo and Mohammedan Law Officers. May 1.
—— 13. Appointment and Duties of Ministerial Officers of Courts of Judicature. May 1.
—— 14. Recovery of Arrears of Revenue. May 1.
—— 15. Rates of Interest to be allowed on Loans and Mortgages. May 1.

Reg. 16. Reference of Suits to Arbitration and to the Nazim. May 1.

—— 17. Power of Landholders to distrain for Rent or Revenue, and restraining the power of inflicting Corporal Punishment. May 1.

—— 18. Preservation of Records, Reports, &c. May 1.

—— 19. Validity of Lakhiraj Titles. May 1.

—— 20. Power of Courts to make Regulations regarding matters coming within their cognisance. May 1.

—— 21. Office for, and Keepers of, Public Records. May 1.

—— 22. Establishment of Police. May 1.

—— 23. Fund for Police Establishment. May 1.

—— 24. Pensions charged on the Land Revenue. May 1.

—— 25. Division of Estates. May 1.

—— 26. Term of Minority of Hindoo and Mohammedan Land Proprietors. May 1.

—— 27. Resumption and Abolition of Sayer. May 1.

—— 28. British subjects, distance of their residence from Calcutta. May 1.

—— 29. Salt Agents. May 1.

—— 30. Illicit Manufacture of Salt. May 1.

—— 31. Conduct of Commercial Agents, Residents. May 1.

—— 32. Opium. May 1.

—— 33. Repair of Dykes, Embankments, &c. May 1.

—— 34. Tax Intoxicating Liquors. May 1.

—— 35. Reform of Gold and Silver Coinage. May 1.

—— 36. Registry of Wills, Deeds, &c. May 1.

—— 37. Grants of Land exempt from the Payment of Public Revenue. May 1.

—— 38. Transactions between Europeans and Natives, with regard to Property, Loans, &c. Covenanted Civil Servants forbidden to Lend Money to Natives, &c. May 1.

—— 39. Appointment and Duties of Cauzies. May 1.

—— 40. Power of Natives to hear and decide Civil Suits. May 1.

—— 41. For forming Regulations into a Code. May 1.

—— 42. Collection of Calcutta Customs. May 1.

REG. 43. Grants of Land to Invalided Native Officers and Soldiers. May 1.

—— 44. Leases, Sale of Lands, &c. May 1.

—— 45. Malguzarry and Lakhiraj Lands. May 1.

—— 46. Admitting certain persons to sue in Courts of Judicature. See Paupers. May 1.

—— 47. Differences of Opinion between Judges. May 1.

—— 48. Formation of Quinquennial Registers. May 1.

—— 49. Affrays arising out of Disputed Boundaries. June 28.

—— 50. Court of Wards to admit Females to manage Estates. December 6.

—— 51. Illicit Manufacture of Intoxicating Liquors. December 27.

1794.

REG. 1. Extension of Penalties for the Illicit Sale or Manufacture of Intoxicating Liquors. Passed January 24.

—— 2. For postponing operation of Sec. 61, Reg. 8, 1793, in the Zillah of Bhaughulpore. March 14.

—— 3. Arrears of Revenue, exemption of certain parties from consequent Confinement, recovery of Public Money from Natives, expediting Settlement of Revenue Accounts, &c.

—— 4. Appointment of Putwarries, exemption of the Zillah of Ramghur from Reg. 8, 1793 ; Rates of Pottahs, &c. March 27.

—— 5. Concerning Appeals from Decisions of the Courts of Dewanny Adawlut. May 30.

—— 6. Parts of Secs. 18, 19, 20, and 23, referring to Silver Coin of Reg. 35, 1793, postponed to April 10, 1795. May 30.

—— 7. Judges and their Circuits. October 17.

—— 8. Registers of Zillah Courts and City, and Power of the latter to refer certain Accounts of Rent and Revenue to Collectors for Report. November 14.

Regulations, first called Acts 1834.

1795.

REG. 1. Concerning permanent settlement of Land Revenue in the province of Benares. Passed March 27.

Reg. 2. Temporary and permanent settlements of the Revenue in the province of Benares. March 27.

—— 3. Collecting Customs in the province of Benares. March 27.

—— 4. Prohibiting collection of Internal Duties in the province of Benares. March 27.

—— 5. Powers and Duties of Collectors of Revenue, Benares. March 27.

—— 6. The process by which the Collector and Tehsildar are to realise Revenue in Benares. March 27.

—— 7. Establishment of Dewanny Adawlut in the cities in the province of Benares. March 27.

—— 8. Modifying Reg. 4, 1793, and concerning certain Exemptions and Privileges of the Rajah of Benares, &c. March 27.

—— 9. Court of Appeal for Benares. March 27.

—— 10. Jurisdiction of the Sudder Dewanny Adawlut in Appeals, Benares. March 27.

—— 11. Hindoo and Mohammedan Law Officers. March 27.

—— 12. Duties of Officers of Civil and Military Courts. March 27.

—— 13. Vakeels in Bengal, Behar, and Orissa; and exemption of Rajah of Benares, &c.

—— 14. Concerning Disputed Boundaries. March 27.

—— 15. Reference of Suits to Nazim and the Rajah of Benares. March 27.

—— 16. Criminal Justice, Benares. March 27.

—— 17. Establishment of Police, Benares. March 27.

—— 18. Preservation of Reports, Benares. March 27.

—— 19. Quinquennial Register of Estates, Benares. March 27.

—— 20. Sale of Mulguzarry and Lakhiraj Lands. March 27.

—— 21. To prevent Female Infanticide, &c., Benares. March 27.

—— 22. Record of Judicial Rules previous to the Judicial Code, Benares. March 27.

—— 23. Paupers in Courts of Civil Judicature, Benares. March 27.

Reg. 24. To extend Reg. 28, 1793, to the province of Benares. March 27.

—— 25. To extend Reg. 47, 1793, concerning Differences of Opinion between Judges and Provincial Courts to Benares. March 27.

—— 26. Estates, Benares. March 27.

—— 27. Rights of Landed Proprietors, Benares. March 27.

—— 28. Registry for Wills, Deeds, &c., Benares. March 27.

—— 29. Concerning power of Courts of Appeal, &c., Benares. March 27.

—— 30. Preservation of Revenue Records, Benares. March 27.

—— 31. Commissions to Natives, Benares. March 27.

—— 32. Opium, Benares. March 27.

—— 33. Cultivation of Indigo by British subjects, Benares. March 27.

—— 34. Pensions, Benares. March 27.

—— 35. Recovery of Arrears of Rent. March 27.

—— 36. Judiciary Repeals, Sec. 7, Reg. 8, 1794.

—— 37. For expediting Justice. March 27.

—— 38. Fees in Courts of Civil Judicature. April 10.

—— 39. Calcutta Customs. May 22.

—— 40. Information on Illicit Manufacture of Salt. June 1.

—— 41. Validity of Lakhiraj Titles, Benares. July 31.

—— 42. Jaghires, Assessment, Grants, &c., Benares. July 31.

—— 43. Grants of Land to discharged Native Officers and Soldiers, Benares. August 28.

—— 44. Succession to Estates of Intestate Land Proprietors, Hindoo and Mohammedan Law. August 28.

—— 45. Recovery of Arrears of Rent, Benares. August 28.

—— 46. Embankments, Watercourses, &c. August 28.

—— 47. Illicit Sale of Intoxicating Liquors. August 28.

—— 48. Covenanted Civil Servants forbidden to lend Money to Native Landowners, Benares. August 28.

Reg. 49. Appointment and Duties of Cauzies, Benares. August 28.
—— 50. Limiting Leases by Zemindars, &c., Benares. August 38.
—— 51. Ryotty Pottahs, Benares. August 28.
—— 52. Importation of Salt. August 28.
—— 53. Illicit Trade in Opium. August 28.
—— 54. Extends Reg. 8, 1794, and Reg. 36, 1795, to Benares, with modifications. September 1.
—— 55. Constitution and Duties of Court of Wards. September 1.
—— 56. Invalids, Heirs of, absence of. September 1.
—— 57. Importation of Grain, Export Duties,. Calcutta. September 28.
—— 58. Collectors, Commission on, resumed, Lakhiraj. September 28.
—— 59. Silver Coin. September 29.
—— 60. Civil Courts Fees. November 13.
—— 61. Collectors to be furnished by the Mint Master with Money-weights.
—— 62. Withdrawal of Mint from Moorshedabad. December 11.

1796.

Reg. 1. Concerning Trial of Hill People for Crimes and Misdemeanours. Passed April 1.
—— 2. Trials of European British Subjects. April 18.
—— 3. Landed Estates and Leases. April 22.
—— 4. Providing for absence of Judges and Magistrates. May 13.
—— 5. Sales of Land. May 20.
—— 6. Pardon of Criminals. July 15.
—— 7. Repeals such parts of Regs. 8 and 10, 1793, as exclude Proprietors of Land from the management of their Estates on account of character. July 22.
—— 8. Fees to be received by Pleaders. September 12.
—— 9. Prisoners' Witnesses. September 23.
—— 10. Difference of opinion in Courts of Justice, as to construction of Regulations. October 7.
—— 11. Resistance to, or evasion of, Justice. October 28.

REG. 12. Deposits on purchase of Lands. December 16.

—— 13. Repeals parts of Regs. 5 and 6, 1793, relating to certain Decrees, and punishing litigious Appeals. December 16.

1797.

REG. 1. Concerning Exports and Imports, Calcutta, and the Importation of Opium. Passed January 2.

—— 2. Police responsibilities of Landholders in the province of Benares. January 27.

—— 3. Single Court of Circuit. January 27.

—— 4. Alteration of Reg. 9, 1793. March 13.

—— 5. Prevention of Dhurnah. March 24.

—— 6. Funds for Public Establishments, Stamp Duties, &c. April 10.

—— 7. Constituting office of Commissioner at Backergunge, Duty on Stills, &c. April 27.

—— 8. Judiciary recovery of Losses by Theft, &c. May 26.

—— 9. Duty on Foreign Indigo. August 11.

—— 10. Licences to be written on Stamped Paper. August 11.

—— 11. Form of Bonds. October 13.

—— 12. Limitation of Appeals. October 27.

—— 13. Powers and Duties of Assistant Magistrates. October 27.

—— 14. Relief to Prisoners, Restitution of Stolen Property, &c. Nov. 10.

—— 15. Fees for Preservation of Native Records and defining of "Jumma." November 24.

—— 16. Appeals to His Majesty in Council. November 24.

—— 17. Perjury. December 1.

—— 18. Reference to Native Commissioners. December 8.

—— 19. Translations, previous Rules rescinded. December 15.

1798.

REG. 1. Concerning the Prevention of Fraud in Conditional Sales. Passed January 19.

Reg. 2. Review of Causes. February 9.
—— 3. Annual Vacations of the Courts. March 2.
—— 4. Summoning of Officers of Salt Chokies. May 4.
—— 5. Security in Appeals and Fees, and Preservation of Records. July 5.

1799.

Reg. 1. Free Trade in Chunam, &c. Passed January 4.
—— 2. For Monthly Jail Deliveries, and concerning escaped Convicts. March 25.
—— 3. Postponement of Sec. 20, Reg. 35, 1793, within the Zillah of Sylhet. April 19.
—— 4. Trial of State Criminals. April 26.
—— 5. Limited interference of Zillah and City Courts, and persons dying intestate. May 3.
—— 6. Opium. July 11.
—— 7. Recovery of Arrears of Revenue. August 29.
—— 8. Mohammedan Law for Murder, and Reg. 21, 1795, and Reg. 5, 1797. October 10.
—— 9. Resistance to process of Civil Courts. October 10.
—— 10. Delay in transmission of Records to the Nizamut Adawlut. October 17.

1800.

Reg. 1. Appointment of Guardians to Minors not subject to jurisdiction of Court of Wards. Passed January 2.
—— 2. Use of Stone Quarries at Chunar, Ghazeepore, and Mirzapore. January 16.
—— 3. Registers of Zillah Judges. February 13.
—— 4. Adulteration of Salt. March 14.
—— 5. Extends Reg. 7, 1799, concerning the Punctual Payment of Rents to the province of Benares. March 27.
—— 6. Taxes on Spirituous Liquors. March 27.
—— 7. Stamp Duties. April 3.
—— 8. Establishment of Pergunnah and other Registers. July 3.
—— 9. Foundation of College, Fort William. July 10.
—— 10. Division of Landed Estates in the Jungle Mehals of Midnapore. December 11.

Reg. 11. Calcutta Customs; abolishes 1 per cent duty established Reg. 1, 1797. December 18.

1801.

Reg. 1. Realisation of Revenue, amending Reg. 7, 1799. Passed January 15.

—— 2. Speedy Justice; powers of single Judges and of Courts of Sudder Dewanny and Nizamut Adawlut. March 12.

—— 3. Perjury by Witnesses in Civil Suits. March 19.

—— 4. College of Fort William. April 11.

—— 5. Re-establishment of Calcutta Town Duties. May 14.

—— 6. Illicit Manufacture and Sale of Salt. July 4.

—— 7. Duty on Coasting Vessels; Gunpowder Ships entering Hooghly. July 16.

—— 8. Mohammedan Law, Accidental Homicide. July 31.

—— 9. Refers to Sec. 15, Reg. 8, 1799, upon persons employed in the Manufacture of Salt, also refers to Sec. 2, Reg. 11, 1796. July 31.

—— 10. Imported Goods, Patna, Dacca, Moorshedabad, Calcutta Town Duties. August 6.

—— 11. Government Customs, Calcutta. August 6.

—— 12. Salt. August 6.

1802.

Reg. 1. Government Customs, Piece Goods. Passed January 28.

—— 2. Duties on Spirits Distilled in the European manner. April 22.

—— 3. Paupers Civil Suits. April 22.

—— 4. Second Court of Appeal for division of Dacca. April 22.

—— 5. Customs Duties, also Town Duties in Bengal, Behar, Orissa, and Benares. July 8.

—— 6. Prevention of Sacrifice of Children, Sangor. August 20.

—— 7. Exemption of certain Articles from Duty. November 8.

1803.

Reg. 1. Concerning the Internal Government of the provinces ceded by the Nawab Vizier. Passed March 24.

REG. 2. Jurisdiction of Zillah Courts in the provinces ceded by the Nawab Vizier. March 24.

—— 3. Trials and Decisions of Civil Suits in ceded provinces of the Nawab Vizier. March 24.

—— 4. Courts of Appeal in provinces ceded by the Nawab Vizier. March 24.

—— 5. Power of Sudder Dewanny Adawlut in provinces ceded by Nawab Vizier. March 24.

—— 6. Powers and Duties of Magistrates in the provinces ceded by the Nawab Vizier. March 24.

—— 7. Courts of Circuit in provinces ceded by the Nawab Vizier. March 24.

—— 8. Jurisdiction the Nizamut Adawlut in the provinces ceded by the Nawab Vizier. March 24.

—— 9. Power of Judges in the various Courts of provinces ceded by the Nawab Vizier, to propose Regulations regarding certain matters. March 24.

—— 10. Appointment of Vakeels in the provinces ceded by the Nawab Vizier. March 24.

—— 11. Appointment of Hindoo and Mohammedan Law Officers in the provinces ceded by the Nawab Vizier. March 24.

—— 12. Appointment of Ministerial Officers in the Civil and Criminal Courts in the provinces ceded by the Nawab Vizier. March 24.

—— 13. Preservation of Reports of Appeals and Public Documents, Records, &c., in the Courts of the provinces ceded by the Nawab Vizier. March 24.

—— 14. Admission of Pauper Suits in the Courts of the provinces ceded by the Nawab Vizier. March 24.

—— 15. In case of Difference of Opinion amongst Judges in the provinces ceded by the Nawab Vizier. March 24.

—— 16. Power of Natives to hear Suits for sums under a certain value in the provinces ceded by the Nawab Vizier. March 24.

—— 17. Registry of Wills, Deeds, &c., in the provinces ceded by the Nawab Vizier. March 24.

REG. 18. Residence of British Subjects, their subjection to the Civil and Criminal Courts, in the provinces ceded by the Nawab Vizier. March 24.

—— 19. Of Government Servants forbidden to Lend Money to, or hold Property from, Natives, or rent Land, &c., in the provinces ceded by the Nawab Vizier. March 24.

—— 20. Procedure against Persons charged with State Crimes in the provinces ceded by the Nawab Vizier. March 24.

—— 21. Arbitration Suits in the provinces. March 24.

—— 22. Difference of Opinion in Courts of Justice as to Construction of Regulations in ceded provinces. March 24.

—— 23. Preservation of Revenue Records in each Zillah in ceded provinces. March 24.

—— 24. Validity of Title to grant Pensions, &c., in the ceded provinces. March 24.

—— 25. Settlement of Land Revenue, Duties of Collectors, Transfer of Estates, &c., in ceded provinces. March 24.

—— 26. Division and Sale of Revenue-paying Lands to ceded provinces. March 24.

—— 27. Realisation of Public Revenue by Tehsildars, &c., in the ceded provinces. March 24.

—— 28. Power of Landholders, &c., in the ceded provinces to distrain for Arrears of Rent or Revenue, and concerning Corporal Punishment. March 24.

—— 29. Duties of Putwarries in the ceded provinces. March 24.

—— 30. Grants of Ryotty Pottahs in the ceded provinces. March 24.

—— 31. Titles of Parties to Lands in the ceded provinces exempted from paying Revenue. March 24.

—— 32. Prevention of Boundary Affrays in the ceded provinces. March 24.

—— 33. Prevention of Embezzlement of Public Money and withholding of Papers in the ceded provinces. March 24.

Reg. 34. Interest on Money on Loans, Mortgages, &c., in ceded provinces. March 24.

—— 35. Police in ceded provinces. March 24.

—— 36. Titles of Persons to Land exempt from Revenue Payment in ceded provinces. March 24.

—— 37. Investment in ceded provinces. March 24.

—— 38. Transit Duties in ceded provinces. March 24.

—— 39. Salt Manufacture, and Sale of, in ceded provinces. March 24.

—— 40. Manufacture and Sale of Intoxicating Liquors, Drugs, &c., in ceded provinces. March 24.

—— 41. Cultivation of the Poppy in ceded provinces. March 24.

—— 42. Register of Zemindaries, &c., in ceded provinces. March 24.

—— 43. Judicial Fees in the Courts in ceded provinces. March 24.

—— 44. Repair of Watercourses, Wells, &c., in ceded provinces. March 24.

—— 45. Gold, Silver, and Copper Coinage in ceded provinces. March 24.

—— 46. Appointment of Head and Town Cauzies in the ceded provinces. March 24.

—— 47. Talooks, Leases, Rents, &c., in the ceded provinces. March 24.

—— 48. Adulteration of Salt. April 14.

—— 49. Occasional Assistant Judges ; Cases of Appeal ; Power of Native Head Commissioners. May 5.

—— 50. Oaths and Attendance of Witnesses, &c. May 5.

—— 51. Power of Nizamut Adawlut in the ceded provinces to take cognisance of certain Cases before the passing of Regulations on March 24.

—— 52. Court of Nurds in the ceded provinces. June 9.

—— 53. Concerning Punishments not defined by Mohammedan Law, and concerning the Definition of certain Crimes. July 21.

—— 54. Postponing the operation of Sec. 20, Reg. 35, 1793, within the Zillah of Chittagong. Nov. 24.

1804.

REG. 1. Invalid Jaghires Pensioned. Passed February 23.

—— 2. Alteration of Periods for Half-yearly Jail Deliveries. February 23.

—— 3. Resistance to the Processes of Zillah Criminal Courts; Female Infanticide. March 8.

—— 4. Administration of Justice extended to Cuttack, as in Bengal, Behar, and Orissa. May 3.

—— 5. Appointment and removal of Native Officials; also concerning Administration of Oaths to Revenue Officers. August 16.

—— 6. Rescinds Reg. 39, 1803, for Levying Duty on Salt, &c. August 25.

—— 7. Importation and Exportation of Salt. October 15.

—— 8. Transferring the Zillahs of Allahabad and Goruckpore from Division of Court of Appeal to Provincial Court of Appeal. November 27.

—— 9. Courts of Circuit and Appeal for ceded provinces. December 14.

—— 10. Power of Governor-General to punish State Offenders by Court-Martial. December 14.

—— 11. Collection of Customs and rescinding Reg. 37, 1803. December 14.

1805.

REG. 1. Concerning Appeals. Passed February 14.

—— 2. Civil Courts, Limitation of Time for Suits, Appeals, &c. February 18.

—— 3. Punishment of Gang-robbery and Theft. March 28.

—— 4. Duty on certain Goods; extending 31, 1793, to Benares. April 25.

—— 5. Land Revenue. April 22.

—— 6. Duties abolished and established. June 27.

—— 7. Exemption of Covenanted Servants from certain Oaths. July 11.

—— 8. Extension of Regulations of 1803 to the conquered provinces. July 11.

—— 9. Causing Proclamation to become a Regulation. July 11.

REG. 10. Courts of Sudder Dewanny Adawlut, Chief Judge of. July 25.

—— 11. Extension of Reg. 45, 1803, to conquered provinces within the Doab and on right bank of Jumna and to ceded provinces; concerning Gold, Silver, and Copper Coin, also concerning Native Officers. August 15.

—— 12. Collection of Public Revenue, Cuttack. September 5.

—— 13. Maintenance of Public Peace in Cuttack. September 5.

—— 14. Civil Justice in Cuttack. September 5.

—— 15. Appointment of Hindoo and Mohammedan Law Officers. September 12.

—— 16. Extending Jurisdiction of Courts of Circuit and of the Court of Nizamut Adawlut. September 19.

—— 17. Management of Joint Undivided Estates. October 24.

—— 18. Magistrates and Zemindars. December 13.

—— 19. Channel of Communication, with a Form of Address to Nazim of Bengal. December 19.

1806.

REG. 1. Abolition of Zillah of Beerbhoom, Moorshedabad. Passed March 27.

—— 2. Modification of Rules of Process in Civil Courts of Judicature. March 27.

—— 3. Silver Coin. March 27.

—— 4. Pilgrim Tax, Juggernauth. April 3.

—— 5. Evasion of Pilgrim Tax. April 17.

—— 6. Repairs of Embankments. April 17.

—— 7. Court of Civil Judicature, vicinity of Calcutta, better known as the Twenty-four Pergunnahs. April 26.

—— 8. Reception of Complaints against European Officers. May 12.

—— 9. Illicit Manufacture and Sale of Salt. June 5.

—— 10. Information against Public Officers, European. June 19.

—— 11. Facilitating progress of Troops and Travellers. July 3.

REG. 12. Annexation of South Sousa and Sahar to the jurisdiction of Agra.

—— 13. Forging Public Stamps or Stamped Paper. July 10.

—— 14. Abolition of Zillah of Seharunpore. July 23.

—— 15. Concerning certain clauses in Sec. 2, Reg. 2, 1796, and Sec. 19, Reg. 6, 1803; and of Rule in Sec. 7, Reg. 5, 1799, relating to European British Subjects. July 24.

—— 16. Address to the Nazim of Bengal. September 4.

—— 17. Loans, Mortgages, Conditional Sales, &c. September 11.

—— 18. Collecting Tolls on the Eastern and other Canals. October 16.

—— 19. Duty on Spirituous Liquors, Leakage, &c. October 16.

—— 20. Manufacture of Spirituous Liquors in European Cantonments. October 23.

—— 21. Office of Tehsildar in Benares and other provinces. December 2.

—— 22. Concerning Pensions charged on the Land Revenue. December 18.

1807.

REG. 1. Powers of single Judge in Provincial Courts of Appeal. Passed January 29.

—— 2. Punishment of Perjury and Forgery. January 29.

—— 3. College at Fort William. February 5.

—— 4. Manner of receiving and issuing Rupees of ceded and conquered provinces. March 19.

—— 5. Cultivation of the Poppy. March 19.

—— 6. Restricting the Partition of small Estates. April 2.

—— 7. Mode of Payment of Revenue by Zemindars, Benares. April 16.

—— 8. Stamped Paper. April 16.

—— 9. Rules of Criminal Process, Police Officers, &c., Calendars and Reports. May 12.

—— 10. Appointment of Commissioner for settlement of ceded and conquered provinces. June 11.

REG. 11. Control of Customs touching Transportation of Arms beyond the Company's Territories. June 11.

—— 12. Ameers of Police, Register of Guards and Watchmen. June 19.

—— 13. Rupees and Gold Mohurs not of established Coinage. June 25.

—— 14. Amending Police System. July 2.

—— 15. Appointment of Judges for the Sudder Dewanny Adawlut Courts and Nizamut Adawlut. July 23.

1808.

REG. 1. Taxes on Taur, Kajoor, and Reared Trees. Passed March 18.

—— 2. Property of Minors subject to the jurisdiction of the European Court at Chandernagore. April 16.

—— 3. Retail of Taury. May 13.

—— 4. Office of Canoongoe. June 17.

—— 5. Settlement of Land Revenue in ceded provinces. July 8.

—— 6. Settlement of Revenue of Cuttack. September 2.

—— 7. Registers of Lakhiraj Lands. September 16.

—— 8. Punishment of Gang Robbery. September 19.

—— 9. Leaders of Robber Gangs. November 4.

—— 10. Superintendent of Police for Calcuttă, Dacca, and Moorshedabad. November 28.

—— 11. Rent payable by the Heirs of invalid Jaghiredars. November 28.

—— 12. Administration of Civil and Criminal Justice in Serampore. December 23.

—— 13. Touching Security for delaying execution of Decrees pending Appeals. December 30.

1809.

REG. 1. Board of Commissioners. Passed February 3.

—— 2. Power of Commander-in-Chief to convene Courts-martial for Bengal Army beyond the sea. February 24.

—— 3. Support of Police in Cantonments and Military Bazaars. March 13.

—— 4. Juggernauth. April 28.

—— 5. Trial of Native Offenders in places beyond the limits of the British Provinces.

Reg. 6. Illicit Cultivation of the Poppy. August 24.
—— 7. Duties on Stamped Paper. August 4.
—— 8. Appointment and removal of Native Officials. August 29.
—— 9. Appeals to Calcutta Provincial Court.
—— 10. Copper Coinage. December 15.

1810.

Reg. 1. Attendance and Functions of the Law Officers of the Courts of Circuit. Passed January 12.
—— 2. Suppression of Robberies, &c., by Cozaucks. January 23.
—— 3. Paupers' Oaths. January 23.
—— 4. Abolition of Office of Commissioner in Cuttack. February 2.
—— 5. Division of Revenue-paying Estates. February 2.
—— 6. Zemindars bound to give information concerning Robberies. February 9.
—— 7. Collection of Tolls between Bootakhana Road and Salt Water Lake. February 9.
—— 8. Superintendent of Police for Patna, Benares, and Bareilly. February 9.
—— 9. Rescinding all old Regulations concerning Customs, and making new ones. April 10.
—— 11. Temple of Juggernauth. April 27.
—— 12. Modifying Rules in Sec. 2, Reg. 7, 1809, and Sec. 6, Reg 10, 1809. May 4.
—— 13. Expedition of Justices; Powers of single Judges of the Sudder Dewanny Adawlut. May 4.
—— 14. Powers of Court of Nizamut Adawlut to remit and mitigate Sentences of Punishment. July 6.
—— 15. House Tax. October 6.
—— 16. Appointment of Magistrates and Assistant Magistrates; Rewards to Police. October 9.
—— 17. Illicit Importation of Salt, &c. October 9.
—— 18. Pilgrim Duties, Allahabad. December 14.
—— 19. Rent for Hindoo Temples, Public Buildings, &c.; disposal of Nuzzool Property. December 14.
—— 20. Camp Followers amenable to Martial Law; Military Bazaars, &c. December 29.

1811.

REG. 1. Punishment of Housebreakers and Purchasers of Stolen Property. Passed February 15.

—— 2. Support of Native invalid Commissioned and Non-commissioned Officers. April 5.

—— 3. Duties on articles of Trade. April 30.

—— 4. Exemption from House Tax. May 28.

—— 5. Duty on Putcherry. May 28.

—— 6. The Holders of Lakhiraj and Malgoozary Lands. June 14.

—— 7. Power of Police Darogahs and Zemindars. June 25.

—— 8. Modifying parts of Regs. 31 and 36, 1803. July 6.

—— 9. Division of Landed Property. July 30.

—— 10. Importation of Slaves prohibited. August 6.

—— 11. Revising Jumma on Lands. August 20.

—— 12. Augmentation of number of Judges. August 27.

—— 13. Discharge of Duties of Board of Revenue. October 18.

—— 14. Punishment by Transportation. December 3.

1812.

REG. 1. Duty on Horses; Exportation of Woollens from Bengal to China. Passed January 13.

—— 2. Duty on Coinage of Silver Bullion. March 21.

—— 3. Preliminary inquiries into Criminal Charges and Apprehension of Criminals. April 18.

—— 4. Conduct of Suits of Native Princes in British Courts. April 24.

—— 5. Collection of Land Revenue. May 1.

—— 6. Alteration of Form of Bond inserted in Clause 5, Sec. 3, Reg. 3, 1811. May 2.

—— 7. Rescinds Regs. 15, 1810, and 4, 1811. May 9.

—— 8. Manufacture of Saltpetre, May 30.

—— 9. Settlements in ceded Provinces not permanent. July 11.

—— 10. Settlement of conquered Provinces on left

banks of the Jumna, and of the Territory ceded by the Peishwa in Bundelcund, and of the district of Cuttack, not to be permanent. July 11.

Reg. 11. Removal of suspicious Immigrants from Foreign Countries. July 18.

—— 12. Time to affix Stamp on Law or Money Papers. July 25.

—— 13. Duty on Licences for the Sale of Spirituous Liquors, &c. July 25.

—— 14. Grants of Leases by Proprietors in ceded Provinces. July 31.

—— 15. Extending certain parts of Reg. 1, 1811, to ceded Provinces and Benares, and rescinding Reg. 2, 1810. August 8.

—— 16. Execution of Judgments passed by the Court of Bequests, Calcutta, by the Judge of the Dewanny Adawlut, by the Twenty-four Pergunnahs. August 15.

—— 17. Modifies Secs. 11 and 12, Reg. 1, 1812. August 29.

—— 18. Explaining Sec. 2, Reg. 5, 1812; rescinding Secs. 3 and 4, Reg. 44, 1793, and Secs. 3 and 4, Reg. 5, 1795, and enacting fresh Rules. September 19.

—— 19. Collection of Government Customs and Town Duties. October 17.

—— 20. Registry of Deeds, &c., and delivery of Indigo. October 17.

—— 21. Rescinds part of Reg. 1, 1811, respecting Licences to certain Trades. October 31.

—— 22. Exempting certain Territories from General Regulations, and annexing certain Lands to the Zillah of Bundelcund. December 5.

1813.

Reg. 1. Modifying Settlement of Cuttack, the Pergunnah of Puttaspore, &c. Passed February 27.

—— 2. Punishment of Native Officers for using Public Money. March 6.

—— 3. Review of Civil Cases appealable. April 3.

—— 4. Boat Tolls. April 3.

—— 5. Cuttack. June 1.

REG. 6. Arbitration Suits; Forcible Dispossession of Land. July 10.

—— 7. Extending to ceded and conquered Provinces Reg. 3, 1801, and Sec. 13, Reg. 8, 1794, and rescinding parts of Secs. 11 and 15, Reg. 1, 1803. July 17.

—— 8. Trial of Offences committed in Foreign Territories. July 24.

—— 9. Restriction of Punishment of Transportation. July 24.

—— 10. Sale of Spirituous Liquors, &c. August 21.

—— 11. Respecting Payment of Pensions. August 28.

—— 12. Collection of Government Customs and Town Duties. September 30.

—— 13. Appointment and Maintenance of Police in Dacca, Patna, and Moorshedabad.

—— 14. Abolishing Duties on Importation of Horses by Sea or through Cuttack. November 6.

—— 15. Abolition of Office of Dewan to the Collectors of Land Revenue. November 13.

—— 16. Rescinds Sec. 10, Reg. 13, 1806. November 13.

—— 17. Inquiries into Charges and Complaints against European Public Officers. December 24.

1814.

REG. 1. Concerning Revenue raised by Stamps. Passed January 1.

—— 2. Trial of Officers for Offences committed in their Official Capacity. January 29.

—— 3. Extending provisions of Reg. 13, 1813, to the Stations at which the Magistrates reside in the Divisions of Dacca, Moorshedabad, Calcutta, and Patna. February 5.

—— 4. Repealing Reg. 8, 1812. March 11.

—— 5. Appointment of Provincial Judges of Courts of Appeal and Circuit. March 19.

—— 6. Modifying specified parts of Reg. 9, 1810, and Reg. 1, 1812, regarding rates of *ad valorem* Duties.

—— 7. Copper Coinage of Benares. April 29.

—— 8. Extending Clause 2, Sec. 4, Reg. 3, 1812, to cases of Murder, Arson, and Theft. May 13.

Reg. 9. Explaining Reg. 13, 1813, and Reg. 3, 1814. May 17.

—— 10. Explaining that part of Reg. 1, 1814, relating to Government Contracts. May 20.

—— 11. Punishment of Housebreaking. May 27.

—— 12. Pensions to invalid Native Officers. May 27.

—— 13. Abolition of the Office of Cutwal in Dacca, Patna, and Moorshedabad. June 10.

—— 14. Twenty-four Pergunnahs formed into two distinct Jurisdictions. June 14.

—— 15. Punishment of Persons convicted of two or more offences. June 21.

—— 16. Extending Reg. 8, 1813, to the Stations at which the Magistrates reside in the Divisions of Benares and Bareilly, except the city of Benares. June 23.

—— 17. Recovery of Arrears due from Persons making or selling Intoxicating Liquors and Drugs. July 29.

—— 18. Arrears of Public Revenue, recovery of the same ; Sale of Land, &c. August 23.

—— 19. Division of Revenue ; paying Estates. September 17.

—— 20. Rescinding Regulation in force respecting College of Fort William. September 27.

—— 21. Prohibiting Judges, Collectors, &c., from employing their Native Creditors on their official Establishments. October 4.

—— 22. Manufacture and Sale of Salt in Cuttack. November 4.

—— 23. Reducing to one Regulation the several Rules respecting Moonsiffs, Native Commissioners, and Sudder Ameens, and for determining the power of these Officers. November 28.

—— 24. Concerning the abolition of the Office of Assistant-Judge in the Zillah and City Court, and the constitution and jurisdiction of these Courts. November 29.

—— 25. Powers of single Judges of Sudder Dewanny Adawlut and Nizamut Adawlut. November 29.

—— 26. Special and Summary Appeals. November 29.

—— 27. For reducing into one Regulation the Rules respecting the Office of Vakeel. November 29.

REG. 28. For reducing into one Regulation the Rules respecting those Persons who sue as Paupers. November 29.

—— 29. Settlement of the Ghautwaullee Mehals in Beerbhoom. December 3.

1815.

REG. 1. Right of British Government to assess certain Lands held under Mocurreree and Istumraree Grants of any preceding Government, on decease of the holders thereof. Passed February 18.

—— 2. For extending Provisions of Clause 7, Sec. 12, Reg. 24, 1814. April 18.

—— 3. Concerning the settlement of Cuttack, the Pergunnah of Puttaspore, and its Dependencies. May 12.

—— 4. Collection of Customs in the territories dependent on Fort William. August 26.

—— 5. Suspending operation of Regulations in the Pergunnah of Bogree. December 29.

1816.

REG. 1. Local Revenue Commission in the Provinces of Benares and Behar. Passed January 5.

—— 2. The Office of Canoongoe, respecting its re-establishment in part of Behar. January 5.

—— 3. For rescinding Reg. 12, 1808. January 12.

—— 4. Prisoners in Civil Suits may petition on unstamped paper; treatment of Prisoners, &c. February 9.

—— 5. For establishing the Office of Canoongoe in Cuttack, Puttaspore, and its Dependencies. February 16.

—— 6. The Settlement of Cuttack, Puttaspore, &c. March 8.

—— 7. Concerning the tenure of certain Lands to be held as an independent Jaghire by his Highness Amrut Rao. March 22.

—— 8. Office of Superintendent and Remembrancer of Legal Affairs. March 29.

—— 9. Commissioner of Revenue in the Sunderbunds. April 26.

—— 10. Exportation and Importation of Saltpetre. April 26.

REG. 11. Right of Inheritance in certain tributary Estates in Cuttack. May 10.

—— 12. Establishment of a Custom-house at Cox's Bazaar. May 17.

—— 13. For reducing into one Regulation Rules about Opium. May 17.

—— 14. Management of Public Jails; also Jail at Alipore, and transportation of Convicts to the Island of Mauritius. May 17.

—— 15. Trial of Civil Suits in which the Native Officers and Soldiers in the Presidency of Fort William may be Parties. June 10.

—— 16. Settlement in those Provinces ceded to the British Government by the Nawab Vizier. July 5.

—— 17. Revision of Police and Jail Establishments, and concerning Police Arrangements generally. July 26.

—— 18. Annexing to the Zillah of Allahabad the Pergunnah of Handya. August 16.

—— 19. Ferries, Tolls, &c. August 23.

—— 20. Modifying parts of Reg. 3, 1811. October 25.

—— 21. Modifying Sec. 43, Reg. 45, 1803, concerning Copper Pice. November 8.

—— 22. Reducing to one Regulation all Rules concerning Chokydars of Police. December 27.

1817.

REG. 1. Extending the Authority of the Commissioners in Behar and Benares to the districts of Ramghur, Bhaugulpore, and Purneah. Passed January 17.

—— 2. Re-establishing Office of Canoongoe. January 17.

—— 3. Diminishing the expense of Appeals. January 31.

—— 4. Annexation of Dehra Doon to the Zillah of Seharunpore. February 28.

—— 5. Discovery of Treasure; Rights of Government and Individuals. February 28.

—— 6. Explaining Sec. 2, Reg. 24, 1803, touching Pensions. April 11.

—— 7. Modifying Sec. 4, Reg. 22, 1816, concerning the Allowances of Chokydars of Police. April 18.

Reg. 8. Modifying Reg. 17, 1813. May 2.

—— 9. Rescinding Reg. 5, 1815, respecting Pergunnah Bogree. July 22.

—— 10. Trial of Persons charged with great Crimes in Kumaon and other territories ceded to H.E.I.C. by the Rajah of Nepaul. July 22.

—— 11. Modifying certain parts of Regs. 19 and 37, 1793, and Regs. 41 and 42, 1795. July 29.

—— 12. Office of Putwaree in ceded Provinces. August 12.

—— 13. Office of Canoongoe extended to certain Provinces, and extending Reg. 12, 1817. August 26.

—— 14. Amending parts of Reg. 2, 1812. September 9.

—— 15. Duty on Foreign Salt. September 9.

—— 16. Duty on Foreign Opium. September 9.

—— 17. The effectual Administration of Criminal Justice in certain cases, Mohammedan Law. September 16.

—— 18. Oaths for Native Judicial Officers, and concerning other Provisions relating to Native Officers and Law Officers of the Civil and Criminal Courts. September 16.

—— 19. Civil Justice, recovery of Arrears of Rent. September 16.

—— 20. Darogahs, &c., concerning evasion of Criminal Process; Assistance given to Police by Owners and Farmers of Land. October 7.

—— 21. Modifying parts of Reg. 4, 1815, and rescinding part of Reg. 9, 1810. October 28.

—— 22. Power of Judge and Magistrate of Cuttack with respect to their Native Ministerial Officers. October 28.

—— 23. Modifying parts of Regs. 19 and 37, 1793, and defining the right of Government to the Revenue of certain Lands. October 28.

—— 24. Constitution of Commission established in Behar, Benares, and other Provinces, for extending that Commission to Dinagepore and Rungpore, concerning Power of a single Member of the Board of Revenue, or a Commission of that Board. December 9.

REG. 25. Pice. December 9.

—— 26. Furruckabad Rupees. December 16.

1818.

REG. 1. For establishing the Office of Canoongoe in certain Provinces, and for extending Reg. 12, 1817, to the same. Passed March 17.

—— 2. Annexing to Bundelcund certain Territories formerly belonging to Nana Govind Rao.

—— 3. For the Confinement of State Prisoners without Judicial Proceedings. April 7.

—— 4. Re-establishing the Dewanny Adawlut of the Northern Division of Seharunpore. April 14.

—— 5. Establishing a Commissioner of Cuttack. April 28.

—— 6. Protracted Confinement of Persons in Criminal Cases, Bail, &c. May 12.

—— 7. Rescinding certain Regulations with respect to Foreign Trade. August 28.

—— 8. For rescinding part of Clause 6, Sec. 2, Reg. 53, 1803, and concerning Security for the good behaviour of Prisoners and their appearance. August 28.

—— 9. Extending for the Period of Five Years the present Settlement to certain conquered Provinces, in certain cases. September 18.

—— 10. For insuring punctual Collections of Revenue in Cuttack. October 9.

—— 11. Modifying parts of Reg. 13, 1816. November 6.

—— 12. Extending the Powers of Magistrates and Joint Magistrates, in cases of Housebreaking, Theft, &c., or in attempts to escape from Jail. November 5.

—— 13. Extending for Three Years the existing Settlement in certain Provinces and under certain circumstances. November 20.

—— 14. Concerning Culcutta Sicca Rupee and Gold Mohur. December 24.

1819.

REG. 1. For replacing Dinagepore and Rungpore under the Board of Revenue, extending the Authority of Board of Commissioners in Behar and Benares to Goruckpore, concerning the Offices of Canoongoes and Putwarry in Bengal, and for modifying certain parts of Reg. 12, 1817. Passed February 5.

REG. 2. Concerning resumption of supposed Lakhiraj Lands. February 12.

—— 3. For extending the Provisions of Sec. 10, Reg. 8, 1818, to Robbers not being Dacoits. April 16.

—— 4. For the establishing of a Board for the Superintendence of the Revenue derived from certain sources. April 22.

—— 5. Concerning Coinage and Mints. June 25.

—— 6. For rescinding Reg. 9, 1816, and replacing other Rules with respect to Ferries. June 25.

—— 7. Concerning Misdemeanours and their Punishments. July 9.

—— 8. Validity of certain Tenures, Sale of Putnee Talooks for Rent, Collection of Rents in Bengal. September 3.

—— 9. Concerning Special Appeals, Powers of the Zillah and City Registers and Registers of Provincial Courts. October 29.

—— 10. Consolidating Salt Regulations. December 7.

—— 11. Concerning Furruckabad and Benares Rupees.

1820.

REG. 1. Concerning Sale of Putnee Talooks for Rent. Passed January 11.

—— 2. Concerning Offences by Natives in Chandernagore and Chinsurah. February 25.

—— 3. Rescinding parts of Reg. 11, 1806, and prohibiting the Pressing of Coolies. March 24.

—— 4. Concerning the Power of the Magistrate to give effect to Military Sentences; the Power of Control of the Courts of Circuit, and for amending Clause 2, Sec. 3, Reg. 12, 1818. July 21.

—— 5. Frontier Duties on Tobacco. August 25.

—— 6. Rescinding Secs. 46, 47, and 48, Reg. 45, 1803. August 25.

—— 7. Alteration of Punishment and form of Trial in cases of Dhurna. December 8.

1821.

REG. 1. Commission concerning Property in ceded and conquered provinces, and the terms, interests, and privileges of the agricultural community. Passed January 13.

—— 2. The powers of Moonsiffs, Sudder Ameens, &c., discharge of additional duties, local jurisdiction of Registers, their Fees, Decrees of Provincial Courts, Appeals, Office of Register of Provincial Courts of Appeal and Circuit abolished. January 19.

—— 3. Assistants to the Magistrates, Hindoo and Mohammedan Law Officers, Period of Appeal in Foujdary cases, rescinding parts of Secs. 12 and 17, Reg. 22, 1816, Collection of Assessment for Chokydars of Police, and concerning Suspected Persons. January 19.

—— 4. Collectors of Land Revenue, and the powers of other Officers to act in that capacity; the duties of the Office. January 19.

—— 5. The Benares and Furruckabad Rupee; its value in payment of the Revenue of Malgoozars. November 23.

1822.

REG. 1. Amending Reg. 49, 1793; Reg. 32, 1803; and Reg. 5, 1809. Passed January 18.

—— 2. Collection of Customs and Town Duties. March 19.

—— 3. Collection of Land Revenue in the Presidency of Fort William. March 19.

—— 4. Providing for the more effectual Administration of Criminal Justice, Mohammedan Law. March 29.

—— 5. Amending some Provisions of Reg. 9, 1808. June 13.

—— 6. Extending Court of Wards to Benares, and concerning the Powers of other Courts of Wards. August 1.

—— 7. Concerning Land Revenue in ceded and conquered Provinces; Leases, Rents, &c. August 8.

—— 8. Place of Trial for those guilty of Crimes and Misdemeanours. September 12.

—— 9. Emigrants, Foreign Tribunals, &c. September 19.

Reg. 10. Exempting Garrow Mountaineers and other Tribes from Regulations, and establishing for them a special system of Government. September 19.

—— 11. Recovery of Revenue ; the Sale of Land for the same ; Government not liable for Errors of Courts of Justice. November 22.

1823.

Reg. 1. Amending part of Reg. 1, 1821. Passed February 20.

—— 2. Effectual Suppression of Affrays. March 20.

—— 3. Licensing of Printing-Presses, and restraining the Liberty of the Press. April 5.

—— 4. Concerning self-convicted Prisoners: Concerning Sec. 14, Reg. 7, 1794, for modifying Clauses 3 and 4 of Sec. 2, Reg. 14, 1811 ; and for rescinding Secs. 4 and 5, Reg. 24, 1814, and Secs. 2 and 4, Reg. 25, 1814. May 29.

—— 5. Rowannahs issued by Officers in the Dehlee Territory, and concerning Transit Duty on Piece Goods. June 19.

—— 6. Summary Suits concerning the Cultivation of Indigo. July 10.

—— 7. Loans from Natives by Covenanted Servants forbidden. October 30.

1824.

Reg. 1. For enabling Officers of Government to obtain Lands for Public Works, and the Manufacture of Salt. Passed January 8.

—— 2. Abolition of Furruckabad Mint and Rupee. February 5.

—— 3. Extension of Jurisdiction of Registers. February 12.

—— 4. Registry of Deeds. February 12.

—— 5. Extending Reg. 6, 1823, to Orissa, Behar, and Benares, and the ceded and conquered Provinces. March 4.

—— 6. Individuals charged with two or more Offences, and modifying Clause 2, Sec. 2, and certain other Provisions of Reg. 12, 1818. March 25.

Reg. 7. Manufacture and Sale of Spirituous Liquors, Opium, &c. March 25.

—— 8. Rescinding Reg. 4 of 1813, and concerning Tolls on certain Rivers. April 8.

—— 9. Extending the existing Settlement in most instances in conquered Provinces and Bundelcund for five years. July 1.

—— 10. Empowering Magistrates to tender Pardon. July 8.

—— 11. Power of Registers or Magistrates' Assistants to make Local Investigation in certain cases. July 15.

—— 12. Reviving Penalties on Revenue Defaulters. July 22.

—— 13. Enlarging Powers of Sudder Ameen. July 22.

—— 14. Summary Suits for Arrears of Rent. July 22.

—— 15. Enabling Magistrates, &c., to act summarily with regard to cases of forcible Dispossession of Land, &c. July 22.

—— 16. Stamp Duties. November 18.

1825.

Reg. 1. Judicial Warrant and Police Officers. Passed January 13.

—— 2. Respecting review of Judgment and Pauper Special Appeals.

—— 3. To empower Courts of Circuit to punish Robbery without appeal.

—— 4. Giving Bail to keep the Peace.

—— 5. Uniting Offices of Judge and Collector.

—— 6. Supply of Troops on march ; modifying Reg. 11, 1806.

—— 7. Attachment and Sales of Land in execution of Decrees.

—— 8. On employment of Public and Private Servants.

—— 9. Extending provisions of Reg. 7, 1822.

—— 10. Defining Duties of Commercial Residents.

—— 11. Concerning Gains and Losses of Land by Floods, &c.

—— 12. Corporal Punishment.

—— 13. Settlement of Resumed Lands.

REG. 14. Validity of Lakhiraj Grants.
—— 15. Duties and Drawbacks.
—— 16. Punishment of Dacoity.
—— 17. Improving various Judicial Circuits.
—— 18. Annexing Chinsurah to Zillah Hooghly.
—— 19. Exercise of Judicial Rights by the Nawab Nazim.
—— 20. Military Courts of Requests.
—— 21. Administration of the Dehra Doon.

1826.

REG. 1. For augmenting the Number of Judges of the Provincial Courts of Appeal and Circuit. Passed March 2.
—— 2. Concerning settlement of Provinces ceded by the Nawab Vizier. April 26.
—— 3. Extending to Dewannee Prisoners some of the Provisions in Reg. 14, 1816; and for modifying Rule in Sec. 3, Reg. 41, 1816. May 11.
—— 4. Expediting Proceedings of Mofussil and Sudder Special Commissions. June 22.
—— 5. Annexing Pergunnah of Goberdhun to Agra. June 22.
—— 6. Constituting Futtehpore a distinct Zillah.
—— 7. Benares Mint. July 13.
—— 8. Contraband Opium. July 13.
—— 9. Customs, Revenue, &c. July 13.
—— 10. Allowing retail sale of Salt, Saline Food, &c. July 13.
—— 11. Appointment of Hindoo and Mohammedan Law-Officers, Vakeels, &c. August 4.
—— 12. Stamp Duties in Calcutta. December 14.*

1827.

—— 1. Administration of Criminal Justice in Bhangulpore. Passed May 17.
—— 2. Criminal Trials in Bareilly. May 17.
—— 3. Punishment of Corruption and Extortion of Officers of the Courts of Judicature.
—— 4. Extending in Special Cases the power of Sudder Ameens. December 27.

Reg. 5. Management of Estates under attachment by Zillah Courts. December 27.

1828.

Reg. 1. Commutation of Sentences by the Governor-General. Passed April 10.

—— 2. Rescinding part of Reg. 1, 1799, concerning freedom of Trade on Sylhet frontier. April 10.

—— 3. Speedy hearing of Appeals with regard to Revenue, Lands, Rents, &c. June 12.

—— 4. Powers of Collectors when making Settlements. August 7.

—— 5. Power of Zillah and City Courts to execute awards of Military Courts in certain Cases. August 28.

—— 6. Explaining Intent and Meaning of parts of Reg. 2, 1823. September 4:

—— 7. Power of the Rajah of Benares. September 12.

—— 8. Punishment of Affrays. October 16.

—— 9. Special or second Appeals *in forma pauperis*. November 27.

1829.

Reg. 1. Administration of Civil and Criminal Justice. Passed January 1.

—— 2. Rescinding Sec. 6, Reg. 15, 1824; Appeal from Magistrates to Commissioners of Circuit. March 10.

—— 3. Judges, Native Law-Officers, &c.; Copyists, Oaths, &c. April 28.

—— 4. Appeals to Special Commissioner; modifying certain former Regulations. May 5.

—— 5. For rescinding parts of Reg. 10, 1817, and parts of Reg. 21, 1825. May 12.

—— 6. Power of Magistrates and Joint-Magistrates in cases of Theft. June 9.

—— 7. Reports, Calendars, Registers, &c., their Forms, &c.; rescinding certain Regulations concerning them. June 9.

—— 8. For amending Reg. 5 of 1809, and Reg. 1 of 1822. June 9.

—— 9. Rescinding parts of Reg. 31, 1793, and concerning the relation of Company's Agents to Natives. June 9.

Reg. 10. For consolidating all Rules concerning Stamp Duties. June 16.

—— 11. Repair of Embankments. July 7.

—— 12. Modifying Provisions of Reg. 12, 1825. July 7.

—— 13. For abolishing Office of Superintendent and Remembrancer of Legal Affairs. July 14.

—— 14. Extending certain Regulations to Persons residing in Foreign Territories. September 1.

—— 15. Valuation of Imported Goods. September 15.

—— 16. Salt Duties. November 24.

—— 17. Concerning abolition of Suttee. December 4.

—— 18. For rescinding Sec. 3, Reg. 4, 1829, and altering Provisions of Reg. 1, 1824, and Reg. 1, 1829. December 8.

1830.

Reg. 1. Rescinding parts of Reg. 1, 1829, with reference to the administration of Justice in the Zillah of Midnapore. Passed January 12.

—— 2. For altering Reg. 7, 1818, and for the regulation of Foreign Trade. January 26.

—— 3. Export Duties, and for altering parts of Reg. 15, 1829. January 26.

—— 4. Explaining Clause 4, Sec. 3, Reg. 1, 1829. March 9.

—— 5. Indigo Contracts. June 9.

—— 6. Subsistence Allowance to Debtors. August 12.

—— 7. Recovery of Arrears of Revenue. September 7.

—— 8. Inquiry by Magistrates, &c., into Criminal Charges. September 7.

1831.

Reg. 1. Rescinding Clause 2, Sec. 3, Reg. 16, 1825. Passed January 8.

—— 2. Doubts of Legality of certain Criminal Trials. May 31.

—— 3. Copper Coins. October 18.

—— 4. Prince of Wales Island, Singapore, and Malacca. October 18.

Reg. 5. Moonsiffs, Sudder Ameens, Vakeels, &c., their Powers and Duties. November 1.

—— 6. Extra Judges and a Sudder Court established in the North-West Provinces. November 1.

—— 7. Power of Zillah and City Judges to hold Monthly Jail Deliveries. November 1.

—— 8. Concerning Suits for Arrears of Rent. November 1.

—— 9. Speedy Administration of Justice. November 1.

—— 10. Concerning Deputation from Sudder Board of Revenue to control Revenue Affairs in the North-West Provinces. November 1.

—— 11. Employment of Tehsildars as Darogahs. November 1.

1832.

Reg. 1. Concerning the Maharajah Bajee Rao Bahadoor. Passed February 7.

—— 2. Administration of Justice in certain cases; Punishment of Police, &c. February 14.

—— 3. Extending Provisions of Reg. 10, 1811; Emancipation of Slaves. March 13.

—— 4. Explaining Sec. 41, Reg. 10, 1819; Transport of Salt. March 13.

—— 5. For annexing Delhi Territory, &c., to the Jurisdiction of the Courts of Sudder Dewanny and Nizamut Adawlut, &c. May 29.

—— 6. Employment of Native Agency by Europeans in certain cases of Administration of Justice; Futwas, &c. July 31.

—— 7. For modifying and adding to certain Provisions of Reg. 5, 1831; uncovenanted Judges in Zillah Courts. October 16.

—— 8. Rescinding Reg. 14, 1814, and establishing Zillah of Twenty-four Pergunnahs. November 20.

Reid, Hon. L. R., Governor of Bombay, August 6, 1846, to January 23, 1847.

Reid, General, succeeded to command of besieging army before Delhi, July 20, 1857.

—— retires from command, August 1, 1857.

REVENUE COUNCIL appointed at Moorshedabad, September 1770.
—— system revised, 1774.
—— permanent settlement determined on, 1793.
REWAH kept quiet during mutiny by British Resident, Lieutenant Osborne, in 1857.
RHOTASGURH surrendered to the British under Colonel Goddard, 1764.
RIPAUD, French captain, shipwrecked off Mangalore, 1797.
—— after inducing Tippoo Sultan to form an alliance with the French, he brought from the Mauritius a small force, April 26, 1798.
ROE, Sir THOMAS, Ambassador from the Court of James I. to the Great Mogul, 1614.
ROHILLA WAR; British troops under Colonel Champion unite with those of the Vizier against the Rohillas, March 1774.
—— Rohillas defeated, April 23, 1774.
—— hostilities terminated, August 16, 1774.
ROMER, JOHN, Governor of Bombay, 1831.
ROSE, Sir HUGH, G.C.B., took command of Central India field-force, December 1857.
—— captured Ratghur, January 29, 1858.
—— captured Garrakota, February 13, 1858.
—— captured Chandairee, March 17, 1858.
—— defeated Tantia Topee at the Betwa, April 1, 1858.
—— stormed Jhansi, April 3, 1858.
—— defeated the enemy at Golowlie, April 22, 1858.
—— captured Calpee, April 23, 1858.
—— defeated the Gwalior Contingent, June 16, 1858.
—— restored Maharajah Scindia, June 20, 1858.
—— assumed command of H.M.'s forces in India, June 4, 1860.
—— disbanded 5th Bengal Fusiliers, November 12, 1860.
RUGOWLEE obtained by the British Government, 1809.
RUMBOLD, THOMAS, Governor of Madras from 1778 to 1780.
RUNGPOOR ceded to E.I.C., 1765.
RUNJEET SINGH, treaty with, April 25, 1809.
—— died July 1839.

RUPEE, changed from Sicca to Company's, December 1835.

—— Sicca ceased to be legal tender in India, January 1838.

RUSSELL, G. E., for two days Governor of Madras, March 1837.

RUTNAGHERRY, abolition of transit duties, 1837; sayer taxes, 1844.

S

SACRIFICE of Children at Saugor prohibited, August 20, 1802.

SALBYE, treaty of, signed May 17, 1782.

SALE, Sir ROBERT, born, September 1780.

—— served in first Burmese war, 1824-1826.

—— commanded at Jellalabad, 1841-42.

—— killed at Moodkee, December 18, 1845.

SALSETTE taken from Portuguese by the Mahrattas, 1739.

—— conquered by the British, 1775.

—— ceded to them by treaty of Salbye, May 17, 1782.

SALT MONOPOLY discontinued by order of the Court of Directors, 1766.

—— resumed on behalf of the Company, 1780.

SALT RIOT, Surat, August 1844.

SAMULCOTTAH ceded by the Nizam to the E.C.I., 1766.

SARUN granted by Shah Allum to the E.I.C., 1765.

SASUNEE captured by General Lake, 1803.

SATTARA PROVINCE annexed to the British dominions, 1848.

SAUGOR and NERBUDDA territories partly ceded to the British Government in 1817, the rest in 1818.

SAUNDERS, THOMAS, Esq., Governor of Madras from 1752 to 1755.

SAVENDROOG FORT taken by British troops, October 1791.

SAWUNTWARREE local corps raised, 1839.

—— taken under immediate British control, 1844.

SCINDIA, MAHADAJEE, rose to power as a general under the Peishwa Bajee Rao, about 1726 ; died, February 12, 1794.

SCINDIA, DOWLUT RAO, treaty with, December 17, 1803 ; and November 23, 1805.

SECUNDRA, battle of, January 5, 1858.

SEETABULDEE, battle of, November 26, 1817.

SEHUNPORE, battle of, December 26, 1857.

SELIMPORE, battle of, September 23, 1858.

SERA (Mysore), occupied by British troops, 1791.

SERAMPORE taken possession of by the Danes, October 8, 1755.

—— sequestered, with other Danish settlements, by the British, 1801.

—— restored to the Danes, July 19, 1802.

—— again occupied by the British, 1808.

—— restored to the Danish Government, 1815.

—— finally sold to the British Government, 1845.

—— Press established, 1800.

SERINGAPATAM, battles of, between the British army and Tippoo Sultan, May 14, 1791, and February 6, 1792.

—— attacked by British troops under Lord Cornwallis and General Abercrombie, February 5, 1792.

—— treaty between English and Tippoo signed, March 18, 1792.

—— fortress taken by the English under Sir David Baird, May 4, 1799.

SEVAJEE, founder of the Mahratta power, died, 1680.

SHAHABAD ceded by treaty to E.I.C.—northern division by the Vizier of Oude, 1775 ; southern division by Shah Allum, 1765.

SHAH ALLUM began to reign, 1707 ; died, 1712.

SHAH JEHAN, Emperor of Delhi, 1628.

SHAHJEHANPORE ceded to the E.I.C., 1801.

—— massacre at, May 31, 1857.

SHOLAPORE, E.I.C. obtained possession, 1818.

SHORE, Sir JOHN (Lord Teignmouth) born, 1751.

—— Governor-General from October 28, 1793, to March 12, 1798.

SHORE, Sir JOHN, died, 1834.

SIAM. First treaty between the Siamese and the British Government was in the reign of Charles II., but superseded by treaty of 1715.

—— provisional treaty, July 31, 1825.

—— political and commercial treaty, June 20, 1826.

SIKH WAR, first, 1845 and 1846 ; second, 1848.

SIKHS become a strong power, 1823.

—— attacked the English on the Sutlej, December 14, 1845.

—— defeated by the British at Moodkee aud Ferozeshah, December 1845.

—— defeated at Aliwal and Sobraon, 1846.

—— Shere Singh strengthened them, 1848.

—— are defeated on the Chenab, 1848.

—— and entirely routed at Chillianwallah and Goojerat, January and February 1849.

—— first incorporated with Indian army, April 1851.

SINDE. Treaty made excluding the French, August 22, 1809.

—— engagement between Sir C. Napier and the Beloochees, February 17, 1843.

—— annexed to the British dominions, April 1843.

SINDWA ceded by Holkar to the English Government, 1818.

SINGAPORE occupied by the English, 1819.

—— ceded by treaty with the Dutch, 1824.

SINGURH surrendered by the Peishwa to the British, 1817.

—— restored to the Peishwa, 1817.

—— finally taken by the English force, March 1, 1818.

SIRDHANA incorporated with British dominions, 1836.

SIRMOUR, Goorkhas expelled from, 1815.

SIRSEE, battle of, April 22, 1858.

SLAVERY, illegal in Travancore, June 1855.

—— abolished, August 1, 1858.

SMITH, CHARLES, Governor of Madras, 1781.

SOBRAON, battle of, February 10, 1846.

SOHAJPOOR, the British Government obtained possession of, by treaty of Nagpore, January 6, 1818.

SONTHAL Rebellion began, July 1855.

SOONDA. One portion of this territory came under Portuguese rule, 1763; the remainder, east of the Ghats, under English domination, 1799.

SOORGAUM, expulsion of hordes of plunderers by British force, 1819.

SOOWURNDROOG FORT fell to E.I.C., 1818.

SPENCER, President of Council, 1764.

STARKE, RICHARD, Esq., Deputy-Governor of Madras from 1750 to 1752.

STEAM communication, monthly, established, 1837.

STEAMER, first, to India, 1825.

STRATON, GEORGE, Esq., Governor of Madras from 1776 to 1777.

SUHARANPORE ceded to E.I.C., 1803.

—— botanical garden formed in, 1817.

SUHEJNEE, action at, September 27, 1858.

SULTANA taken and destroyed, May 4, 1858.

SULTANPORE, battle of, February 23, 1858.

SUMATRA discovered by Portuguese, 1510.

SUMBULPORE reunited to British possessions, 1849.

SURAJ-OO-DOWLAH, Nabob of Bengal, took Calcutta, June 18, 1756.

SURAT, English establish a factory, 1612.

—— inundated, 1837.

—— English obtain possession of the castle, 1759.

—— English assume the reins of government, 1799.

—— title of Nawab extinct, 1842.

SUTARA, Rajah of, abolished suttee, 1839.

SUTLEJ campaigns, 1845, 1846, 1848, and 1849.

SUTTEE, practice of, abolished by law, December 7, 1829.

—— abolished in the Punjab, Rajpootana, &c., December 1847.

SWEDISH INDIA COMPANY formed, 1731.

T

TAL-BEHUT FORT captured by Sir Hugh Rose, March 14, 1858.

TANJORE, first treaty between the Rajah and British Government, 1781.

—— surrendered to the Danish Government by the Danish E.I.C., 1624.

—— transferred to British rule, 1855.

—— District of Karical bought by the French, 1739.

TANNAH RAILWAY opened, April 16, 1853.

TANTIA TOPEE hanged, April 18, 1859.

TAX, pilgrim, imposed, 1805.

—— abolished, 1840.

TEIGNMOUTH, Lord, born 1751; Governor-General, 1793; died 1834.

TELEGRAPH, ELECTRIC, lines commenced, 1852.

—— first opened in India, December 1851.

—— between Sardinia and Malta, first used for accelerating news to India, November 24, 1857.

—— submarine, laid between India and Ceylon, September 14, 1858.

—— between Kurrachee and Suez, 1860; finished, October 12.

TELLICHERRY attacked by Hyder Ali, and relieved by Major Abington, 1782.

TENASSERIM provinces ceded to the British, February 26, 1826.

THAUNADARREE introduced, 1792.

THOMASON, Mr JAMES, Lieutenant-Governor of the North-west Provinces, November 9, 1843.

—— died September 27, 1853.

THORNTON, A., Chairman of the Court of Directors, 1813.

THUNNESIR (Sirhind), partly escheated to British Government in 1833 and 1851, and since wholly confiscated.

TIJARA; the English obtained political supremacy, 1803.

TIMOUR or TAMERLANE, born, May 7, 1336.

—— invaded India, 1397.

TIMOUR or TAMERLANE takes Delhi, 1399.

TIPPOO succeeded to the throne of Mysore, January 2, 1783.

—— the Nizam and Mahrattas united to overthrow his power, 1786.

—— attacked Travancore and was defeated, December 29, 1789.

—— he successfully renewed the attempt, 1790.

—— treaty of peace, March 18, 1792.

—— fresh misunderstandings, November 8, 1798.

—— war declared, February 1799.

—— action at Malavilly in which the Sultan's troops were defeated, March 6, 1799.

—— Seringapatam taken; death of Tippoo, May 4, 1799.

TIRHOOT granted to E.I.C., 1765.

TOLLS established throughout India, July 4, 1850.

TOOLA RAM SENAHPUTTEE'S country annexed to British dominions, 1852.

TRAMWAY first opened, May 5, 1851.

TRANQUEBAR sold to the British Government by the Danes, 1845.

—— settlement founded by Danes, 1618.

TRANSIT DUTIES abolished in Bengal, April 1, 1836.

TRAVANCORE, tributary to E.I.C., 1797.

—— virtually governed by British Resident from 1809 to 1832.

TREATIES—

—— between the E.I.C. and the Rajah of Mysore, dated July 8, 1799.

—— additional articles added to the above treaty, January 29, 1807.

—— between the E.I.C. and the Nizam, October 12, 1800; and December 12, 1822.

—— between the E.I.C and the Peishwa, called the treaty of Bassein, bearing date December 31, 1802.

—— between E.I.C. and the Peishwa, June 13, 1817.

—— between the E.I.C. and the Rajah of Macherry, November 14, 1803; an engagement strengthening former treaty, July 16, 1811.

TREATIES—*continued.*

—— between the E.I.C. and the Rajah of Berar, called the treaty of Deogaun, December 17, 1803, August 24, 1806, and May 27, 1816.

—— between H.E.I.C. and Dowlut Rao Scindiah, styled the treaty of Serjee Aujengaum, December 30, 1803, November 22, 1805, and November 5, 1817.

—— between H.E.I.C. and the Rajah of Travancore, January 12, 1805.

—— between the H.E.I.C. and the Rajah of Bhurtpore, April 17, 1805.

—— between the H.E.I.C. and Amind Rao Quicowar, April 21, 1805.

—— supplementary to the above, November 6, 1817; additional article to supplementary treaty, bears date November 28, 1818.

—— between the British Government and Jeswunt Rao Holkar, December 24, 1805; declaratory article annexed to the above, bears date February 2, 1806.

—— between the H.E.I.C. and Mulhar Rao Holkar, January 6, 1818.

—— between the H.E.I.C. and the Rana of Gohud, or the Rajah of Dholepore, Baree, and Rajah Kerra, January 10, 1806.

—— or engagement with the British Government, entered into by the agents of Bunga Singh, April 1, 1806.

—— between the British Government and the Rajah of Lahore, April 25, 1809.

——between the H.E.I.C. and the Rajah of Cochin, May 6, 1809.

—— between the British Government and the King of Cabul, June 17, 1809.

—— between the H.E.I.C. and the Ameers of Scinde, August 22, 1809.

—— between the H.E.I.C. and Futteh Mahomed of Cutch, 1809.

—— between the H.E.I.C. and the Rao of Cutch, January 16, 1816; a supplementary treaty, June 18, 1816.

TREATIES—*continued.*

—— between the H.E.I.C. and the Rajah of Cutch, October 13, 1819, and May 21, 1822.

—— or engagement between Dewan Hunsraj of Mandavie, October 28, 1809.

—— between the H.E.I.C. and the Vizier of Oude, January 14, 1812.

—— between the Vizier of Oude and the British Government, May 1, 1816.

—— or engagement between the above parties, July 12 and August 3, 1814.

—— between the Rajah of Colapore and the British Government, October 1, 1812.

—— or agreement between the Sir Dessaye of Sawuntwarree and the H.E.I.C., October 3, 1812.

—— between the Regency of Sawuntwarree and the H.E.I.C., February 17, 1819, and February 17, 1820.

—— between the Rajah of Rewah and the British Government, October 5, 1812; June 2, 1813; and March 11, 1814.

—— between the Rajah of Tehree and the British Government, December 23, 1812.

—— between the Rajah of Nepaul and the E.I.C., December 2, 1815.

—— between the Rajah of Sikkim and the H.E.I.C., February 10, 1817.

—— or engagement between the British Government and Nana Govind Rao, November 1, 1817.

—— between the Rajah of Kerowlee and the H.E.I.C., November 9, 1817.

—— or engagement between Ameer Khan and the British Government, November 9, 1817.

—— or engagement between the Rajah of Sumpthur and the British Government, November 12, 1817.

—— between the Soubadar of Jhansi and the British Government, November 17, 1817.

—— between the Rajah of Kotah and the H.E.I.C., December 26, 1817.

TREATIES—*continued.*

—— between the Rajah of Nagpore and the British Government, January 6, 1818.

—— between the Rajah of Joudpore and the H.E.I.C., January 6, 1818.

—— between the Rajah of Oudipore and the H.E.I.C., January 13, 1818.

—— between the Rajah of Boondee and the H.E.I.C., February 10, 1818.

—— between the Rajah of Bhopaul and the H.E.I.C., February 26, 1818.

—— between the Rajah of Bickaneer and the H.E.I.C., March 9, 1818.

—— between the Rajah of Kishengurh and the H.E.I.C., March 26, 1818.

—— between the Rajah of Jyepore and the H.E.I.C., April 2, 1818.

—— between the Rajah of Dutteeah and the British Government, July 31, 1818.

—— between the Rajah of Banswarra and the H.E.I.C., September 16, 1818 ; and December 25, 1818.

—— between the Rajah of Dowleah and Purtaubgurh and the H.E.I.C., October 5, 1818.

—— between the Rajah of Doongerpore and the H.E.I.C., December 11, 1818.

—— between the Rajah of Jusselmere and the H.E.I.C., December 12, 1818.

—— between the chiefs of Dewass and the H.E.I.C., December 12, 1818.

—— between the Rajah of Dhar and the H.E.I.C., January 10, 1819 ; and December 18, 1821.

—— between the King of Acheen and the H.E.I.C., April 22, 1819.

—— between the Rajah of Sattarah and the H.E.I.C., September 25, 1819.

—— between the Arab tribes of the Persian Gulf and the British Government, January 8, 1820.

—— perpetual treaty of peace, May 4, 1853.

TREATIES—*continued.*

—— between the Ameers of Scinde and the H.E.I.C., November 9, 1820.

—— between the Imaum of Seiana and the British Government, January 15, 1821.

—— between Raghojee Angria of Colaba and the H.E.I.C., July 1822.

—— with the Imaum of Muscat, August 29, 1822.

—— with the Nizam, December 12, 1822.

—— with the Regent of Serohee, October 31, 1823.

—— with Raja Govind Chunder of Cachar, March 6, 1824.

—— with Raja Ram Singh of Jynteea, March 10, 1824.

—— agreement with the King of Oude, August 17, 1825.

—— with the King of Oude, May 1, 1829; and September 11, 1837.

—— treaty of peace with King of Ava, February 24, 1826.

—— commercial treaty with King of Ava, November 23, 1826.

—— with Ragi of Nagpore, December 1, 1826.

—— revised engagement with Rajah of Nagpore, December 25, 1829.

—— Indus Toll treaty with Maharajah Runjeet Singh, December 26, 1832.

—— supplementary treaty with Maharajah Runjeet Singh, January 24, 1835.

—— tripartite treaty between the British Government, Maharajah Runjeet Singh, and Shah Shoojah-ool-Moolk, June 26, 1838.

—— Indus Toll treaty with Ameers of Scinde, October 12, 1834.

—— commercial treaty with Ameers of Scinde, November 28, 1836.

—— with Ameers of Scinde, April 20, 1838; and March 11, 1839.

—— with King of Cabul, September 30, 1839.

—— with State of Lahore, March 9, 1849.

TREATIES—*continued.*

—— agreement with Lahore Durbar, March 11, 1846; and December 16, 1846.

—— with Maharajah Gholab Singh of Cashmere, March 16, 1846.

—— with the Nizam, May 21, 1853.

—— agreement with the Nizam, May 21, 1860.

—— extradition treaty with Maharajah of Nepaul, February 10, 1855.

—— Treaty of Peace between her Majesty the Queen and the Shah of Persia, March 4, 1857.

TRICHINOPOLY besieged by the French and relieved by Captain Calliaud, 1757.

TRINCOMALEE taken from the Dutch by the English, 1781.

—— by the French, 1782.

—— restored to the Dutch, 1783.

—— again taken by the English, 1795.

—— confirmed to them by treaty, 1802.

TRINOMALLEE, battle of, 1767.

—— naval engagements between French and English off, March 17, and April 12, 1782.

—— taken by Tippoo Sultan, 1791.

TUCKER, Chairman of the Court of Directors, 1834 and 1847.

TULLYGAUN, English defeated at, by the Mahrattas, January 11, 1779.

TURNER, J. M., bishop of Calcutta from 1829; died, 1831.

TWEEDDALE, the most noble the Marquess of, Governor of Madras from September 24, 1842, to February 23, 1848.

TWENTY-FOUR PERGUNNAHS granted by Nabob Jaffier Ally Khan, 1757.

U

UDIAMPUR, persecution of Syrian Christians by Don Alexis de Menezes, Archbishop of Goa, 1599.

UMRITSUR FORTRESS, built by Runjeet Singh, 1809.

UNIVERSITY, Calcutta, established, January 24, 1857.

UNIVERSITY, Bombay, established, July 18, 1857.
—— Madras, established, September 5, 1857.

V

VANSITTART, President of Council, July 27, 1760.
—— left Calcutta, 1764.
VAUX, JOHN, Governor of Bombay, 1690.
VELLORE, mutiny at, July 10, 1806.
VERNACULAR languages used for public business, 1837.
VICTORIA POINT ceded by the Mahrattas in exchange for Gheriah, 1756.
VOLUNTEER CORPS, Calcutta, raised June 12, 1857.
—— Rifle Corps sanctioned, September 12, 1860.
VOYAGE, first, round the Cape in sailing-ship by Vasco de Gama, 1498.
—— first, round the Cape in steam-ship, by Captain Johnson, 1825.

W

WAGHERS, operations against, 1860-61.
WAGHORN, Lieutenant, born 1801 ; succeeded in taking Bombay Mail overland to England in thirty days, 1845; died, 1850.
WAITE, Sir NICHOLAS, Governor of Bombay, 1702.
WALKER, Lieutenant-General Sir G. T., Commander-in-Chief, Madras, March 3, 1826, to May 11, 1831.
WANDEWASH, battle of, January 21, 1760.
WARD, WILLIAM, born, October 20, 1769 ; died, March 7, 1823.
WARI taken by British troops, 1819.
WATSON, Admiral CHARLES, destroyed the stronghold of Angria in conjunction with Clive, 1756.
—— assisted him in taking Calcutta, 1756.
WEER surrendered to the English, 1826.
WELLESLEY, ARTHUR.—*See* WELLINGTON.
WELLESLEY, Marquess, born June 20, 1760.

WELLESLEY, Governor-General, May 1798, to July 30, 1805.

—— Lord of the Treasury, 1786.

—— Commissioner for the Affairs of India, 1793 to 1798.

—— died, September 26, 1842.

WELLESLEY PROVINCE ceded to the British, 1802.

WELLINGTON, Duke of, born 1769.

—— sent, when Arthur Wellesley, to India.

—— appointed Commandant of Seringapatam 1799.

—— had command of an army in the Mahratta war, 1803.

—— took Poonah and Ahmednugger, August 12, 1803.

—— gained the victory of Assaye, September 23, 1803.

—— defeated Scindiah and the Rajah of Berar at Argaum, November 28, 1803.

—— again at Gawulghur, December 13.

—— compelled them to make peace, and returned to England, December 30.

WHISH, General, raised the siege of Mooltan, September 15, 1848; Moultan city stormed January 2, 1849; died, 1853.

WHITEHILL, JOHN, Esq., Governor of Madras, from 1777 to 1778, and from 1780 to 1781.

WILSON, General Sir ARCHIBALD, K.C.B., succeeded to command of army before Delhi, August 1, 1857.

—— stormed Delhi, September 14 to September 20, 1857.

WILSON, DANIEL, Bishop of Calcutta, November 1832; died, January 2, 1858.

WINDHAM, General C., defeated at Cawnpore, November 27, 1857.

WUZEEREES, two expeditions against, 1860.

WYNCH, ALEXANDER, Governor of Bombay from 1773 to 1775.

—— recalled on account of his conquest of Travancore.

X

XAVIER, FRANCIS, established Christianity in India, 1522; died, 1552.

Y

YALE, ELIHU, Esq., Governor of Madras from 1687 to 1692.

YANDABOO, Treaty of, February 26, 1826.

Z

ZAMORIN, the, of Calicut, graciously received Vasco de Gama, 1498.

ZANZIBAR, discovered by Albuquerque, 1503.

ZEMAUN SHAH, threatened invasion of Hindostan, 1797; dethroned and deprived of sight, 1801.

THE END.

THE DISCOVERY OF THE SOURCE OF THE NILE:

A JOURNAL. By JOHN HANNING SPEKE, Captain H.M. Indian Army. With a Map of Eastern Equatorial Africa by Captain SPEKE; numerous Illustrations, chiefly from Drawings by Captain GRANT; and Portraits, engraved on Steel, of Captains SPEKE and GRANT. 8vo, 21s.

"The volume which Captain Speke has presented to the world possesses more than a geographical interest. It is a monument of preseverance, courage, and temper, displayed under difficulties which have perhaps never been equalled."—*Times.*

WHAT LED TO THE DISCOVERY OF THE NILE

SOURCE. By JOHN HANNING SPEKE, Captain H.M. Indian Army. 8vo, with Maps, &c., 14s.

"Will be read with peculiar interest, as it makes the record of his travels complete, and at the same time heightens, if possible, our admiration of his indomitable perseverance, as well as tact."—*Dispatch.*

A WALK ACROSS AFRICA;

Or, Domestic Scenes from my Nile Journal. By JAMES AUGUSTUS GRANT, Captain H.M. Bengal Army, Fellow and Gold-Medallist of the Royal Geographical Society. 8vo, with Map, 15s.

"Captain Grant's frank, manly, unadorned narrative."—*Daily News.*

"Captain Grant's book will be doubly interesting to those who have read Captain Speke's. He gives, as his special contribution to the story of their three years' walk across Africa, descriptions of birds, beasts, trees, and plants, and all that concerns them, and of domestic scenes throughout the various regions. The book is written in a pleasant, quiet, gentlemanly style, and is characterised by a modest tone. . . . . The whole work is delightful reading."—*Globe.*

STRAY LEAVES FROM AN ARCTIC JOURNAL;

Or, Eighteen Months in the Polar Regions in Search of Sir John Franklin's Expedition in 1850-51. To which is added, THE CAREER, LAST VOYAGE, AND FATE OF CAPTAIN SIR JOHN FRANKLIN. By CAPTAIN SHERARD OSBORN, C.B. A new Edition, in crown 8vo, with a Map, 5s.

CAXTONIANA:

A Series of Essays on LIFE, LITERATURE, and MANNERS. By SIR EDWARD BULWER LYTTON, Bart. 2 vols. crown 8vo, 21s.

"It would be very possible to fill many pages with the wise bright things of these volumes."—*Eclectic.*

"Gems of thought, set upon some of the most important subjects that can engage the attention of men."—*Daily News.*

THE CAIRNGORM MOUNTAINS.

By JOHN HILL BURTON. In crown 8vo, 3s. 6d.

"One of the most complete as well as most lively and intelligent bits of reading that the lover of works of travel has seen for many a day."—*Saturday Review.*

ESSAYS ON SOCIAL SUBJECTS.

From the 'Saturday Review.' Crown 8vo, 7s. 6d. Third Edition.

"In their own way of simple, straightforward reflection upon life, the present century has produced no essays better than these."—*Examiner.*

"We shall welcome the author again if he has more to say on topics which he treats so well."—*Guardian.*

THE SCOT ABROAD,

AND THE ANCIENT LEAGUE WITH FRANCE. By JOHN HILL BURTON, Author of 'The Book-Hunter,' &c. 2 vols. crown 8vo, in Roxburghe binding, 15s.

"Mr Burton's lively and interesting 'Scot Abroad,' not the least valuable of his contributions to the historical literature of his country."—*Quarterly Review.*

"An excellent book, that will interest Englishmen and fascinate Scotchmen."—*Times.*

"No amount of selections, detached at random, can give an adequate idea of the varied and copious results of reading which are stored up in the compact and pithy pages of 'The Scot Abroad.'"—*Saturday Review.*

"A charming book."—*Spectator.*

THE GREAT GOVERNING FAMILIES OF ENGLAND.

By J. LANGTON SANFORD and MEREDITH TOWNSEND.

CONTENTS:—The Percies—The Greys of Howick—The Lowthers—The Vanes or Fanes—The Stanleys of Knowsley—The Grosvenors—The Fitzwilliams—The Cavendishes—The Bentincks—The Clintons—The Stanhopes—The Talbots—The Leveson-Gowers—The Pagets—The Manners—The Montagus—The Osbornes—The Fitzroys—The Spencers—The Grenvilles—The Russells—The Cecils—The Villiers—The Barings—The Petty-Fitzmaurices—The Herberts—The Somersets—The Berkeleys—The Seymours—The Lennoxes—The Howards.

2 vols. 8vo, £1, 8s. in extra binding, with richly-gilt cover.

BIOGRAPHICAL SKETCHES OF EMINENT SOLDIERS

OF THE LAST FOUR CENTURIES. By the late MAJOR-GENERAL JOHN MITCHELL, Author of 'Life of Wallenstein,' the 'Fall of Napoleon,' &c. Edited, with a Memoir of the Author, by LEONHARD SCHMITZ, LL.D. In Post 8vo, 9s.

ELEMENTS OF MODERN GEOGRAPHY.

For the Use of Junior Classes. By the REV. ALEX. MACKAY, A.M., F.R.G.S. In crown 8vo, pp. 304, 3s.

"There is no work of the kind, in the English or any other language, known to me, which comes so near my *ideal* of perfection in a school-book, on the important subject of which it treats. In arrangement, style, selection of matter, clearness, and thorough accuracy of statement, it is without a rival; and knowing, as I do, the vast amount of labour and research bestowed on its production, I trust it will be so appreciated as to insure, by an extensive sale, a well-merited reward."—*A. Keith Johnston, Esq., F.R.S.E., F.R.G.S., H.M. Geographer for Scotland; Author of the 'Physical Atlas,' &c. &c.*

"The best geography we have ever met with."—*Spectator.*

ADVANCED TEXT-BOOK OF PHYSICAL GEOGRAPHY.

By DAVID PAGE, F.R.S.E., F.G.S., Author of 'Introductory and Advanced Text-Books of Geology,' &c. Crown 8vo, with a Glossary of Terms and numerous Illustrations, 5s.

"Mr Page's volume is aptly entitled, and meets the wants of earnest and systematic students."—*Athenæum.*

"A thoroughly good Text-Book of Physical Geography."—*Saturday Review.*

THE ECONOMY OF CAPITAL:

GOLD AND TRADE. By R. H. PATTERSON, Author of 'The New Revolution,' &c. In 1 thick vol. crown 8vo, 12s. cloth.

FAMILY PRAYERS FOR TWO WEEKS.

Prepared by the Committee of the General Assembly of the Church of Scotland on Aids to Devotion. In crown 8vo, 1s. 6d. bound in cloth, red edges.

IN THE PRESS.

THE HISTORY OF SCOTLAND
From Agricola's Invasion to the Revolution of 1688. By JOHN HILL BURTON, Author of 'The Scot Abroad,' &c.

ETONIANA.
Originally published in 'Blackwood's Magazine.' 1 vol. fcap. 8vo.

THE OPERATIONS OF WAR EXPLAINED AND ILLUSTRATED. By COLONEL E. B. HAMLEY, R.A., late Professor of Military History, Strategy, and Tactics at the Staff College. In 1 vol. 4to, with Plans.

THE ILIAD OF HOMER.
Translated into English Verse in the Spenserian Stanza, by PHILIP STANHOPE WORSLEY, M.A., Fellow of Corpus Christi College, Oxford. Uniform with the 'Odyssey,' Translated by the Same.

ESSAYS ON SOCIAL SUBJECTS.
From the 'Saturday Review.' A Second Series, uniform with the First.

THE HANDY HORSE BOOK;
Or. Practical Instructions on Riding, Driving, and the General Care and Management of Horses. By a CAVALRY OFFICER.

DICTIONARY OF BRITISH INDIAN DATES:
Being a Compendium of all the Dates essential to the Study of the History of British Rule in India, Legal, Historical, and Biographical. Intended for Students about to face Examinations for the Indian Services.

COMPARATIVE GEOGRAPHY.
By CARL RITTER, Professor of Geography in the University of Berlin. Translated by W. L. GAGE. In crown 8vo, 3s. 6d.

DEFINITIONS IN ASTRONOMY AND NAVIGATION MADE EASY. By the REV. J. HARBORD, M.A., R.N., Author of 'Glossary of Navigation.'

CATALOGUE
OF
MESSRS BLACKWOOD AND SONS'
PUBLICATIONS.

HISTORY OF EUROPE,
From the Commencement of the French Revolution in 1789 to the Battle of Waterloo. By SIR ARCHIBALD ALISON, Bart., D.C.L.

A NEW LIBRARY EDITION (being the Tenth), in 14 vols. demy 8vo, with Portraits, and a copious Index, £10, 10s.

ANOTHER EDITION, in crown 8vo, 20 vols., £6.

A PEOPLE'S EDITION, 12 vols., closely printed in double columns, £2, 8s., and Index Volume, 3s.

"An extraordinary work, which has earned for itself a lasting place in the literature of the country, and within a few years found innumerable readers in every part of the globe. There is no book extant that treats so well of the period to the illustration of which Mr Alison's labours have been devoted. It exhibits great knowledge, patient research, indefatigable industry, and vast power."—*Times, Sept. 7, 1850.*

CONTINUATION OF ALISON'S HISTORY OF EUROPE,
From the Fall of Napoleon to the Accession of Louis Napoleon. By SIR ARCHIBALD ALISON, Bart., D.C.L. In 9 vols., £6, 7s. 6d. Uniform with the Library Edition of the previous work.

EPITOME OF ALISON'S HISTORY OF EUROPE.
For the Use of Schools and Young Persons. Fifteenth Edition, 7s. 6d., bound.

ATLAS TO ALISON'S HISTORY OF EUROPE;
Containing 109 Maps and Plans of Countries, Battles, Sieges, and Sea-Fights. Constructed by A. KEITH JOHNSTON, F.R.S.E. With Vocabulary of Military and Marine Terms. Demy 4to. Library Edition, £3, 3s.; People's Edition, crown 4to, £1, 11s. 6d.

LIVES OF LORD CASTLEREAGH AND SIR CHARLES STEWART, Second and Third Marquesses of Londonderry. From the Original Papers of the Family, and other sources. By SIR ARCHIBALD ALISON, Bart., D.C.L. In 3 vols. 8vo, £2, 5s.

ANNALS OF THE PENINSULAR CAMPAIGNS.
By CAPT. THOMAS HAMILTON. A New Edition. Edited by F. HARDMAN, Esq. 8vo, 16s.; and Atlas of Maps to illustrate the Campaigns, 12s.

A VISIT TO FLANDERS AND THE FIELD OF WATERLOO.
By JAMES SIMPSON, Advocate. A Revised Edition. With Two Coloured Plans of the Battle. Crown 8vo, 5s.

WELLINGTON'S CAREER:
A Military and Political Summary. By LIEUT.-COL. E. BRUCE HAMLEY, Professor of Military History and Art at the Staff College. Crown 8vo, 2s.

THE STORY OF THE CAMPAIGN OF SEBASTOPOL.
Written in the Camp. By LIEUT.-COL. E. BRUCE HAMLEY. With Illustrations drawn in Camp by the Author. 8vo, 21s.

"We strongly recommend this 'Story of the Campaign' to all who would gain a just comprehension of this tremendous struggle. Of this we are perfectly sure, it is a book unlikely to be ever superseded. Its truth is of that simple and startling character which is sure of an immortal existence; nor is it paying the gallant author too high a complement to class this masterpiece of military history with the most precious of those classic records which have been bequeathed to us by the great writers of antiquity who took part in the wars they have described."—*The Press.*

THE INVASION OF THE CRIMEA:
Its Origin, and Account of its Progress down to the Death of Lord Raglan. By ALEXANDER WILLIAM KINGLAKE, M.P. Vols. I. and II., bringing the Events down to the Close of the Battle of the Alma. Fourth Edition. Price 32s. To be completed in 4 vols. 8vo.

TEN YEARS OF IMPERIALISM IN FRANCE.
Impressions of a "Flâneur." Second Edition. In 8vo, price 9s.

"There has not been published for many a day a more remarkable book on France than this, which professes to be the impressions of a Flaneur. . . . It has all the liveliness and sparkle of a work written only for amusement; it has all the solidity and weight of a State paper; and we expect for it not a little political influence as a fair, full, and masterly statement of the Imperial policy—the first and only good account that has been given to Europe of the Napoleonic system now in force."—*Times.*

FLEETS AND NAVIES.
By CAPTAIN CHARLES HAMLEY, R.M. Originally published in 'Blackwood's Magazine.' Crown 8vo, 6s.

HISTORY OF GREECE UNDER FOREIGN DOMINATION.
By GEORGE FINLAY, LL.D., Athens—viz.;

GREECE UNDER THE ROMANS. B.C. 146 to A.D. 717. A Historical View of the Condition of the Greek Nation from its Conquest by the Romans until the Extinction of the Roman Power in the East. Second Edition, 16s.

HISTORY OF THE BYZANTINE EMPIRE, A.D. 716 to 1204; and of the Greek Empire of Nicæa and Constantinople, A.D. 1204 to 1453. 2 vols., £1, 7s. 6d.

MEDIEVAL GREECE AND TREBIZOND. The History of Greece, from its Conquest by the Crusaders to its Conquest by the Turks, A.D. 1204 to 1566; and the History of the Empire of Trebizond, A.D. 1204 to 1461. 12s.

GREECE UNDER OTHOMAN AND VENETIAN DOMINATION. A.D. 1453 to 1821. 10s. 6d.

HISTORY OF THE GREEK REVOLUTION. 2 vols. 8vo, £1, 4s.

"His book is worthy to take its place among the remarkable works on Greek history, which form one of the chief glories of English scholarship. The history of Greece is but half told without it."—*London Guardian.*

THE NATIONAL CHARACTER OF THE ATHENIANS.
By JOHN BROWN PATTERSON. Edited from the Author's revision, by PROFESSOR PILLANS, of the University of Edinburgh. With a Sketch of his Life. Crown 8vo, 4s. 6d.

STUDIES IN ROMAN LAW.
With Comparative Views of the Laws of France, England, and Scotland. By LORD MACKENZIE, one of the Judges of the Court of Session in Scotland. 8vo, 12s. Second Edition.

"We know not in the English language where else to look for a history of the Roman law so clear, and, at the same time, so short. . . . More improving reading, both for the general student and for the lawyer, we cannot well imagine; and there are few, even among learned professional men, who will not gather some novel information from Lord Mackenzie's simple pages."—*London Review.*

THE EIGHTEEN CHRISTIAN CENTURIES.
By the REV. JAMES WHITE. Fourth Edition, with an Analytical Table of Contents, and a Copious Index. Post 8vo, 7s. 6d.

THE MONKS OF THE WEST,
From St Benedict to St Bernard. By the COUNT DE MONTALEMBERT. Authorised Translation. 2 vols. 8vo, 21s.

HISTORY OF FRANCE,

From the Earliest Period to the Year 1848. By the REV. JAMES WHITE, Author of 'The Eighteen Christian Centuries.' Second Edition. Post 8vo, 9s.

"An excellent and comprehensive compendium of French history, quite above the standard of a school-book, and particularly well adapted for the libraries of literary institutions."—*National Review.*

LEADERS OF THE REFORMATION:

LUTHER, CALVIN, LATIMER, and KNOX. By the REV. JOHN TULLOCH, D.D., Principal, and Primarius Professor of Theology, St Mary's College, St Andrews. Second Edition, crown 8vo, 6s. 6d.

ENGLISH PURITANISM AND ITS LEADERS:

CROMWELL, MILTON, BAXTER, and BUNYAN. By the REV. JOHN TULLOCH, D.D. Uniform with the 'Leaders of the Reformation.' 7s. 6d.

HISTORY OF THE FRENCH PROTESTANT REFUGEES.

By CHARLES WEISS, Professor of History at the Lycée Buonaparte. Translated by F. HARDMAN, Esq. 8vo, 14s.

HISTORY OF THE CHURCH OF SCOTLAND,

From the Reformation to the Revolution Settlement. By the Very REV. JOHN LEE, D.D., LL.D., Principal of the University of Edinburgh. Edited by the Rev. WILLIAM LEE. 2 vols. 8vo, 21s.

HISTORY OF SCOTLAND FROM THE REVOLUTION

To the Extinction of the last Jacobite Insurrection, 1689-1748. By JOHN HILL BURTON, Esq., Advocate. 2 vols. 8vo, reduced to 15s.

LIVES OF THE QUEENS OF SCOTLAND,

And English Princesses connected with the Regal Succession of Great Britain. By AGNES STRICKLAND. With Portraits and Historical Vignettes. Post 8vo, £4, 4s.

"Every step in Scotland is historical; the shades of the dead arise on every side; the very rocks breathe. Miss Strickland's talents as a writer, and turn of mind as an individual, in a peculiar manner fit her for painting a historical gallery of the most illustrious or dignified female characters in that land of chivalry and song."—*Blackwood's Magazine.*

MEMORIALS OF THE CASTLE OF EDINBURGH.

By JAMES GRANT, Esq. A New Edition. In crown 8vo, with 12 Engravings, 3s. 6d.

MEMOIRS OF SIR WILLIAM KIRKALDY OF GRANGE,

Governor of the Castle of Edinburgh for Mary Queen of Scots. By JAMES GRANT, Esq. Post 8vo, 10s. 6d.

MEMOIRS OF SIR JOHN HEPBURN,

Marshal of France under Louis XIII., &c. By JAMES GRANT, Esq. Post 8vo, 8s.

WORKS OF THE REV. THOMAS M'CRIE, D.D.

A New and Uniform Edition. Edited by Professor M'CRIE. 4 vols. crown 8vo, 24s. Sold separately—viz.:

LIFE OF JOHN KNOX. Containing Illustrations of the History of the Reformation in Scotland. Crown 8vo, 6s.

LIFE OF ANDREW MELVILLE. Containing Illustrations of the Ecclesiastical and Literary History of Scotland in the Sixteenth and Seventeenth Centuries. Crown 8vo, 6s.

HISTORY OF THE PROGRESS AND SUPPRESSION OF THE REFORMATION IN ITALY IN THE SIXTEENTH CENTURY. Crown 8vo, 4s.

HISTORY OF THE PROGRESS AND SUPPRESSION OF THE REFORMATION IN SPAIN IN THE SIXTEENTH CENTURY. Crown 8vo, 3s. 6d.

THE BOSCOBEL TRACTS;

Relating to the Escape of Charles the Second after the Battle of Worcester, and his subsequent Adventures. Edited by J. HUGHES, Esq., A.M. A New Edition, with additional Notes and Illustrations, including Communications from the Rev. R. H. BARHAM, Author of the 'Ingoldsby Legends.' In 8vo, with Engravings, 16s.

"'The Boscobel Tracts' is a very curious book, and about as good an example of single subject historical collections as may be found. Originally undertaken, or at least completed, at the suggestion of the late Bishop Copplestone, in 1827, it was carried out with a degree of judgment and taste not always found in works of a similar character."—*Spectator.*

LIFE OF JOHN DUKE OF MARLBOROUGH.

With some Account of his Contemporaries, and of the War of the Succession. By SIR ARCHIBALD ALISON, Bart., D.C.L. Third Edition. 2 vols. 8vo, Portraits and Maps, 30s.

THE NEW 'EXAMEN;'

Or, An Inquiry into the Evidence of certain Passages in 'Macaulay's History of England' concerning—THE DUKE OF MARLBOROUGH—THE MASSACRE OF GLENCOE—THE HIGHLANDS OF SCOTLAND—VISCOUNT DUNDEE—WILLIAM PENN. By JOHN PAGET, Esq., Barrister-at-Law. In crown 8vo, 6s.

"We certainly never saw a more damaging exposure, and it is something worth notice that much of it appeared in 'Blackwood's Magazine' during the lifetime of Lord Macaulay, but he never attempted to make any reply. The charges are so direct, and urged in such unmistakable language, that no writer who valued his character for either accuracy of fact or fairness in comment would let them remain unanswered if he had any reason to give."—*Gentleman's Magazine.*

AUTOBIOGRAPHY OF THE REV. DR CARLYLE,

Minister of Inveresk. Containing Memorials of the Men and Events of his Time. Edited by JOHN HILL BURTON. In 8vo. Third Edition, with Portrait, 14s.

"This book contains by far the most vivid picture of Scottish life and manners that has been given to the public since the days of Sir Walter Scott. In bestowing upon it this high praise, we make no exception, not even in favour of Lord Cockburn's 'Memorials'—the book which resembles it most, and which ranks next to it in interest."—*Edinburgh Review.*

MEMOIR OF THE POLITICAL LIFE OF EDMUND BURKE.

With Extracts from his Writings. By the REV. GEORGE CROLY, D.D. 2 vols. post 8vo, 18s.

CURRAN AND HIS CONTEMPORARIES.

By CHARLES PHILLIPS, Esq., A.B. A New Edition. Crown 8vo, 7s. 6d.

"Certainly one of the most extraordinary pieces of biography ever produced. . . . . . No library should be without it."—*Lord Brougham.*

"Never, perhaps, was there a more curious collection of portraits crowded before into the same canvass."—*Times.*

MEMOIR OF MRS HEMANS.

By her SISTER. With a Portrait. Fcap. 8vo, 5s.

LIFE OF THE LATE REV. JAMES ROBERTSON, D.D.,

F.R.S.E., Professor of Divinity and Ecclesiastical History in the University of Edinburgh. By the REV. A. H. CHARTERIS, M.A., Minister of Newabbey. With a Portrait. 8vo, price 10s. 6d.

ESSAYS; HISTORICAL, POLITICAL, AND MISCELLANEOUS.

By SIR ARCHIBALD ALISON, Bart. 3 vols. demy 8vo, 45s.

ESSAYS IN HISTORY AND ART.

By R. H. PATTERSON. Viz.:

COLOUR IN NATURE AND ART—REAL AND IDEAL BEAUTY—SCULPTURE—ETHNOLOGY OF EUROPE—UTOPIAS—OUR INDIAN EMPIRE—THE NATIONAL LIFE OF CHINA—AN IDEAL ART-CONGRESS—BATTLE OF THE STYLES—GENIUS AND LIBERTY—YOUTH AND SUMMER—RECORDS OF THE PAST: NINEVEH AND BABYLON—INDIA: ITS CASTES AND CREEDS—"CHRISTOPHER NORTH:" IN MEMORIAM. In 1 vol. 8vo, 12s.

NORMAN SINCLAIR.
By W. E. AYTOUN, D.C.L., Author of 'Lays of the Scottish Cavaliers,' &c. &c. In 3 vols. post 8vo, 31s. 6d.

THE OLD BACHELOR IN THE OLD SCOTTISH VILLAGE.
By THOMAS AIRD. Fcap. 8vo, 4s.

SIR EDWARD BULWER LYTTON'S NOVELS.
Library Edition. Printed from a large and readable type. In Volumes of a convenient and handsome form. 8vo, 5s. each—viz.:

THE CAXTON NOVELS, 10 Volumes:

The Caxton Family. 2 vols.
My Novel. 4 vols.
What will he do with it? 4 vols.

HISTORICAL ROMANCES, 11 Volumes:

Devereux. 2 vols.
The Last Days of Pompeii. 2 vols.
Rienzi. 2 vols.
The Siege of Grenada. 1 vol.
The Last of the Barons. 2 vols.
Harold. 2 vols.

ROMANCES, 5 Volumes:

The Pilgrims of the Rhine. 1 vol.
Eugene Aram. 2 vols.
Zanoni. 2 vols.

NOVELS OF LIFE AND MANNERS, 15 Volumes:

Pelham. 2 vols.
The Disowned. 2 vols.
Paul Clifford. 2 vols.
Godolphin. 1 vol.
Ernest Maltravers—First Part. 2 vols.
Ernest Maltravers — Second Part (*i.e.* Alice.) 2 vols.
Night and Morning. 2 vols.
Lucretia. 2 vols.

"It is of the handiest of sizes; the paper is good; and the type, which seems to be new, is very clear and beautiful. There are no pictures. The whole charm of the presentment of the volume consists in its handiness, and the tempting clearness and beauty of the type, which almost converts into a pleasure the mere act of following the printer's lines, and leaves the author's mind free to exert its unobstructed force upon the reader."—*Examiner.*

"Nothing could be better as to size, type, paper, and general get-up."—*Athenæum.*

JESSIE CAMERON: A HIGHLAND STORY.
By the LADY RACHEL BUTLER. Second Edition. Small 8vo, with a Frontispiece, 2s. 6d.

SOME PASSAGES IN THE LIFE OF ADAM BLAIR,
And History of Matthew Wald. By the Author of 'Valerius.' Fcap. 8vo, 4s. cloth.

CAPTAIN CLUTTERBUCK'S CHAMPAGNE:
A West Indian Reminiscence. Post 8vo, 12s.

SCENES OF CLERICAL LIFE.
The Sad Fortunes of Amos Barton—Mr Gilfil's Love-Story—Janet's Repentance. By GEORGE ELIOT. 2 vols. fcap. 8vo, 12s.

ADAM BEDE.
By GEORGE ELIOT. 2 vols. fcap. 8vo, 12s.

THE MILL ON THE FLOSS.
By GEORGE ELIOT. 2 vols. fcap. 8vo, 12s.

SILAS MARNER: THE WEAVER OF RAVELOE.
By GEORGE ELIOT. Fcap. 8vo, 6s.

THE NOVELS OF GEORGE ELIOT.
Cheap Edition, complete in 3 vols., price 6s. each—viz.:

ADAM BEDE.
THE MILL ON THE FLOSS.
SCENES OF CLERICAL LIFE, and SILAS MARNER.

ANNALS OF THE PARISH, AND AYRSHIRE LEGATEES.
By JOHN GALT. Fcap. 8vo, 4s. cloth.

SIR ANDREW WYLIE.
By JOHN GALT. Fcap. 8vo, 4s. cloth.

THE PROVOST, AND OTHER TALES.
By JOHN GALT. Fcap. 8vo, 4s. cloth.

THE ENTAIL.
By JOHN GALT. Fcap. 8vo, 4s. cloth.

THE YOUTH AND MANHOOD OF CYRIL THORNTON.
By CAPTAIN HAMILTON. Fcap. 8vo, 4s. cloth.

LADY LEE'S WIDOWHOOD.
By LIEUT.-COL. E. B. HAMLEY. Crown 8vo, with 13 Illustrations by the Author. 6s.

THE LIFE OF MANSIE WAUCH,
Tailor in Dalkeith. By D. M. MOIR. Fcap. 8vo, 3s. cloth.

NIGHTS AT MESS, SIR FRIZZLE PUMPKIN, AND OTHER TALES. Fcap. 8vo, 3s. cloth.

KATIE STEWART: A TRUE STORY.
By MRS OLIPHANT. Fcap. 8vo, with Frontispiece and Vignette. 4s.

PEN OWEN.
Fcap. 8vo, 4s. cloth.

PENINSULAR SCENES AND SKETCHES.
Fcap. 8vo, 3s. cloth.

REGINALD DALTON.
By the Author of 'Valerius.' Fcap. 8vo, 4s. cloth.

LIFE IN THE FAR WEST.
By G. F. RUXTON, Esq. Second Edition. Fcap. 8vo, 4s.

TOM CRINGLE'S LOG.
A New Edition. With Illustrations by STANFIELD, WEIR, SKELTON, WALKER, &c., Engraved by WHYMPER. Crown 8vo, 6s.

"Everybody who has failed to read 'Tom Cringle's Log' should do so at once. The 'Quarterly Review' went so far as to say that the papers composing it, when it first appeared in 'Blackwood,' were the most brilliant series of the time, and that time one unrivalled for the number of famous magazinists existing in it. Coleridge says, in his 'Table Talk,' that the 'Log' is most excellent; and these verdicts have been ratified by generations of men and boys, and by the manifestation of Continental approval which is shown by repeated translations. The engravings illustrating the present issue are excellent."—*Standard.*

TOM CRINGLE'S LOG.
Fcap. 8vo, 4s. cloth.

THE CRUISE OF THE MIDGE.
By the Author of 'Tom Cringle's Log.' Fcap. 8vo, 4s. cloth.

CHAPTERS ON CHURCHYARDS.
By MRS SOUTHEY. Fcap. 8vo, 7s. 6d.

THE SUBALTERN.
By the Author of the 'The Chelsea Pensioners.' Fcap. 8vo, 3s. cloth.

CHRONICLES OF CARLINGFORD: SALEM CHAPEL.
Second Edition. Complete in 1 vol., price 5s.

"This story, so fresh, so powerfully written, and so tragic, stands out from among its fellows like a piece of newly-coined gold in a handful of dim commonplace shillings. Tales of pastoral experience and scenes from clerical life we have had in plenty, but the sacred things of the conventicle, the relative position of pastor and flock in a Nonconforming 'connection,' were but guessed at by the world outside, and terrible is the revelation."—*Westminster Review.*

CHRONICLES OF CARLINGFORD: THE RECTOR, AND THE DOCTOR'S FAMILY. Post 8vo, 12s.

TALES FROM BLACKWOOD.
Complete in 12 vols., bound in cloth, 18s. The Volumes are sold separately, 1s. 6d.; and may be had of most Booksellers, in Six Volumes, handsomely half-bound in red morocco.

CONTENTS.

VOL. I. The Glenmutchkin Railway.—Vanderdecken's Message Home.—The Floating Beacon.—Colonna the Painter.—Napoleon.—A Legend of Gibraltar.—The Iron Shroud.

VOL. II. Lazaro's Legacy.—A Story without a Tail.—Faustus and Queen Elizabeth.—How I became a Yeoman.—Devereux Hall.—The Metempsychosis.—College Theatricals.

VOL. III. A Reading Party in the Long Vacation.—Father Tom and the Pope.—La Petite Madelaine.—Bob Burke's Duel with Ensign Brady.—The Headsman: A Tale of Doom.—The Wearyful Woman.

VOL. IV. How I stood for the Dreepdaily Burghs.—First and Last.—The Duke's Dilemma: A Chronicle of Niesenstein.—The Old Gentleman's Teetotum.—"Woe to us when we lose the Watery Wall."—My College Friends: Charles Russell, the Gentleman Commoner.—The Magic Lay of the One-Horse Chay.

VOL. V. Adventures in Texas.—How we got Possession of the Tuileries.—Captain Paton's Lament.—The Village Doctor.—A Singular Letter from Southern Africa.

VOL. VI. My Friend the Dutchman.—My College Friends—No. II.: Horace Leicester.—The Emerald Studs.—My College Friends—No. III.: Mr W. Wellington Hurst.—Christine: A Dutch Story.—The Man in the Bell.

VOL. VII. My English Acquaintance.—The Murderer's Last Night.—Narration of Certain Uncommon Things that did formerly happen to Me, Herbert Willis, B.D.—The Wags.—The Wet Wooing: A Narrative of '98.—Ben-na-Groich.

VOL. VIII. The Surveyor's Tale. By Professor Aytoun.—The Forrest Race Romance.—Di Vasari: A Tale of Florence.—Sigismund Fatello.—The Boxes.

VOL. IX. Rosaura: A Tale of Madrid.—Adventure in the North-West Territory.—Harry Bolton's Curacy.—The Florida Pirate.—The Pandour and his Princess.—The Beauty Draught.

VOL. X. Antonio di Carara.—The Fatal Repast.—The Vision of Cagliostro.—The First and Last Kiss.—The Smuggler's Leap.—The Haunted and the Haunters.—The Duellists.

VOL. XI. The Natolian Story-Teller.—The First and Last Crime.—John Rintoul.—Major Moss.—The Premier and his Wife.

VOL. XII. Tickler among the Thieves!—The Bridegroom of Barna.—The Involuntary Experimentalist.—Lebrun's Lawsuit.—The Snowing-up of Strath Lugas.—A Few Words on Social Philosophy.

THE WONDER-SEEKER;
Or, The History of Charles Douglas. By M. FRASER TYTLER, Author of 'Tales of the Great and Brave,' &c. A New Edition. Fcap. 8vo, 3s. 6d.

VALERIUS: A ROMAN STORY.
Fcap. 8vo, 3s. cloth.

THE DIARY OF A LATE PHYSICIAN.
By SAMUEL WARREN, D.C.L. 1 vol. crown 8vo, 5s. 6d.

TEN THOUSAND A-YEAR.
By SAMUEL WARREN, D.C.L. 2 vols. crown 8vo, 9s.

NOW AND THEN.
By SAMUEL WARREN, D.C.L. Crown 8vo, 2s. 6d.

THE LILY AND THE BEE.
By SAMUEL WARREN, D.C.L. Crown 8vo, 2s.

MISCELLANIES.
By SAMUEL WARREN, D.C.L. Crown 8vo, 5s.

WORKS OF SAMUEL WARREN, D.C.L.
Uniform Edition. 5 vols. crown 8vo, 24s.

WORKS OF PROFESSOR WILSON.
Edited by his Son-in-Law, Professor FERRIER. In 12 vols. crown 8vo, £3, 12s.

RECREATIONS OF CHRISTOPHER NORTH.
By PROFESSOR WILSON. In 2 vols. crown 8vo, 12s.

THE NOCTES AMBROSIANÆ.
By PROFESSOR WILSON. With Notes and a Glossary. In 4 vols. crown 8vo, 24s.

A CHEAP EDITION OF THE NOCTES AMBROSIANÆ.
In 12 Parts, price 1s. each, forming Four Volumes at 4s. each in cloth.

LIGHTS AND SHADOWS OF SCOTTISH LIFE.
By PROFESSOR WILSON. Fcap. 8vo, 3s. cloth.

THE TRIALS OF MARGARET LYNDSAY.
By PROFESSOR WILSON. Fcap. 8vo, 3s. cloth.

THE FORESTERS.
By PROFESSOR WILSON. Fcap. 8vo, 3s. cloth.

TALES.
By PROFESSOR WILSON. Comprising 'The Lights and Shadows of Scottish Life;' 'The Trials of Margaret Lyndsay;' and 'The Foresters.' In 1 vol. crown 8vo, 6s. cloth.

ESSAYS, CRITICAL AND IMAGINATIVE.
By PROFESSOR WILSON. 4 vols. crown 8vo, 24s.

THE BOOK-HUNTER, ETC.

By JOHN HILL BURTON. New Edition. In crown 8vo, 7s. 6d.

"A book pleasant to look at and pleasant to read—pleasant from its rich store of anecdote, its geniality, and its humour, even to persons who care little for the subjects of which it treats, but beyond measure delightful to those who are in any degree members of the above-mentioned fraternity."—*Saturday Review.*

"We have not been more amused for a long time: and every reader who takes interest in typography and its consequences will say the same, if he will begin to read; beginning, he will finish, and be sorry when it is over."—*Athenæum.*

"Mr Burton has now given us a pleasant book, full of quaint anecdote, and of a lively bookish talk. There is a quiet humour in it which is very taking, and there is a curious knowledge of books which is really very sound."—*Examiner.*

HOMER AND HIS TRANSLATORS,

And the Greek Drama. By PROFESSOR WILSON. Crown 8vo, 6s.

"But of all the criticisms on Homer which I have ever had the good fortune to read, in our own or any language, the most vivid and entirely genial are those found in the 'Essays, Critical and Imaginative,' of the late Professor Wilson."—*Mr Gladstone's Studies on Homer.*

THE SKETCHER.

By the REV. JOHN EAGLES. Originally published in 'Blackwood's Magazine.' 8vo, 10s. 6d.

"This volume, called by the appropriate name of 'The Sketcher,' is one that ought to be found in the studio of every English landscape-painter. . . . . More instructive and suggestive readings for young artists, especially landscape-painters, can scarcely be found."—*The Globe.*

ESSAYS.

By the REV. JOHN EAGLES, A.M. Oxon. Originally published in 'Blackwood's Magazine.' Post 8vo, 10s. 6d.

CONTENTS:—Church Music, and other Parochials.—Medical Attendance, and other Parochials.—A few Hours at Hampton Court.—Grandfathers and Grandchildren.—Sitting for a Portrait.—Are there not Great Boasters among us?—Temperance and Teetotal Societies.—Thackeray's Lectures: Swift.—The Crystal Palace.—Civilisation: The Census.—The Beggar's Legacy.

ESSAYS; HISTORICAL, POLITICAL, AND MISCELLANEOUS.

By SIR ARCHIBALD ALISON, Bart., D.C.L. Three vols., demy 8vo, 45s.

LECTURES ON THE POETICAL LITERATURE OF THE PAST HALF-CENTURY. By D. M. MOIR. Third Edition. Fcap. 8vo, 5s.

"Exquisite in its taste and generous in its criticisms."—*Hugh Miller.*

LECTURES ON THE HISTORY OF LITERATURE,

Ancient and Modern. From the German of F. SCHLEGEL. Fcap., 5s.

"A wonderful performance—better than anything we as yet have in our own language."—*Quarterly Review.*

THE GENIUS OF HANDEL,

And the distinctive Character of his Sacred Compositions. Two Lectures. Delivered to the Members of the Edinburgh Philosophical Institution. By the VERY REV. DEAN RAMSAY, Author of 'Reminiscences of Scottish Life and Character.' In crown 8vo, 3s. 6d.

BLACKWOOD'S MAGAZINE,

From Commencement in 1817 to December 1861. Numbers 1 to 554, forming 90 Volumes. £31, 10s.

INDEX TO THE FIRST FIFTY VOLUMES OF BLACKWOOD'S MAGAZINE. 8vo, 15s.

LAYS OF THE SCOTTISH CAVALIERS,

And other Poems. By W. EDMONDSTOUNE AYTOUN, D.C.L., Professor of Rhetoric and English Literature in the University of Edinburgh. Fourteenth Edition. Fcap. 8vo, 7s. 6d.

"Professor Aytoun's 'Lays of the Scottish Cavaliers'—a volume of verse which shows that Scotland has yet a poet. Full of the true fire, it now stirs and swells like a trumpet-note—now sinks in cadences sad and wild as the wail of a Highland dirge."—*Quarterly Review.*

BOTHWELL: A POEM.

By W. EDMONDSTOUNE AYTOUN, D.C.L. Third Edition. Fcap. 8vo, 7s. 6d.

"Professor Aytoun has produced a fine poem and an able argument, and 'Bothwell' will assuredly take its stand among the classics of Scottish literature."—*The Press.*

THE BALLADS OF SCOTLAND.

Edited by Professor AYTOUN. Second Edition. 2 vols. fcap. 8vo, 12s.

"No country can boast of a richer collection of Ballads than Scotland, and no Editor for these Ballads could be found more accomplished than Professor Aytoun. He has sent forth two beautiful volumes which range with 'Percy's Reliques'—which, for completeness and accuracy, leave little to be desired—which must henceforth be considered as the standard edition of the Scottish Ballads, and which we commend as a model to any among ourselves who may think of doing like service to the English Ballads."—*Times.*

POEMS AND BALLADS OF GOETHE.

Translated by Professor AYTOUN and THEODORE MARTIN. Second Edition. Fcap. 8vo, 6s.

"There is no doubt that these are the best translations of Goethe's marvellously-cut gems which have yet been published."—*Times.*

THE BOOK OF BALLADS.

Edited by BON GAULTIER. Seventh Edition, with numerous Illustrations by DOYLE, LEECH, and CROWQUILL. Gilt edges, post 8vo, 8s. 6d.

FIRMILIAN; OR, THE STUDENT OF BADAJOS.

A Spasmodic Tragedy. By T. PERCY JONES. In small 8vo, 5s.

"Humour of a kind most rare at all times, and especially in the present day, runs through every page, and passages of true poetry and delicious versification prevent the continual play of sarcasm from becoming tedious."—*Literary Gazette.*

POETICAL WORKS OF THOMAS AIRD.

Fourth Edition. In 1 vol. fcap. 8vo, 6s.

POEMS.

By the LADY FLORA HASTINGS. Edited by her SISTER. Second Edition, with a Portrait. Fcap., 7s. 6d.

THE POEMS OF FELICIA HEMANS.

Complete in 1 vol. royal 8vo, with Portrait by FINDEN. Cheap Edition, 12s. 6d. *Another Edition,* with MEMOIR by her SISTER. Seven vols. fcap., 35s. *Another Edition,* in 6 vols., cloth, gilt edges, 24s.

The following Works of Mrs HEMANS are sold separately, bound in cloth, gilt edges, 4s. each:—

RECORDS OF WOMAN. FOREST SANCTUARY. SONGS OF THE AFFECTIONS. DRAMATIC WORKS. TALES AND HISTORIC SCENES. MORAL AND RELIGIOUS POEMS.

THE ODYSSEY OF HOMER.

Translated into English Verse in the Spenserian Stanza. By PHILIP STANHOPE WORSLEY, M.A., Scholar of Corpus Christi College. 2 vols. crown 8vo, 18s.

"Mr Worsley,—applying the Spenserian stanza, that beautiful romantic measure, to the most romantic poem of the ancient world—making the stanza yield him, too (what it never yielded to Byron), its treasures of fluidity and sweet ease—above all, bringing to his task a truly poetical sense and skill,—has produced a version of the 'Odyssey' much the most pleasing of those hitherto produced, and which is delightful to read."—*Professor Arnold on Translating Homer.*

POEMS AND TRANSLATIONS.
By PHILIP STANHOPE WORSLEY, M.A., Scholar of Corpus Christi College, Oxford. Fcap. 8vo, 5s.

POEMS.
By ISA. In small 8vo, 4s. 6d.

POETICAL WORKS OF D. M. MOIR.
With Portrait, and Memoir by THOMAS AIRD. Second Edition. 2 vols. fcap. 8vo, 12s.

LECTURES ON THE POETICAL LITERATURE OF THE PAST HALF-CENTURY. By D. M. MOIR (Δ). Second Edition. Fcap. 8vo, 5s.

"A delightful volume."—*Morning Chronicle.*
"Exquisite in its taste and generous in its criticisms."—*Hugh Miller.*

THE COURSE OF TIME: A POEM.
By ROBERT POLLOK, A.M. Twenty-third Edition. Fcap. 8vo, 5s.

"Of deep and hallowed impress, full of noble thoughts and graphic conceptions—the production of a mind alive to the great relations of being, and the sublime simplicity of our religion."—*Blackwood's Magazine.*

AN ILLUSTRATED EDITION OF THE COURSE OF TIME.
In large 8vo, bound in cloth, richly gilt, 21s.

"There has been no modern poem in the English language, of the class to which the 'Course of Time' belongs, since Milton wrote, that can be compared to it. In the present instance the artistic talents of Messrs FOSTER, CLAYTON, TENNIEL, EVANS, DALZIEL, GREEN, and WOODS, have been employed in giving expression to the sublimity of the language, by equally exquisite illustrations, all of which are of the highest class."—*Bell's Messenger.*

POEMS AND BALLADS OF SCHILLER.
Translated by Sir EDWARD BULWER LYTTON, Bart. Second Edition. 8vo, 10s. 6d.

ST STEPHEN'S;
Or, Illustrations of Parliamentary Oratory. A Poem. *Comprising*—Pym—Vane—Strafford—Halifax—Shaftesbury—St John—Sir R. Walpole—Chesterfield—Carteret—Chatham—Pitt—Fox—Burke—Sheridan—Wilberforce—Wyndham—Conway—Castlereagh—William Lamb (Lord Melbourne)—Tierney—Lord Grey—O'Connell—Plunkett—Shiel—Follett—Macaulay—Peel. Second Edition. Crown 8vo, 5s.

LEGENDS, LYRICS, AND OTHER POEMS.
By B. SIMMONS. Fcap., 7s. 6d.

SIR WILLIAM CRICHTON—ATHELWOLD—GUIDONE:
Dramas by WILLIAM SMITH, Author of 'Thorndale,' &c. 32mo, 2s. 6d.

THE BIRTHDAY, AND OTHER POEMS.
By MRS SOUTHEY. Second Edition, 5s.

ILLUSTRATIONS OF THE LYRIC POETRY AND MUSIC OF SCOTLAND. By WILLIAM STENHOUSE. Originally compiled to accompany the 'Scots Musical Museum,' and now published separately, with Additional Notes and Illustrations. 8vo, 7s. 6d.

PROFESSOR WILSON'S POEMS.
Containing the 'Isle of Palms,' the 'City of the Plague,' 'Unimore,' and other Poems. Complete Edition. Crown 8vo, 6s.

POEMS AND SONGS.
By DAVID WINGATE. Second Edition. Fcap. 8vo, 5s.

"We are delighted to welcome into the brotherhood of real poets a countryman of Burns, and whose verse will go far to render the rougher Border Scottish a classic dialect in our literature."—*John Bull.*

THE PHYSICAL ATLAS OF NATURAL PHENOMENA.
By ALEXANDER KEITH JOHNSTON, F.R.S.E., &c., Geographer to the Queen for Scotland. A New and Enlarged Edition, consisting of 35 Folio Plates, and 27 smaller ones, printed in Colours, with 135 pages of Letterpress, and Index. Imperial folio, half-bound morocco, £8, 8s.

"A perfect treasure of compressed information."—*Sir John Herschel.*

THE PHYSICAL ATLAS.
By ALEXANDER KEITH JOHNSTON, F.R.S.E., &c. Reduced from the Imperial Folio. This Edition contains Twenty-five Maps, including a Palæontological and Geological Map of the British Islands, with Descriptive Letterpress, and a very copious Index. In imperial 4to, half-bound morocco, £2, 12s. 6d.

"Executed with remarkable care, and is as accurate, and, for all educational purposes, as valuable, as the splendid large work (by the same author) which has now a European reputation."—*Eclectic Review.*

A GEOLOGICAL MAP OF EUROPE.
By Sir R. I. MURCHISON, D.C.L., F.R.S., &c., Director-General of the Geological Survey of Great Britain and Ireland; and JAMES NICOL, F.R.S.E., F.G.S., Professor of Natural History in the University of Aberdeen. Constructed by Alexander Keith Johnston, F.R.S.E., &c. Four Sheets imperial, beautifully printed in Colours. In Sheets, £3, 3s.; in a Cloth Case, 4to, £3, 10s.

GEOLOGICAL AND PALÆONTOLOGICAL MAP OF THE BRITISH ISLANDS, including Tables of the Fossils of the different Epochs, &c. &c., from the Sketches and Notes of Professor Edward Forbes. With Illustrative and Explanatory Letterpress. 21s.

GEOLOGICAL MAP OF SCOTLAND.
By JAMES NICOL, F.R.S.E., &c., Professor of Natural History in the University of Aberdeen. With Explanatory Notes. The Topography by Alexander Keith Johnston, F.R.S.E., &c. Scale, 10 miles to an inch. In Cloth Case, 21s.

INTRODUCTORY TEXT-BOOK OF PHYSICAL GEOGRAPHY.
By DAVID PAGE, F.R.S.E., &c. With Illustrations and a Glossarial Index. Crown 8vo, 2s.

INTRODUCTORY TEXT-BOOK OF GEOLOGY.
By DAVID PAGE, F.R.S.E., F.G.S. With Engravings on Wood and Glossarial Index. Fifth Edition, 1s. 9d.

"It has not often been our good fortune to examine a text-book on science of which we could express an opinion so entirely favourable as we are enabled to do of Mr Page's little work."—*Athenæum.*

ADVANCED TEXT-BOOK OF GEOLOGY,
Descriptive and Industrial. By DAVID PAGE, F.R.S.E., F.G.S. With Engravings and Glossary of Scientific Terms. Third Edition, revised and enlarged, 6s.

"It is therefore with unfeigned pleasure that we record our appreciation of his 'Advanced Text-Book of Geology.' We have carefully read this truly satisfactory book, and do not hesitate to say that it is an excellent compendium of the great facts of Geology, and written in a truthful and philosophic spirit."—*Edinburgh Philosophical Journal.*

HANDBOOK OF GEOLOGICAL TERMS AND GEOLOGY.
By DAVID PAGE, F.R.S.E., F.G.S. In crown 8vo, 6s.

THE PAST AND PRESENT LIFE OF THE GLOBE:
Being a Sketch in Outline of the World's Life-System. By DAVID PAGE, F.R.S.E., F.G.S. Crown 8vo, 6s. With Fifty Illustrations, drawn and engraved expressly for this Work.

"Mr Page, whose admirable text-books of geology have already secured him a position of importance in the scientific world, will add considerably to his reputation by the present sketch, as he modestly terms it, of the Life-System, or gradual evolution of the vitality of our globe. In no manual that we are aware of have the facts and phenomena of biology been presented in at once so systematic and succinct a form, the successive manifestations of life on the earth set forth in so clear an order, or traced so vividly from the earliest organisms deep-buried in its stratified crust, to the familiar forms that now adorn and people its surface."—*Literary Gazette.*

THE GEOLOGICAL EXAMINATOR:
A Progressive Series of Questions adapted to the Introductory and Advanced Text-Books of Geology. Prepared to assist Teachers in framing their Examinations, and Students in testing their own Progress and Proficiency. By DAVID PAGE, F.R.S.E., F.G.S. Second Edition, 6d.

THE GEOLOGY OF PENNSYLVANIA:
A Government Survey; with a General View of the Geology of the United States, Essays on the Coal-Formation and its Fossils, and a Description of the Coal-Fields of North America and Great Britain. By PROFESSOR HENRY DARWIN ROGERS, F.R.S., F.G.S., Professor of Natural History in the University of Glasgow. With Seven large Maps, and numerous Illustrations engraved on Copper and on Wood. In 3 vols. royal 4to, £8, 8s.

SEA-SIDE STUDIES AT ILFRACOMBE, TENBY, THE SCILLY ISLES, AND JERSEY. By GEORGE HENRY LEWES. Second Edition. Crown 8vo, with Illustrations, and a Glossary of Technical Terms, 6s. 6d.

PHYSIOLOGY OF COMMON LIFE.
By GEORGE HENRY LEWES, Author of 'Sea-side Studies,' &c. Illustrated with numerous Engravings. 2 vols., 12s.

CHEMISTRY OF COMMON LIFE.
By PROFESSOR J. F. W. JOHNSTON. A New Edition. Edited by G. H. LEWES. With 113 Illustrations on Wood, and a Copious Index. 2 vols. crown 8vo, 11s. 6d.

NOMENCLATURE OF COLOURS,
Applicable to the Arts and Natural Sciences, to Manufactures, and other Purposes of General Utility. By D. R. HAY, F.R.S.E. 228 Examples of Colours, Hues, Tints, and Shades. 8vo, £3, 3s.

NARRATIVE OF THE EARL OF ELGIN'S MISSION TO CHINA AND JAPAN. By LAURENCE OLIPHANT, Private Secretary to Lord Elgin. Illustrated with numerous Engravings in Chromo-Lithography, Maps, and Engravings on Wood, from Original Drawings and Photographs. Second Edition. In 2 vols. 8vo, 21s.

"The volumes in which Mr Oliphant has related these transactions will be read with the strongest interest now, and deserve to retain a permanent place in the literary and historical annals of our time."—*Edinburgh Review.*

RUSSIAN SHORES OF THE BLACK SEA
In the Autumn of 1852. With a Voyage down the Volga and a Tour through the Country of the Don Cossacks. By LAURENCE OLIPHANT, Esq. 8vo, with Map and other Illustrations. Fourth Edition, 14s.

EGYPT, THE SOUDAN, AND CENTRAL AFRICA:
With Explorations from Khartoum on the White Nile to the Regions of the Equator. By JOHN PETHERICK, F.R.G.S., Her Britannic Majesty's Consul for the Soudan. In 8vo, with a Map, 16s.

NOTES ON NORTH AMERICA:
Agricultural, Economical, and Social. By PROFESSOR J. F. W. JOHNSTON. 2 vols. post 8vo, 21s.

"Professor Johnston's admirable Notes. . . . The very best manual for intelligent emigrants, whilst to the British agriculturist and general reader it conveys a more complete conception of the condition of these prosperous regions than all that has hitherto been written."—*Economist.*

A FAMILY TOUR ROUND THE COASTS OF SPAIN AND PORTUGAL during the Winter of 1860-1861. By LADY DUNBAR, of Northfield. In post 8vo, 5s.

THE ROYAL ATLAS OF MODERN GEOGRAPHY.

In a Series of entirely Original and Authentic Maps. By A. KEITH JOHNSTON, F.R.S.E., F.R.G.S., Author of the 'Physical Atlas,' &c. With a complete Index of easy reference to each Map, comprising nearly 150,000 Places contained in this Atlas. Imperial folio, half-bound in russia or morocco, £5, 15s. 6d. (Dedicated by permission to Her Majesty.)

"No one can look through Mr Keith Johnston's new Atlas without seeing that it is the best which has ever been published in this country."—*The Times.*

"Of the many noble atlases prepared by Mr Johnston and published by Messrs Blackwood & Sons, this Royal Atlas will be the most useful to the public, and will deserve to be the most popular."—*Athenæum.*

"We know no series of maps which we can more warmly recommend. The accuracy, wherever we have attempted to put it to the test, is really astonishing."—*Saturday Review.*

"The culmination of all attempts to depict the face of the world appears in the Royal Atlas, than which it is impossible to conceive anything more perfect."—*Morning Herald.*

"This is, beyond question, the most splendid and luxurious, as well as the most useful and complete, of all existing atlases."—*Guardian.*

"There has not, we believe, been produced for general public use a body of maps equal in beauty and completeness to the Royal Atlas just issued by Mr A. K. Johnston."—*Examiner.*

"An almost daily reference to, and comparison of it with others, since the publication of the first part some two years ago until now, enables us to say, without the slightest hesitation, that this is by far the most complete and authentic atlas that has yet been issued."—*Scotsman.*

"Beyond doubt the greatest geographical work of our time."—*Museum.*

INDEX GEOGRAPHICUS:

Being an Index to nearly ONE HUNDRED AND FIFTY THOUSAND NAMES OF PLACES, &c.; with their LATITUDES and LONGITUDES as given in KEITH JOHNSTON'S 'ROYAL ATLAS;' together with the COUNTRIES and SUBDIVISIONS OF THE COUNTRIES in which they are situated. In 1 vol. large 8vo., 21s.

A NEW MAP OF EUROPE.

By A. KEITH JOHNSTON, F.R.S.E. Size, 4 feet 2 inches by 3 feet 5 inches. Cloth Case, 21s.

ATLAS OF SCOTLAND.

31 Maps of the Counties of Scotland, coloured. Bound in roan, price 10s. 6d. Each County may be had separately, in Cloth Case, 1s.

KEITH JOHNSTON'S SCHOOL ATLASES:—

GENERAL AND DESCRIPTIVE GEOGRAPHY, exhibiting the Actual and Comparative Extent of all the Countries in the World, with their present Political Divisions. A New and Enlarged Edition. With a complete Index. 26 Maps. Half-bound, 12s. 6d.

PHYSICAL GEOGRAPHY, illustrating, in a Series of Original Designs, the Elementary Facts of Geology, Hydrology, Meteorology, and Natural History. A New and Enlarged Edition. 19 Maps, including coloured Geological Maps of Europe and of the British Isles. Half-bound, 12s. 6d.

CLASSICAL GEOGRAPHY, comprising, in Twenty Plates, Maps and Plans of all the important Countries and Localities referred to by Classical Authors; accompanied by a pronouncing Index of Places, by T. HARVEY, M.A. Oxon. A New and Revised Edition. Half-bound, 12s. 6d.

ASTRONOMY. Edited by J. R. HIND, Esq., F.R.A.S., &c. Notes and Descriptive Letterpress to each Plate, embodying all recent Discoveries in Astronomy. 18 Maps. Half-bound, 12s. 6d.

ELEMENTARY SCHOOL ATLAS OF GENERAL AND DESCRIPTIVE GEOGRAPHY for the Use of Junior Classes. A New and Cheaper Edition. 20 Maps, including a Map of Canaan and Palestine. Half-bound, 5s.

"They are as superior to all School Atlases within our knowledge, as were the larger works of the same Author in advance of those that preceded them."—*Educational Times.*

"Decidedly the best School Atlases we have ever seen."—*English Journal of Education.*

"The best, the fullest, the most accurate and recent, as well as artistically the most beautiful atlas that can be put into the schoolboy's hands."—*Museum, April* 1863.

A MANUAL OF MODERN GEOGRAPHY:

Mathematical, Physical, and Political. Embracing a complete Development of the River-Systems of the Globe. By the REV. ALEX. MACKAY, F.R.G.S. With Index. 7s. 6d., bound in leather.

THE BOOK OF THE FARM.

Detailing the Labours of the Farmer, Farm-Steward, Ploughman, Shepherd, Hedger, Cattle-man, Field-worker, and Dairymaid, and forming a safe Monitor for Students in Practical Agriculture. By HENRY STEPHENS, F.R.S.E. 2 vols. royal 8vo, £3, handsomely bound in cloth, with upwards of 600 Illustrations.

"The best book I have ever met with."—*Professor Johnston.*

"We have thoroughly examined these volumes; but to give a full notice of their varied and valuable contents would occupy a larger space than we can conveniently devote to their discussion; we therefore, in general terms, commend them to the careful study of every young man who wishes to become a good practical farmer."—*Times.*

"One of the completest works on agriculture of which our literature can boast."—*Agricultural Gazette.*

THE BOOK OF FARM IMPLEMENTS AND MACHINES.

By JAMES SLIGHT and R. SCOTT BURN. Edited by HENRY STEPHENS, F.R.S.E. Illustrated with 876 Engravings. Royal 8vo, uniform with the 'Book of the Farm,' half-bound, £2, 2s.

THE BOOK OF FARM BUILDINGS:

Their Arrangement and Construction. By HENRY STEPHENS, F.R.S.E., and R. SCOTT BURN. Royal 8vo, with 1045 Illustrations. Uniform with the 'Book of the Farm.' Half-bound, £1, 11s. 6d.

THE BOOK OF THE GARDEN.

By CHARLES M'INTOSH. In 2 large vols. royal 8vo, embellished with 1353 Engravings.

Each Volume may be had separately—viz.:

I. ARCHITECTURAL AND ORNAMENTAL.—On the Formation of Gardens—Construction, Heating, and Ventilation of Fruit and Plant Houses, Pits, Frames, and other Garden Structures, with Practical Details. Illustrated by 1073 Engravings, pp. 766. £2, 10s.

II. PRACTICAL GARDENING.—Directions for the Culture of the Kitchen Garden, the Hardy-fruit Garden, the Forcing Garden, and Flower Garden, including Fruit and Plant Houses, with Select Lists of Vegetables, Fruits, and Plants. Pp. 868, with 279 Engravings. £1, 17s. 6d.

"We feel justified in recommending Mr M'Intosh's two excellent volumes to the notice of the public." —*Gardeners' Chronicle.*

PRACTICAL SYSTEM OF FARM BOOK-KEEPING:

Being that recommended in the 'Book of the Farm' by H. STEPHENS. Royal 8vo, 2s. 6d. Also, SEVEN FOLIO ACCOUNT-BOOKS, printed and ruled in accordance with the System, the whole being specially adapted for keeping, by an easy and accurate method, an account of all the transactions of the Farm. A detailed Prospectus may be had from the Publishers. Price of the complete set of Eight Books, £1, 4s. 6d. Also, A LABOUR ACCOUNT OF THE ESTATE, 2s. 6d.

"We have no hesitation in saying that, of the many systems of keeping farm accounts which are now in vogue, there is not one which will bear comparison with this."—*Bell's Messenger.*

AINSLIE'S TREATISE ON LAND-SURVEYING.

A New and Enlarged Edition. Edited by WILLIAM GALBRAITH, M.A., F.R.A.S. 1 vol. 8vo, with a Volume of Plates in Quarto, 21s.

"The best book on surveying with which I am acquainted."—W. RUTHERFORD, LL.D., F.R.A.S., *Royal Military Academy, Woolwich.*

THE FORESTER:

A Practical Treatise on the Planting, Rearing, and Management of Forest Trees. By JAMES BROWN, Wood Manager to the Earl of Seafield. Third Edition, greatly enlarged, with numerous Engravings on Wood. Royal 8vo, 31s. 6d.

"Beyond all doubt this is the best work on the subject of Forestry extant."—*Gardeners' Journal.*

"The most useful guide to good arboriculture in the English language."—*Gardeners' Chronicle.*

HANDBOOK OF THE MECHANICAL ARTS,

Concerned in the Construction and Arrangement of Dwellings and other Buildings; Including Carpentry, Smith-work, Iron-framing, Brick-making, Columns, Cements, Well-sinking, Enclosing of Land, Road-making, &c. By R. SCOTT BURN. Crown 8vo, with 504 Engravings on Wood, 6s. 6d.

PROFESSOR JOHNSTON'S WORKS:—

EXPERIMENTAL AGRICULTURE. Being the Results of Past, and Suggestions for Future, Experiments in Scientific and Practical Agriculture. 8s.

ELEMENTS OF AGRICULTURAL CHEMISTRY AND GEOLOGY. Eighth Edition, 6s. 6d.

A CATECHISM OF AGRICULTURAL CHEMISTRY AND GEOLOGY. Fifty-seventh Edition. Edited by Dr VOELCKER. 1s.

ON THE USE OF LIME IN AGRICULTURE. 6s.

INSTRUCTIONS FOR THE ANALYSIS OF SOILS. Fourth Edition, 2s.

THE RELATIVE VALUE OF ROUND AND SAWN TIMBER,

Shown by means of Tables and Diagrams. By JAMES RAIT, Land-Steward at Castle-Forbes. Royal 8vo, 8s. half-bound.

THE YEAR-BOOK OF AGRICULTURAL FACTS.

1859 and 1860. Edited by R. SCOTT BURN. Fcap. 8vo, 5s. each. 1861 and 1862, 4s. each.

ELKINGTON'S SYSTEM OF DRAINING:

A Systematic Treatise on the Theory and Practice of Draining Land, adapted to the various Situations and Soils of England and Scotland, drawn up from the Communications of Joseph Elkington, by J. JOHNSTONE. 4to, 10s. 6d.

JOURNAL OF AGRICULTURE, AND TRANSACTIONS OF THE HIGHLAND AND AGRICULTURAL SOCIETY OF SCOTLAND.

OLD SERIES, 1828 to 1843, 21 vols.	£3	3	0
NEW SERIES, 1843 to 1851, 8 vols.	2	2	0

THE RURAL ECONOMY OF ENGLAND, SCOTLAND, AND IRELAND.

By LEONCE DE LAVERGNE. Translated from the French. With Notes by a Scottish Farmer. In 8vo, 12s.

"One of the best works on the philosophy of agriculture and of agricultural political economy that has appeared."—*Spectator.*

DAIRY MANAGEMENT AND FEEDING OF MILCH COWS;

Being the recorded Experience of MRS AGNES SCOTT, Winkston, Peebles. Second Edition. Fcap., 1s.

ITALIAN IRRIGATION:

A Report addressed to the Hon. the Court of Directors of the East India Company, on the Agricultural Canals of Piedmont and Lombardy; with a Sketch of the Irrigation System of Northern and Central India. By LIEUT.-COL. BAIRD SMITH, C.B. Second Edition. 2 vols. 8vo, with Atlas in folio, 30s.

THE ARCHITECTURE OF THE FARM:

A Series of Designs for Farm Houses, Farm Steadings, Factors' Houses, and Cottages. By JOHN STARFORTH, Architect. Sixty-two Engravings. In medium 4to, £2, 2s.

"One of the most useful and beautiful additions to Messrs Blackwood's extensive and valuable library of agricultural and rural economy."—*Morning Post.*

THE YESTER DEEP LAND-CULTURE:

Being a Detailed Account of the Method of Cultivation which has been successfully practised for several years by the Marquess of Tweeddale at Yester. By HENRY STEPHENS, Esq., F.R.S.E., Author of the 'Book of the Farm.' In small 8vo, with Engravings on Wood, 4s. 6d.

A MANUAL OF PRACTICAL DRAINING.

By HENRY STEPHENS, F.R.S.E., Author of the 'Book of the Farm.' Third Edition, 8vo, 5s.

A CATECHISM OF PRACTICAL AGRICULTURE.

By HENRY STEPHENS, F.R.S.E., Author of the 'Book of the Farm,' &c. In crown 8vo, with Illustrations, 1s.

HANDY BOOK ON PROPERTY LAW.

By LORD ST LEONARDS. The Seventh Edition. To which is now added a Letter on the New Laws for obtaining an Indefeasible Title. With a Portrait of the Author, engraved by HOLL. 3s. 6d.

"Less than 200 pages serve to arm us with the ordinary precautions to which we should attend in selling, buying, mortgaging, leasing, settling, and devising estates. We are informed of our relations to our property, to our wives and children, and of our liability as trustees or executors, in a little book for the million,—a book which the author tenders to the *profanum vulgus* as even capable of 'beguiling a few hours in a railway carriage.'"—*Times.*

THE PLANTER'S GUIDE.

By SIR HENRY STEUART. A New Edition, with the Author's last Additions and Corrections. 8vo, with Engravings, 21s.

STABLE ECONOMY:

A Treatise on the Management of Horses. By JOHN STEWART, V.S. Seventh Edition, 6s. 6d.

"Will always maintain its position as a standard work upon the management of horses."—*Mark Lane Express.*

ADVICE TO PURCHASERS OF HORSES.

By JOHN STEWART, V.S. 18mo, plates, 2s. 6d.

A PRACTICAL TREATISE ON THE CULTIVATION OF THE GRAPE VINE. By WILLIAM THOMSON, Gardener to His Grace the Duke of Buccleuch, Dalkeith Park. Third Edition. 8vo, 5s.

"When books on gardening are written thus conscientiously, they are alike honourable to their author and valuable to the public."—*Lindley's Gardeners' Chronicle.*

"Want of space prevents us giving extracts, and we must therefore conclude by saying, that as the author is one of the very best grape-growers of the day, this book may be stated as being the key to his successful practice, and as such, we can with confidence recommend it as indispensable to all who wish to excel in the cultivation of the vine."—*The Florist and Pomologist.*

THE CHEMISTRY OF VEGETABLE AND ANIMAL PHYSIOLOGY. By DR J. G. MULDER, Professor of Chemistry in the University of Utrecht. With an Introduction and Notes by Professor JOHNSTON. 22 Plates. 8vo, 30s.

THE MOOR AND THE LOCH.

Containing Minute Instructions in all Highland Sports, with Wanderings over Crag and Correi, Flood and Fell. By JOHN COLQUHOUN, Esq. Third Edition. 8vo, with Illustrations, 12s. 6d.

SALMON-CASTS AND STRAY SHOTS:

Being Fly-Leaves from the Note-Book of JOHN COLQUHOUN, Esq., Author of 'The Moor and the Loch,' &c. Second Edition. Fcap. 8vo, 5s.

COQUET-DALE FISHING SONGS.

Now first collected by a North-Country Angler, with the Music of the Airs. 8vo, 5s.

THE ANGLER'S COMPANION TO THE RIVERS AND LOCHS OF SCOTLAND. By T. T. STODDART. With Map of the Fishing Streams and Lakes of Scotland. Second Edition. Crown 8vo, 3s. 6d.

"Indispensable in all time to come, as the very strength and grace of an angler's tackle and equipment in Scotland, must and will be STODDART'S ANGLER'S COMPANION."—*Blackwood's Magazine.*

RELIGION IN COMMON LIFE:
A Sermon preached in Crathie Church, October 14, 1855, before Her Majesty the Queen and Prince Albert. By the REV. JOHN CAIRD, D.D. Published by Her Majesty's Command. Bound in cloth, 8d. Cheap Edition, 3d.

SERMONS.
By the REV. JOHN CAIRD, D.D., Professor of Divinity in the University of Glasgow, and one of Her Majesty's Chaplains for Scotland. In crown 8vo, 5s. This Edition includes the Sermon on 'Religion in Common Life,' preached in Crathie Church, Oct. 1855, before Her Majesty the Queen and the late Prince Consort.

"They are noble sermons; and we are not sure but that, with the cultivated reader, they will gain rather than lose by being read, not heard. There is a thoughtfulness and depth about them which can hardly be appreciated, unless when they are studied at leisure; and there are so many sentences so felicitously expressed that we should grudge being hurried away from them by a rapid speaker, without being allowed to enjoy them a second time."—*Fraser's Magazine.*

THE BOOK OF JOB.
By the late REV. GEORGE CROLY, LL.D., Rector of St Stephen's, Walbrook. With a Memoir of the Author by his SON. Fcap. 8vo, 4s.

LECTURES IN DIVINITY.
By the late REV. GEORGE HILL, D.D., Principal of St Mary's College, St Andrews. Stereotyped Edition. 8vo, 14s.

"I am not sure if I can recommend a more complete manual of Divinity."—*Dr Chalmers.*

THE MOTHER'S LEGACIE TO HER UNBORNE CHILDE.
By MRS ELIZABETH JOCELINE. Edited by the Very Rev. Principal LEE. 32mo, 4s. 6d.

"This beautiful and touching legacie."—*Athenæum.*

"A delightful monument of the piety and high feeling of a truly noble mother."—*Morning Advertiser.*

ANALYSIS AND CRITICAL INTERPRETATION OF THE HEBREW TEXT OF THE BOOK OF GENESIS. Preceded by a Hebrew Grammar, and Dissertations on the Genuineness of the Pentateuch, and on the Structure of the Hebrew Language. By the REV. WILLIAM PAUL, A.M. 8vo, 18s.

PRAYERS FOR SOCIAL AND FAMILY WORSHIP.
Prepared by a COMMITTEE OF THE GENERAL ASSEMBLY OF THE CHURCH OF SCOTLAND, and specially designed for the use of Soldiers, Sailors, Colonists, Sojourners in India, and other Persons, at Home or Abroad, who are deprived of the Ordinary Services of a Christian Ministry. *Published by Authority of the Committee.* Third Edition. In crown 8vo, bound in cloth, 4s.

PRAYERS FOR SOCIAL AND FAMILY WORSHIP.
Being a Cheap Edition of the above. Fcap. 8vo, 1s. 6d.

THE CHRISTIAN LIFE,
In its Origin, Progress, and Perfection. By the VERY REV. E. B. RAMSAY, LL.D., F.R.S.E., Dean of the Diocese of Edinburgh. Crown 8vo, 9s.

THEISM: THE WITNESS OF REASON AND NATURE TO AN ALL-WISE AND BENEFICENT CREATOR. By the REV. JOHN TULLOCH, D.D., Principal and Professor of Theology, St Mary's College, St Andrews; and one of Her Majesty's Chaplains in Ordinary in Scotland. In 1 vol. 8vo, 10s. 6d.

ON THE ORIGIN AND CONNECTION OF THE GOSPELS OF MATTHEW, MARK, AND LUKE; With Synopsis of Parallel Passages, and Critical Notes. By JAMES SMITH, Esq. of Jordanhill, F.R.S., Author of the 'Voyage and Shipwreck of St Paul.' Medium 8vo, 16s.

INSTITUTES OF METAPHYSIC: THE THEORY OF KNOWING AND BEING. By JAMES F. FERRIER, A.B. Oxon., Professor of Moral Philosophy and Political Economy, St Andrews. Second Edition. Crown 8vo, 10s. 6d.

"We have no doubt, however, that the subtlety and depth of metaphysical genius which his work betrays, its rare display of rigorous and consistent reasonings, and the inimitable precision and beauty of its style on almost every page, must secure for it a distinguished place in the history of philosophical discussion."—*Tulloch's Burnett Prize Treatise.*

LECTURES ON METAPHYSICS.
By SIR WILLIAM HAMILTON, Bart., Professor of Logic and Metaphysics in the University of Edinburgh. Edited by the Rev. H. L. MANSEL, B.D., LL.D., Waynflete Professor of Moral and Metaphysical Philosophy, Oxford; and JOHN VEITCH, M.A., Professor of Logic, Rhetoric, and Metaphysics, St Andrews. Third Edition. 2 vols. 8vo, 24s.

LECTURES ON LOGIC.
By SIR WILLIAM HAMILTON, Bart. Edited by Professors MANSEL and VEITCH. In 2 vols., 24s.

THORNDALE; OR, THE CONFLICT OF OPINIONS.
By WILLIAM SMITH, Author of 'A Discourse on Ethics,' &c. Second Edition. Crown 8vo, 10s. 6d.

"The subjects treated of, and the style—always chaste and beautiful, often attractively grand—in which they are clothed, will not fail to secure the attention of the class for whom the work is avowedly written. . . . . It deals with many of those higher forms of speculation characteristic of the cultivated minds of the age."—*North British Review.*

GRAVENHURST; OR, THOUGHTS ON GOOD AND EVIL.
By WILLIAM SMITH, Author of 'Thorndale,' &c. In crown 8vo, 7s. 6d.

"One of those rare books which, being filled with noble and beautiful thoughts, deserves an attentive and thoughtful perusal."—*Westminster Review.*

A DISCOURSE ON ETHICS OF THE SCHOOL OF PALEY.
By WILLIAM SMITH, Author of 'Thorndale.' 8vo, 4s.

ON THE INFLUENCE EXERTED BY THE MIND OVER THE BODY, in the Production and Removal of Morbid and Anomalous Conditions of the Animal Economy. By JOHN GLEN, M.A. Crown 8vo, 2s. 6d.

DESCARTES ON THE METHOD OF RIGHTLY CONDUCTING THE REASON, and Seeking Truth in the Sciences. Translated from the French. 12mo, 2s.

DESCARTES' MEDITATIONS, AND SELECTIONS FROM HIS PRINCIPLES OF PHILOSOPHY. Translated from the Latin. 12mo, 3s.

SPECULATIVE PHILOSOPHY:
An INTRODUCTORY LECTURE delivered at the Opening of the Class of Logic and Rhetoric in the University of Glasgow, Nov. 1, 1864. By JOHN VEITCH, M.A., Professor of Logic and Rhetoric in the University of Glasgow. 1s.

Published by

Facsimile Publisher
Ashok Vihar, Delhi-110052 (India)
Website: www.facsimilepublisher.com

Distributed by

Gyan Books Pvt. Ltd.
5, Ansari Road, Daryaganj, New Delhi-110002 (India)
E-mail: books@gyanbooks.com, Website: www.gyanbooks.com

2 222000 010300